© A.R.T. Publishing House – London
eMail: *art.publishinghouse@ssaemea.com*
Web: *www.ssaemea.com/art*
Translation by Roberta Baima and Martin De Sa Pinto
Editing by Martin De Sa Pinto
Public relations by Roberta Baima
Art direction by Roberto Grigoletto

ISBN: 9781800490833

First Edition: December 2020

Dania Mondini
Claudio Loiodice

The Modigliani racket

Afterword *by Pietro Grasso*

A.R.T.
Publishing House London

Sommario

THE MODIGLIANI RACKET

To Giordano Bruno, revolutionary heretic

There will come a day when man will wake from oblivion and finally understand who he really is and to whom has he handed over the reins of his existence, to a fallacious, lying mind which enslaves him and keeps him enslaved... Man has no limits and when one day he realises it, he will be free in this world, too.

Giordano Bruno, *The Expulsion of the Triumphant Beast*

The authors declare that all information, news items and interviews reported in this book have been strictly documented. The documentation is in their custody, and will be made available in the case of disputes.

This Book

Anarchic, insane, violent, alcoholic, drug-crazed, troublemaking, despotic, short-tempered, womanising, irresponsible, self-centred. These are just some of the derogatory epithets applied to the greatest of the twentieth century Italian painters. It was a narrow-minded view, often based on nothing but shame, jealousy or envy. We, who have analysed the details of his life through a primarily criminological, but also historical, social and psychological reconstruction, believe conversely that Amedeo Modigliani was a genius who possessed the freedom of spirit to express his heresy towards an arrogant society, which tended to restrict the fields of freedom and expression according to its own questionable parameters.

It is the profile of a social misfit, created ad hoc for the benefit of those who, even then, thought they could profit by inferring pathological meanings to the personality of an artist who was on closer inspection sensitive, aristocratic, candid, educated, multilingual, refined and generous, but also restless and inclined to self-harm. The perverse charm falsely attributed to a painter who dies young (he was thirty-five years old), poor and sick, would have buoyed the price of his works, as was indeed the case, enabling many to get rich, through many decades.

This Modigliani "racket" continues today, and it is more lucrative than ever. This book is an act of accusation. There have been too many plots, too many mysteries, errors, omissions. There has been an often deliberate superficiality that enabled the misdeeds that engulfed the person and works of Modigliani, and his family. The many texts published to date shed light almost exclusively on the historical and artistic details of his life and works; and personal testimonies are often contradictory.

Prior to this book, no one had collected and summarised the existing material in criminological terms, based on an investigation born from meticulous research of the details, of complicit parties and neglected particulars, of ongoing legal cases and of judgements already passed, of the personalities of the actors and their sometimes less-than-solid explanations. Evidence blackened by the chimney of time's crematorium.

Scams, exhibitions with fake paintings, prolific forgers, foundations created from nothing. Internal wars that revolve around art critics, self-appointed experts or common criminals who made their fortune in recent decades by linking their name to that of Amedeo Modigliani. Powerful people who with their overbearing influence could intimidate poor souls with a fragile family history. Merchants willing to do anything, only interested in profit. Artworks that acquire an immense value, sometimes increasing tenfold within a few years. Chinese taxi drivers who suddenly take on the role of billionaire art lovers and collectors. A business with a value we estimated to be at least 11 billion Euro, something which hasn't escaped organised crime or international money launderers.

Our story spans a hundred years of history, following a path that, step by step, transformed that talented child into a young rebel, an imaginative artist, a tormented genius at times insecure, perfectionist, arrogant and tender. We will meet characters who have left an indelible mark in the history of modern art, such as Pablo Picasso. We will wander the streets and alleys of the Paris of the early twentieth century and we will stay there for seventy years; later, we will arrive in Italy as we track the sombre and criminal destiny of all the great protagonists in this story who fascinated us and who, we are sure, will also win over many readers.

There are six main characters in this long mystery: Amedeo Modigliani, his partner and muse Jeanne Hébuterne (who tragically passed away on January 26, 1920, two days after the artist's death); their daughter Jeanne and her daughter Laure; the eccentric Piedmontese archivist Christian Parisot, and, last but not least, the tenacious standard bearer and "forgery hunter" Carlo Pepi. Many supporting actors and a number of extras move around the main characters on the stage: magistrates, lawyers, businessmen, collectors, art critics, criminals.

Behind the scenes, malicious and refined puppet masters pull the levers of a complex and lucrative mechanism. For each of them we took a picture as precise as possible, inserting them as players in a drama we have drawn out by moving virtually to the scene of each crime. Eight chapters, as many "crime scenes"[1] that led us to visit several Italian cities (Leghorn, Rome,

---

[1] The title of "crime scenes" refers exclusively to the places that we visited while writing the book, not to the characters.

Genoa, Palermo ...) in our effort to collect precious testimonies and documents, many of which are revealed here for the first time.

In Paris, we reconstructed the events surrounding the mysterious death of Modgliani's daughter. In Geneva, we were allowed exclusive access to the opening of the Amedeo Modigliani Legal Archives, which we helped bring back to Europe from New York during the drafting of this book. In London, we visited the Tate Modern, which houses an exhibition dedicated to Modigliani, in the company of Isabella Quattrocchi, currently among the most authoritative and accredited court experts in cases involving fakes and forgers in the art world. In her judgment, there are doubts about several of the paintings housed at the Tate Modern. All these events followed the sensational premature closure of the July 2017 exhibition at the Palazzo Ducale in Genoa, after more than twenty paintings were impounded by the Police. This and much more, in an investigation that reveals for the first time the illicit plots and interests in the shadow of the great "Modì".

As with the centenary of his birth, on July 12, 1984, the period surrounding the hundredth anniversary of his death (January 24, 2020) is marked by a number of momentous occasions, with the preparation of a multitude of projects seeking to showcase the international fame which Modigliani conquered only after his untimely death. Starting from July, 24, 1984, the city of Leghorn and a phalanx of art experts put together a farcical collection of works that effectively rendered absurd efforts to celebrate the centenary with dignity and honour. Sculptures were found which many, in haste or greed, had attributed to the artist from Leghorn. The extent to which these antics were staged for commercial purposes cannot be gauged precisely, but we collected evidence that could at least give rise to the suspicion of a broad conspiracy behind the story, and perhaps even the connivance of a country beyond the ocean.

Three days after the discovery of the fake Modigliani sculpted heads, when Leghorn was invaded by the world's media circus, Jeanne Modigliani, the painter's daughter, passed away in Paris under suspicious circumstances. She was found dying in her apartment in a working class tower block in Porte d'Italie and two days later, she died in hospital. Jeanne's death was the result of a violent blow, at the time considered accidental, but disturbing questions emerged soon afterwards. We worked on the details and on the statements of some of those close to her at the time, reconstructing new scenarios enveloped in mystery. We wondered who might have an interest in silencing a voice that was both authoritative and inconvenient. So, "following the money," we tried to identify the likely motive for a possible murder.

The focal point of this untrammelled flow of interests, the cornerstone on which the entire system rests, are in fact the disputed and mysterious Amedeo Modigliani Legal Archives, compiled thanks to the tireless work of the artist's daughter Jeanne, and for years at the centre of international intrigue. The Archives represent the basis for making the certifications on the authenticity of the art works attributed to Modigliani. Whoever controls them controls a business worth millions. We then asked ourselves where they are, what they contain and also who legally owns them.

We looked for answers. In some cases, we believe we found them, even if false trails, which seem to be a constant in this story, often muddy the picture. We confine ourselves to the facts, and analyse them by lining up all the details. What is certain is that this is not an affair managed in compliance with ethical principles or, as many would have us believe, only for the sake of art. No, there is a hidden motive here for which Amedeo did not care at all: the obsession with money.

With this investigation, we want to send a signal, to lay bare the squalid dealing that pervades the exhibitions, sponsored in some cases by public bodies. This book also contains hypotheses of crime, which we will not keep to ourselves: the first copies, in fact, will be delivered to the competent prosecutors, in Italy and abroad.

We want to restore dignity to the artist and to the cultural heritage of our country. We were inspired by the shared values of legality that unites us in the Antonino Caponnetto Foundation[2]. Today more than ever there are people who continue to profit from the life and works of that "damned" artist, one who died in absolute poverty, and possibly not just as a result of his illness.

---

[2] The foundation is named after the Italian Antimafia magistrate who died in December 2002

First Crime Scene: Place Denfert-Rochereau, Paris
Amedeo Clemente Modigliani, death of an artist[3]

CHARACTERS

Jeanne Hébuterne – painter, last companion of the artist, mother of Jeanne Modigliani.

Lunia Czechowska – friend, confidant, in love with Amedeo. Model in many famous paintings.

Simone Thiroux – Amedeo's lover and mother of Gerald, the male son who the artist never acknowledged.

---

[3] This chapter, dedicated to the death and to the last days of Modigliani's life, is based on documents contained in the Modigliani Legal Archives and is the result of the study and analysis of other works dedicated to the artist. The contents of the loving correspondence between Amedeo and his mother, the letters sent by the Jewish merchant Léopold Zborowski to Emanuele Modigliani after the death of his brother, the rare correspondence that testifies to the bond with Jeanne Hébuterne, including the marriage engagement and the certificates (from his birth in Leghorn to his death in Paris) which mark Amedeo's life all come from the Archives. The search for details related to Modì's life and our "detective's eye" allowed us to reread the sources from a fresh perspective. The investigation began with the text published by Jeanne Modigliani in various updated editions: *Modigliani racconta Modigliani*. A number of books were also fundamental: Aldo Santini, *Modigliani. Leghorn Parigi ultima Bohème*, Rizzoli, Milan 1987; Corrado Augias, *Modigliani, l' ultimo romantico*, Oscar Mondadori, Milan 1998; Meryle Secrest, *Modigliani, l'uomo e il mito*, Mondadori, Milan 2012; Enzo Maiolino, *Modigliani, dal vero. Testimonianze inedite e rare raccolte e annotate da Enzo Maiolino*, De Ferrari, Genova 2017.

Beatrice Hastings – English journalist, Amedeo's lover. She is the one who
introduces Amedeo to the use of drugs. Amedeo's years of rebellion
begin with Beatrice.

Paul Alexandre – doctor, friend, patron, passionate collector of art

Léopold Zborowski – Polish Jew, Modigliani's main merchant. He follows
Modigliani closely in the last years of his life: he will be behind the
first international successes of the Italian painter.

Pablo Picasso – Spanish painter, intellectual and a rival of Modigliani.

Guillaume Chéron – Modigliani's first merchant, described by friends as a
ruthless "tyrant". He was the first person to pay Amedeo to paint.

Paul Guillaume – French gallery owner and art collector.

Eugenia Garsin and Flaminio Modigliani – Amedeo's parents. Both
Sephardic Jews.

Isacco Garsin – Amedeo's maternal grandfather. He introduced Amedeo to
the study of philosophy and languages from an early age.

The last days of Amedeo and Jeanne

January 10, 1920. Place Denfert-Rochereau. It is a very cold and wet
night. It has been raining for hours. The Lion of Belfort, from the Bartholdi
monument that presides over the square, reigns impassively amid the
downpour and puddles. The dim light of the street lamps reveals the
outlines of a group of men who arrive out of breath. Many metres behind,
Amedeo shuffles along. He wanted to follow them to the home of their
mutual friend and designer Benito, but he could not keep up with the
others: he is too weak, his pace is unsteady. However, he seems almost
heedless of the water soaking him. He does not go into the house with
them. He stops, looks at the bronze lion and rails against the statue. He
talks to it, or he talks to someone who is not there. In fact, he is not really
there either. He is not himself; he has drunk himself senseless, once again,
to quell the pains that have been building up for days.

The others had invited him to enter the house, but in vain. They did not
even manage to convince him to at least take a taxi back to the two rooms

that he shares with Jeanne in rue de la Grande Chaumière, not far away. Nobody can convince him. He remains alone in the square in the company of the shadows and the ghosts in his mind. He wanders around the monument for a while. We do not know what thoughts overwhelm him. Probably memories: the blurred images of Leghorn, of Jeanne, of his daughter, and then terrible monsters that assail his mind; he vents his anger by throwing a few punches at the night. Memories emerge of his quarrels with Picasso, of the drinks with Utrillo, of the nights in the attic with Soutine singing Jewish songs along with the models, Dante's verses, the colours, the caresses of his mother, the sculptures and Brancusi, the numbers of the Kabbalah and Nostradamus.

Everything loses substance. Suddenly it seems to him that someone is yelling at him, that he is under attack, so he returns the punches blindly. But he falls under the blows that come from behind: on his kidneys, his ribs. They knock him down; they leave him breathless in the rain that he does not feel, in the frost of that Parisian January so different from the mild winter nights of his home town of Leghorn. Amedeo collapses against the door of Benito's apartment building. When his friends come down after a few hours, they find him yelling at a police officer, without fully understanding what has happened in the meantime. Emilio Lascano Tegui, who was there, will recall that evening as his last meeting with Modì. Eventually, the friends manage to persuade the gendarme to spare the poor man from spending yet another night in a cell for disturbing the peace. Amedeo cannot stand up on his own but he still rails against them, his own friends, calling them traitors. Then he sits on a bench near the church of Saint-Pierre de Montrouge, inviting the others to do the same. In his frenzy he believes he is standing on a pier, and speaks of a ghost ship, ready to sail. These hallucinations perhaps come to him from very far away in time and space, from when he discussed philosophy with his grandfather Isacco, in the late nineteenth century, strolling in the port of Leghorn between the rocks and the walkways by the sea. In the meantime, without knowing it, he received his most tragic legacy: paranoid neurosis.

He will not tell anyone if he was attacked that night, nor will he say what happened to him. Maybe he does not even realise what happened and he thinks it was just one of his usual nightmares, of his paranoid hallucinations. When asked about the severe illness that assails him he only replies that he "stumbled and fell while returning home", thus justifying the bruises and the pain. However, something terrible has happened, probably in those few hours in the rain, if not some days before: something that provoked a sudden deterioration of his health. Forty-eight hours after that terrible night he begins to feel unbearable pain in his kidneys. This is what Léopold Zborowski, poet and art merchant, will write in a letter to Emanuele Modigliani: "No one could foresee such an imminent tragedy: he had an appetite, he could walk and he was in a good mood, he never complained of any pain. Ten days before his death he took to his bed complaining of a severe ache in his kidneys. The doctor came and said it was nephritis."

On the easel, his last unfinished painting. That portrait of Mario Varvogli will remain unfinished. Below, the painter wrote a prophetic line: *Hic incipit vita nova* here begins a new life. The room is as messy as ever. Bottles scattered everywhere and a pile of rubbish, leftovers of food that Amedeo ate with paint-smeared hands. On that pallet which serves as bed, and despite his high fever, the painter amazes friends with his physical and mental endurance, and this seems at odds with the diagnosis after his death.

His condition gets rapidly worse. Another doctor, summoned by his friend Manuel Ortiz de Zárate when it was already too late, comes every day to check the bleeding, but in fact, he is preparing to certify his death.

"I only have a tiny piece of brain left; I know the end has come." This is how Modigliani takes leave from his love and from those few friends who are with him in his last hours. Then he loses consciousness. On January 22, he is taken to the Hôpital de la Charité. He slips into a coma on January 24, then, in the evening, "at 8.50, he passed away without suffering and without regaining consciousness", as Zborowski writes in the letter sent to the artist's brother Emanuele Modigliani. In reality, his sufferings had overwhelmed him. However, Zborowski wants to avoid further and unnecessary pain to the family. Even so, Zborowski, who had been close to him for years and had always supported him economically after the doctor Paul Alexandre had departed for the war, had taken his distance in those fateful days, excusing himself because of an alleged illness. On some occasions, Zborowski sent his wife to check on Modigliani, but perhaps his presence and his own intervention would have been crucial.

Jeanne had stayed close to her man for days. Heavily pregnant, she moved around with difficulty; she was due to give birth soon. She was paralysed by fear, unable to believe what was happening to him; she was unable to look after him but she always relied on him, even in his last few hours. Maybe too much, thus negating her own personality. Dazed by the pain of seeing him slowly fading away, too small compared to that big man, she did not have the strength to make him take care of himself, and she could not force him to live. Ortiz de Zárate returned from a trip and passed by to get news from them; he had to break down the door to enter the small apartment. He said he found them in a state of complete abandonment, "like two beings waiting together for death".

Perhaps it is death calling her. Two days after Amedeo's demise, she embraces her own end and, her mind probably dulled and racked by pain, decides to free herself from the enormous weight that her body had become. With a jump from fifteen meters, Jeanne takes her life and the life of the child that she was carrying at dawn, on January 26.

She was unable to accompany her man to the hospital, although the doctor wanted to take her in too, concerned as he was by her health conditions. She does not want to go. She stays home, pregnant and alone. On the morning of the 25th, she arrives at the Hôpital de la Charité on the arm of her father, Achille. The scene before her is dramatic and disturbing: Amedeo is rigid, cold and pale. His friend Moïse Kisling is trying to make a mortuary plaster mask from his face. He will report that, after a terrified cry, the woman bent down to kiss the lifeless body on the mouth, "with such passion as to overwhelm her, forcing her to back off". A few minutes later Jeanne leaves the room, walking backwards without ever taking her eyes from her beloved. She reaches her father at the door. All witnesses recall a woman who was from that moment detached from any emotion, apathetic, heedless to any words of comfort, isolated in her pain. Apparently calm and silent, she is actually already dead inside. That night she returns to her parents for the first time in many months, to that house she had left to go and live with Amedeo, her doomed lover. Her brother André does not leave her side until almost dawn. But, just before sunrise, from the window of her room, she surrenders to the emptiness she now has inside.

For several hours she took refuge in the heart wrenching memories of those two years spent with the most beloved, most envied, most admired and loneliest man in Montparnasse. She remembered their meeting at the Colarossi Academy, where Amedeo was teaching. Very talented and perhaps with some ambition, she fell under the spell of the bewitching expression and seductive manner of the Italian. For her that meeting froze time. For him, she challenged the social conventions of the Parisian Catholic middle class. Her father, an accountant, certainly did not see Modigliani as a good match for his daughter. His reputation as a womaniser and as a rebellious, unreliable, excessive Jew made him a man that any respectable family girl should avoid. Jeanne was only nineteen when she met him; she turned twenty-one when she killed herself. In three years, she threw her life away for a lover who was already thirty-three when they met.

For Amedeo the woman was his muse, but also the illusion of a family, the welcoming and stable love around which he could rebuild himself as a new man, a new artist. From 1917 to his death, Modigliani's genius excelled, both in quality and in the number of art works he produced. He finally found his style and his way of expression. Scenes, snapshots of a life that perhaps flow through Jeanne's mind moments before she crashes into the courtyard of the building on rue Amyot. An epilogue worthy of a Greek tragedy.

But the drama did not end there. According to Chantal Quenneville, a friend from the Colarossi Academy who went to clean up the apartment in rue de la Grande Chaumière after the death of the couple, Jeanne had already considered suicide. "I found drawings in which Jeanne portrayed herself in the act of stabbing herself in the chest with a long blade."

Moreover, Chantal recalled the events in the hours following the tragedy. André, in order to spare their mother from the sight of his sister's ravaged body, initially told her that she was only injured and that she was at the hospital. In fact, he asked a worker to load her onto a wheelbarrow and to take her body to the apartment where she lived with Amedeo. The story she told got increasingly grim. When the worker arrives at his destination, he is stopped by the concierge - it is the painter who rented the apartment; that woman is not his wife and officially she does not live in the building.

The worker feels pity for that poor disfigured body which nobody wants, and goes to the Police Station to say what has happened. Only after the intervention of the police does the concierge allow Jeanne's body to be laid on the bed she had shared with her lover. Chantal arrives at the apartment with another friend, Jeannette Léger. "Jeannette went to the hospital to find a nurse to help her dress the body while I was left alone in front of that terrible scene," Quenneville would write. "Her head, white and strewn with green spots, still bore traces of that life she had heroically given up. She had had a baby from Modigliani and she was expecting another one: her belly emerged from the tattered blanket. One leg seemed to have been broken in the fall."

There was no mention of visits by family members. No flowers from the parents. Not even André, with whom Jeanne was very close, would visit her for the last time. They are only concerned with limiting the scandal. The body is wrapped in a Russian tablecloth donated by Marie Vassilieff. Two of Amedeo's friends, one of them Wacław Zawadowski (or Zawado to his friends), will stay and watch over her for the night.

The day after, on January 27, the city is preparing to celebrate the funeral of Modigliani in grand style. The hearse, pulled by horses, crosses Montparnasse, many people look on, come out of their gates, fall silent and take off their hats as a sign of respect. The parade of Parisian artists, including Picasso, follow the procession as one, mourning the most generous of them all.

Modì would have never imagined being the lead player in such a grandiose ceremony. His friend Kisling collected the money to pay for that solemn funeral. The Modigliani family was unable to send the money from Leghorn in time. His brother Emanuele, despite being a senator, would get a passport to leave Italy only a month later. Once in Paris, he would return the money to everyone, right up to the last cent. He will thank the communities of Montparnasse and Montmartre for their heartfelt tribute to Amedeo Clemente.

The crowd that swelled behind the coffin included some unscrupulous speculators. Like carrion birds, they were preparing to snap up anything on offer from the artist's acquaintances and friends, offering thousands of francs for works they had not wanted to buy for just a few dozen francs the day before.

The next day a nondescript van retraces those same streets with Jeanne's body. This time only her closest friends along with their spouses and her classmates take part in the almost clandestine ceremony. Some taxis slowly follow behind the scant procession. The parents and the brother of the suicide hide inside in the shadows. For her, no flowers, no visible pain.

The artists who witnessed the love story between Amedeo and Jeanne want to reunite them in the cemetery of Père-Lachaise, where Modigliani was buried the day before. Nevertheless, there is no chance of that: the relatives want to condemn her to loneliness and to oblivion even in death, placing her in an anonymous corner of the Parisian cemetery of Bagneux.[4] A few years later, thanks to Emanuele Modigliani's persistence, the two lovers will find a common burial ground.

Today, on a grey stone slab, a landmark where lovers lay their tributes, can be seen, written in Italian:

AMEDEO MODIGLIANI
PAINTER
BORN IN LEGHORN ON JULY 12, 1884
DIED IN PARIS ON JANUARY 24, 1920
DEATH TOOK HIM
WHEN HE ATTAINED GLORY
JEANNE HEBUTERNE
BORN IN PARIS ON APRIL 6, 1898
DIED IN PARIS ON JANUARY 25,[5] 1920
DEVOTED COMPANION
OF AMEDEO MODIGLIANI
UNTIL HER ULTIMATE SACRIFICE

---

[4] Translator's note: While Jeanne's Catholic family was likely hostile towards Modigliani, who was a Jew, it should also be noted that the Catholic Church refused burial on consecrated ground to murderers (Jeanne had killed her unborn child) and especially to suicides, as the latter would have no chance to repent and hence to be redeemed. Emanuele may have ultimately received some sort of dispensation which allowed Amedeo and Jeanne to share a common burial ground.

[5] The gravestone shows the date of the 25th because the recollection of events placed Jeanne's death before midnight. Later her death was adjudged to have occurred at the dawn of the 26th.

The "Ultimate Sacrifice"

The ultimate sacrifice was not her death by suicide, but her life itself. Amongst Modigliani's significant relationships, the one with Jeanne was certainly the most complete, the one that expressed all the shades of his palette, right up to the black of mourning. But what was Amedeo for her? Certainly her great love, but also her obsession.

Although she was very young and she came from a conservative family, at the age of nineteen Jeanne had already had relationships with other men, such as the Japanese Tsuguharu Foujita, a painter and a friend of Amedeo. She had also been his model. Her friends describe her as shy but firm and resolute. She must have been a determined woman in order to resist to Amedeo's dynamic, tender but also fickle temper. She was tiny, graceful, with slender legs and lithe body. She had a loyal and passionate look, the look of a sweet, newly blossomed girl. This is how her classmates at the Colarossi Academy will remember her.

Jeanne wanted to be a painter just like her brother André and that is why she studies and spends time with the artists of Montparnasse. Falling in love with Amedeo, who is not only dirt poor, but Jewish to boot, means cutting her ties with the rest of her world. She decides to dedicate herself to him unconditionally, no regrets. Emancipation for French women, unlike the English, is still a mirage. Though she yet hopes for marriage, Jeanne breaks society's rules and goes against everything and everyone. Being a model, posing naked, dancing can-can at Moulin Rouge means being a "whore", indecent. However, the confinements of gender do not concern artists, who instead find in freedom, cultural change and rebellion their purpose in life.

The personality of the young girl changes abruptly from her very first meeting with her "damned" lover. The price she pays is enormous. The estrangement from her family will be permanent. Things will not change even with the birth of little Jeanne, the daughter born from sin, who the maternal grandparents will not want to take in even after the death of her parents.

Amedeo becomes her only reference point, her obsession. Modigliani has a complex and cumbersome personality which is entirely his own. She gives herself over completely to him, not without suffering over his girlfriends and his models, his drinking, his attitude to squandering the little money he earns and his boundless pride. Over the years, she must have developed a serious form of depression, exacerbated by her two pregnancies which were clearly unwanted and too close to each other. The first birth, in the November 1918, certainly increased her mental discomfort, very likely because of what is now known as postnatal depression.

Jeanne Modigliani was born in Nice, where her mother had gone in the company of her grandmother Eudoxie, who seems to be open to a reconciliation. Modì joined her to recover from the umpteenth relapse of his tuberculosis. The months spent in the South of France give new serenity to the small family: the child, however, is immediately entrusted to a Calabrian nurse. Modi recovers, the sea air helps, and now begins his most intense and accomplished period of production. There are a few extra francs to spend in the house.

But the relationships between the lovers is perhaps strained, also because of the continuous quarrels between Amedeo and his lover's mother, who despises him. It may even be possible to think that the young muse started to see the new-born baby as an obstacle: a sort of sentimental barrier that stands between her and her man. This may explain why she does not take care of her daughter from the beginning. When, a few months later, she discovers that she is pregnant again, her compulsive thoughts will become more serious. As she approaches death she does not think at all of the baby she is carrying in her womb and perhaps, if she had had custody of the eldest child, she would not have hesitated to take her first born, too, with her in the depths of her despair.

It is a pain that the surviving daughter, Jeanne Modigliani, will in her turn transform into resentment. So much so that she never referred to her as "mother", recalling her only in the third person and nursing throughout her life a never-healed rift with the woman who bore her, and with her mother's family.

The painter understood that great love of his life, and tried to protect it however he could. But he did not understand that the only person from whom he could not have saved her was himself, Amedeo Clemente Modigliani, aka Modì. Nor did he want her psychological subjugation, this was rather something she herself sought, or perhaps it was the only way she could conceive of being with that man, a man you had to take or you leave as he was. After all Modigliani was a Jew and an Italian, and society at the turn of the century offered few other options.

A model wife had to stand two steps behind her husband. Anselmo Bucci, a painter friend of the couple, tells of one evening at dinner:

> *The bride joined us there; and he, eating very little like all alcoholics, never ceased to caress her, to question her, to take care of her in an almost ostentatious manner. And we left, well-refreshed naturally, for the Rotonde.*
>
> *In the middle of the Raspail-Montparnasse intersection, he parted ways with his wife, embracing and kissing her with affection, continuing to wave goodbye from afar. And perceiving my surprise, he explained to me: "We two go to the Cafe. My wife goes home. The Italian way. This is how we do things."*

Jeanne felt she was Amedeo's wife and he treated her as such. "I am Mrs. Modigliani" she would introduce herself to the Italian friends who knocked at the door of their house.

There is only one sketch of her naked. It was used for the poster of the first personal exhibition that Modi held at the Berthe Weill gallery in December 1917. But she certainly inspired him, with her long white neck and auburn hair, her pregnancies and her soft curves, to give a colour to expressions, to give soul to those colours, to those piercing eyes, almost devoid of an iris which often appear in the faces of the artist's portraits.

But then with her silences, her sadness, her resignation, her speechless presence, despite or precisely because of her great love, Jeanne takes on the consistency of a burden, a responsibility that Modigliani wants, but which at the same time weighs on him in his life as an émigré. The woman returns to Paris accompanied by her mother and her little daughter at the end of June 1919; she is pregnant again. The Hébuterne family is exasperated: they must fix that umpteenth scandal.

Modigliani had already returned to the capital months before and is doing well, "He doesn't drink, he doesn't overindulge, he seems to have found a new balance," says his friend Lunia Czechowska, with whom he spent the summer walking in the Jardin du Luxembourg and who is one of his favourite models in that period. However, the new pregnancy is a problem for him too. With the return of the family from Nice, that magical and carefree moment, marked by his moderation and his philosophical reflections with Lunia, ends and gives way to his looming responsibilities. When Amedeo drinks, it is not to go wild, but to numb the increasingly acute physical pain, as well as his psychological torments. Vice does not dominate him; it is fear that rules him.

Perhaps his partner feels this same anguish too. She had suddenly told him she was coming back from Nice. Jeanne had just found out she was expecting another child and she probably longed to share the news with her partner. Nevertheless, the pregnancy also provoked her anxiety, knowing that Amedeo was alone in Paris, highly susceptible to feminine charm and always in the company of Lunia. Meanwhile, the Hébuterne family was pushing for him to make a commitment, to take responsibility through a "reparatory marriage". Maybe Jeanne is fed up with that situation which isolates her from everything and everyone.

Already in Nice Amedeo had left her alone with her mother, because he could no longer bear the constant arguments with his "mother-in-law". He had rented a room in a small hotel away from his family, later even moving to Cagnes-sur-Mer. A few weeks after the birth of his daughter, Amedeo left them. When in those months he writes to his mother, Eugenia Garsin, to thank her for the love shown to his child born "out of legitimate wedlock", he does not spare a word for his companion. A picture that may indicate a possible crisis between the couple. In consideration of this overall situation, it is no surprise that she wanted something more on her return.

"I am committed, today July 7 1919, to marrying Miss Jane [sic] Hébuterne as soon as the documents are ready. Amedeo Modigliani." This is the promise, the solemn commitment that Amedeo seals in front of his friends, opening a new perspective in the mind of the young mother. She hopes that the consolidation of a family union would shelter her in the not unlikely event of the death of the man she loves (she is among the very few, perhaps the only one, to know about the true health conditions of her loved one). She and her children will be able have social recognition.

However, that wedding will be never celebrated. Who knows if Amedeo had asked his family in Leghorn to prepare the necessary documents? Not only they will not be delivered to Paris, but his mother Eugenia, who meticulously writes down everything in her diary, never even mentions such a request. Maybe he forgot about it, as he had forgotten before to register the birth of his daughter Jeanne, whom he also wanted to acknowledge, at the registry office. His partner's hopes of getting to the altar, which would also reconcile her with her family, soon fade. This is when that bewildering aspect of her personality takes over: inertia, apathy or inability to take decisions, to do at least something as Amedeo's health gets worse.

"You remember, Pablo, that day when I came to your place and you painted a portrait of me? You wanted to make me immortal that evening, I do not know if you will succeed, but I know that only Modigliani has been able to portray my soul. Nobody else has ever succeeded; my soul belongs to him." This is what, in her delirium just a few hours before taking her own life, Jeanne is said to have told Picasso when he asked how she was feeling.

The most elegant man in Paris

"I can only admit it: that Italian knows how to dress!" Pablo Picasso is at a table at the Rotonde when he sees Amedeo Clemente arriving with his flamboyant manner and the air of defiance that he shows off with his best smile every time he meets the Spaniard.

"He always wore corduroy trousers, a plaid shirt and a red waistband, like a labourer. His thick hair was always matted." This is how Foujita describes him.

And Paul Guillaume, one of the first authors to describe Modigliani as an artist in an essay published in 1920 in "Les Arts à Paris" and one of the first dealers in his works, reaffirms: "Even in his strange way of dressing like a ragamuffin, he possessed an undoubted elegance, a surprising and sometimes alarming quality."

In that Paris, where schools of thought and art were born, Modigliani could not be pigeonholed, nor did he want to be linked to any art movement. He only wanted to be Modì. He broke the rational and conservative norms of his time, even at the risk of seeming arrogant and presumptuous. He emerged from a body of Leghorn artists who lacked the courage to measure themselves against the outside world: his old colleagues preferred to compete with each other in a small but reassuring cocoon. Amedeo conversely wanted to test himself in the city that in that moment was the centre of the world.

In leaving Leghorn, he became a heretic for the Macchiaioli, so devoted to their master Giovanni Fattori, and he certainly had no intention of arriving in Paris to end up in Picasso's court. The great Andalusian painter represented the alpha male of the French intellectual community, the undisputed and unreachable ruler of the art scene in those years. Modigliani is aware of the greatness of his rival, because he is a rival, and he intends to challenge him, but not to take his place. He is not interested in taking Picasso's crown. He rather wants to affirm his psychological and artistic independence.

It is actually Picasso who fears him, misunderstanding his anarchic nature. He however respects the Italian and his heroism in the search for his own limits; he respects Modigliani's spiritual preparation and his refined culture. Maybe he is even a bit envious of the attraction, greater than his own, that Amedeo has for the opposite sex, and not only them. He admires the pride and the aristocratic grace that Modigliani maintains despite his abject poverty. With a pinch of superciliousness, Picasso invites him many times to visit his studio, and with every refusal, he cannot help feeling embarrassed in the face of such dignity.

Modigliani, for his part, admires the intelligence of the Spaniard, his expressive ability and his artistic gymnastics, even if he sometimes is wary of them, considering them excessively intellectual. But he does not appreciate Picasso as a man, and keeps his distance.

There is however a clear common trait between the two rivals, the metaphysical place where they meet and clash: sexuality and their resulting vision of the feminine body. They fall in love easily. In the wake of such feeling, the great transport and turmoil of the soul, they start afresh with ever-changing impetus; they reach new discoveries, both personal and external. They are both aware of this, enough to articulate it in scathing lines that will remain in the history of those years and that convey their erotic dream wonderfully.

"The future of art resides in the face of a woman ... Picasso, how do you make love made with a cube?" This is how the passionate and at times playfully ironic Italian provoked his rival in 1919, challenging him to present himself at the Salon des Artistes with his virile, pragmatic, geometric impact.

"I do try to understand. I try, for example to put myself in the place of a chap who has been painting the same picture for years and years. It is a problem that torments me. What can he be thinking of? He must be bored to death!" Picasso in his turn joked, being careful not to refer directly to Modigliani because he never wanted to comment explicitly on his works or his art. The Andalusian was keen to point out that Amedeo always painted the same nudes, all alike, in a continuous search for a perfect balance between colour, sensuality, love and poetry.

The Leghorn painter is well aware that in order to prevail, he must choose his battles: if he stayed on that ground, the ground of reason, of straight lines and of precise angles, he would only attain a place alongside countless others in the flock of lackeys that surrounded his rival. Instead, he brings his philosophical, abstract heritage, his exaggerated sensitivity with an uncommon knack for introspection. "To draw is to possess, a deeper and more concrete act of knowledge and of possession than sexual intercourse, which only dreams or death can bestow." Osvaldo Licini, an artist from Italy's Marches region who was often in Modigliani's company in France, recalls the words the artist used to describe his creative drive.

There were many rumours about the bitterness between the two artistic giants that criss-crossed the narrow streets of Montparnasse and Montmartre. Stories that they themselves fed when they met each other in cafes and restaurants. "I'm Modigliani, I'm Italian and I'm Jewish!" this was his provocative opening gambit each time. With bitter sarcasm, his adversary invited him to be less boastful, and on one occasion, they almost came to blows. One evening, however, Modigliani took Picasso by the collar of the jacket, tightening his grip and pushing him against a wall: the Spaniard had called him "Jew" in an implicitly derogatory manner. Violence accompanied by a warning: "Don't do it ever again". Picasso understood the threat was for real, and did not repeat the slur.

But Modì did not forget. In the ups and downs of the lives of the artists the wheel of fortune sometimes turns quickly. It is said in fact that when Amedeo still had some money in his pocket, when he had just arrived in the French capital, he had met a penniless Picasso and had given him five francs so that he could eat. A few years later and the Spaniard is living in great comfort, while life is increasingly difficult for the Tuscan. Picasso visits him, gives him 100 francs and when leaving says to him: "I have come to give you back the money you lent me". The other, following him, responds with a clear reference to the past offence: "Do not expect the change; I have to remember that I'm a Jew!".

A dialectical duel that the Montparnasse artists could neither ignore nor forget, often at the tip of a paintbrush, but which sometimes risked getting physical. Pablo Picasso never compared himself with his friends in Montmartre; his narcissism placed him above everyone. It is said that the Spaniard presented himself at an art exhibition with portrait of Jeanne Hébuterne; it had been painted without Amedeo knowing about it. Legend has it that Amedeo destroyed it as soon as he saw it, under the terrified and yet hostile gaze of the author.

Shortly after revenge is served. A billboard hangs at the Salon d'Automne. Who wants to take part in the painting competition should add his name. The prize is 5000 francs. Neither Modì nor Picasso usually take part in such competitions, but this time they do. Thus begins the challenge that will remain in the annals of art history, one which continues to this day in the art auctions of the world's most important art houses, from London to New York.

It is a cold late November night in 1919, Modigliani only has two months left of his tormented yet majestic existence. The art contest judge announces the top six classified. Soutine is in sixth place. Rivera is fifth. Kisling is fourth. Utrillo is third. The second place, surprisingly, goes to the canvas painted by Picasso: a splendid tribute to that Italian who is as foolish as he is charming. Amedeo is portrayed with as many edges as there are in the roughness of his personality. At this point the auctioneer raises the sheet that reveals the name of the winner: Modigliani, with the masterpiece that will for the last time immortalise Jeanne and her tormented soul.

It is the chance of a lifetime. But he is not there at the award ceremony. In the front, row Jeanne sits alone. And where is the prize winner? In the street, the victim of a group of thugs who attacked him to take away the money he bragged about, without yet having it in his pocket. Someone, moreover, claims that his enemies sent the thugs: the in-laws? Picasso? Or some betrayed husband? Even the film director Mick Davis, in the 2004 film *The Colours of the Soul*, wanted to offer his own opinion. He puts the death of the Italian painter in the context of his bitter rivalry with the great Spaniard. Our own conclusion is that a number of people who had good reason to hate him may have been behind the would-be assassins.

Happiness is an angel with a stern face

"Happiness is an angel with a stern face," Modigliani wrote in 1913 in a postcard to Paul Alexandre. Amedeo looks for the stern face of that angel in the features of a dark-haired girl, white complexion, deep green eyes and long braids flowing across her chest. A talented painter full of hopes when she met him, a ghost of herself when he gives her his last farewell on his deathbed. In between, three years of a troubled love story and two children.

By a strange twist of fate, Modigliani's name will forever be bound to his last love, Jeanne, and he will seal his greatness in those three final years of his life spent with her. With her and perhaps because of her, he found his unique place in the art universe. It was to her that the last chance fell to save him from himself. But it was for nought.

Amedeo had always frequented many women: intellectuals, models, high-society women. The curly "head of Antinoo" and his dark eyes, his kindness, elegance and nobility of manners, but also his sheer brazenness, made his charm irresistible. The "prince of Montparnasse" comes through those love affairs carrying heavy burdens: drug abuse, alcohol, and the violence of tumultuous relationships, an unruly life, and a child which he does not wish to acknowledge from a woman who he does not love, along with canvases in which his style is still uncertain. He has yet to find himself, or has only partially done so, and gives vent to his rebellious character and his deepest contradictions, while casting aside his values.

In order to understand why Modigliani chooses Jeanne Hébuterne or, better, why events lead him to choose her, it is necessary to retrace some steps that punctuate his development. First of all the affectionate and constant attachment to his mother Eugenia. Despite his revolutionary, heretical and subversive spirit, Dedo nonetheless remains very attached to his origins. Other important figures from his mother's side of the family, such as his grandfather Isaac Garsin, his uncle Giuseppe and especially Aunt Laura, help that talented child slowly develop into a man who, contrary to what may emerge from a superficial character analysis, is well aware of the importance of the role of the family.

The English artist Christopher Nevinson, who shared a studio with Modi for a period, says, "He was a quiet man with fascinating manners [...]. Modigliani should have been a family man. He was kind, assiduous, correct and thoughtful: a bourgeois Jew [...]. Women seemed to instinctively know that they were in the presence of a great man, albeit a poor one."

His Jewish heritage, cultural rather than religious, also helped develop within him the psychological importance of procreation as a continuation of the family lineage. The warm and welcoming fireplace where he comes from forms in the young Amedeo Clemente the belief that home is always, and in all ways, a place where he can return when he needs rest and peace. And at a certain moment in Paris, and quite unexpectedly, it is peace he will need: a domestic serenity that becomes his new fulcrum.

For this to happen, however, the chosen woman must be devoted, prepared to give herself to him completely. At the time this feminine trait is not at all rare, indeed, it is common. The women of that generation know how to carve out spaces that are tiny but at the same time immense, becoming a vital reference point for the growth of offspring and for the economy of the nuclear family. A man like Modigliani is rather rare indeed. He is so particular as to demand not only devotion, but also a heroic kind of love verging on martyrdom, because the artist from Leghorn himself feeds on suffering and self-punishment.

In meeting Jeanne, the two conflicting souls within him find peace. Amedeo takes possession of first the emerald green eyes, then the soul of the young woman. From the first moment, her own needs and personality are subsumed into his.

However, Modigliani's gaze in those years was not focused only on Jeanne. In 1917, perhaps simultaneously with the blossoming of the love with his muse, he keeps up a relationship from which a male child is born. Simone Thiroux. This is the name of the woman who begs him to acknowledge the child only a few days before the tragic passing of the painter. For her never even a letter, nor a word of comfort.

Just a year earlier, in 1916, the most elegant and lonely man of Montparnasse had crossed the path of the young Polish woman who would remain an enigma for his friends and for those who remember him. Maybe he imagined he could find his muse in her, too. Lunia Czechowska, will after many years recall that day at the Rotonde in her memoirs. "It was mutual love at first sight". He wandered through the avenues with his pencils and notebook always in hand. He was looking for subjects who could embody his ideal.

His attention was directed almost exclusively to women, all different, each with their own particular beauty. It was this way before Jeanne, but also during their relationship.

Lunia is only twenty-two when she meets Amedeo; she is twenty-six when he dies. Four years of an intense and mysterious relationship, with great understanding and complicity, perhaps only a platonic love or maybe even a love never-confessed. There are ten portraits of Lunia painted by Modigliani, as well as numerous drawings. Like Jeanne, there are no nudes of Lunia. Right behind one portrait of the young Polish woman the painter writes one of his most famous and most cryptic messages: "Life is a gift / of the few to the many / of those who know and have / to those who do not know and do not have".

Their walks in the Jardin du Luxembourg and their summer night conversations that lasted through to dawn are well-known. In the meantime, his "wife" is still in Nice and already expecting their second child.

It was complicity made of dreams and hopes. When he joins Lunia he is never high, when they are together he does not drink nor takes or drugs, he takes more care of himself. With her he does not talk about painting, he talks about his desire to return to Italy, to be close to his mother, to improve his health conditions, to raise his daughter in Leghorn. Lunia is not in Paris when Modigliani dies. She also suffers from tuberculosis and had decided to spend that winter on the French Riviera, near the sea. For many months, nobody will have the heart to tell her of his death. Their mutual friend Zborowski will explain Amedeo's silence by telling her that he has returned to Leghorn.

But later she will say that when she received the news, it was only a confirmation. "I had a strange dream. I was in the spa park from which I had recently returned. It was autumn and the meadows were covered with a carpet of chestnut leaves. I was walking slowly with Amedeo. There was no one around. Modigliani had something in his hand that looked like a magazine. Suddenly he opened it and said, "Look here, Lunia. They say I'm dead. Don't you think they are exaggerating? I'm not dead. You can see that too." In that moment Lunia noticed Jeanne Hébuterne coming towards them, with a very sad look, and she said: "There is Jeanne. Let's call her". Modigliani stopped her: "No, no. In a moment." But Lunia was so happy to see her that she called to her. Then she woke up. "When they told me what had happened, and how, I understood everything."

It was July 1985 when the brothers Giorgio and Guido Guastalla, art gallery owners from Leghorn, rang at the door of a modest apartment in

Nice, on the top floor of an austere building. The writer Aldo Santini was with them. A ninety-two year old lady, still bright and neat-looking welcomed them. On her face, you could see the features of an ancient beauty. Lunia was the only living person to witness to the completion of nearly all the paintings of Amedeo, and yet she did not own any of them. Her pension was her only means of support and perhaps she had accepted that interview to raise some money. "She showed me an invoice of the upholsterer. She had to redo the curtains and she didn't have the money to pay for it," Guido Guastalla told us. "We paid for it." "Her eyes lit up as with the brightness of youth," Aldo Santini wrote in the interview. "She says Modigliani in the Italian way, without the emphasis on the final i."

> *I wasn't a model and I never posed naked for him nor for other painters. I belonged to the circle of his best friends. And for the portraits, that's the difference, he only used his friends, they didn't cost him anything and he knew them well. Because Modigliani tried to portray not only our faces, but also our characters, what we had inside our hearts, in our souls. We must understand this to enter his poetic world.*
>
> *I had arrived in Paris in 1914 with a couple of friends from Warsaw, then I had met my husband, a compatriot, and we got married in France. It was June 1916 when I met Modigliani. Zborowski took us to his exhibition. He introduced us at the Rotonde. My husband was on leave because in the meantime he had enlisted... His (Modigliani's) face, despite the regularity of his features, was not remarkable. His hands, however, were very beautiful. I was fascinated by his distinct manner and by his eyes. He was very simple and at the same time, you know, very noble. A man unlike anyone I knew. He sat down next to me and wanted to draw immediately... He invited me to have dinner with him. I said I was with my husband: but that made no impression on him at all. He insisted... Then he asked me to pose for him the next day.*

Modigliani does not notice that the beautiful girl sitting at the table of the cafe is in the company of her husband. When they introduce him, Amedeo almost shows irritation, but he continues to trace the graphite lines of his drawing. He finishes it, signs it, which he never does, gets up and gives it to her. For him, she is no longer a stranger, even if they have only just met. The passionate looks that they exchange bind them as if they had spent a lifetime together. Their first date is in the apartment that Zborowski

occupies in the boulevard de Port-Royal. A painting that Lunia remembers
with these words:

> *For him I was the ideal woman, I only understood it later. He lit a*
> *cigarette. He poured himself some grappa, keeping the bottle nearby.*
> *Apart from those simple gestures, I did not understand anything he*
> *said. He spoke to himself in Italian. I learned at the next day's sitting*
> *that he was quoting verses of the Divine Comedy. For three*
> *afternoons, I had to listen to Dante Alighieri's verses. And he*
> *continued to drink the grappa that Zbó put for him on the table [...].*
> *He drank but he was not an alcoholic nor was he a drug addict. The*
> *cursed legend of Modigliani the drug addict is totally invented [...].*
> *In the long period in which I frequented him, from 1916 until 1919,*
> *just before he died, I never saw him under the influence of drugs, and*
> *he drank periodically, preferably red wine. Whoever says that*
> *Modigliani found inspiration in alcohol is writing poor literature.*
> *Modigliani drank because he was in bad health, because he was*
> *unsuccessful, because he was always broke; but he had the education*
> *of a real gentleman. The wine helped him forget his troubles.*

That first portrait of Lunia is now kept in the Musée de Grenoble. The
canvas conserves a fragment of Amedeo's fatalistic character. For him all
events are the result of an inevitable force. Fate is fate; it is useless to try to
change its course, like illness. As he removes the canvas from the easel, it
falls on the ground and a match remains attached to the colour. He does not
remove it. Fate has wished it so.

Amedeo's respect and Lunia's discretion will take to their graves the
secret of their love. She is, like Jeanne, a woman of her time, but
conversely, she does not challenge convention. She is already married
when she meets the painter. When she loses her husband in the war,
Amedeo is now tied to Jeanne and her womb. Modigliani is sure of that
love, he knows he can trust it. And if Jeanne is jealous of Lunia, the latter
does not hide what she thinks of the other. "I couldn't do much, since he
had a wife," she says years later in a conversation with the art critic and
great Modigliani expert Ambrogio Ceroni. "My principles, not those of the
bourgeoisie but simple honest morality towards another woman, prevented
me from interfering." She suggests that Jeanne should have done more and
better to take care of her man. Modi entrusts the little Jeanne, "Modigliani's

joy", to Lunia herself when he realises he can't count on her natural mother when she returned from Nice, unreliable and psychologically unstable.

Beatrice Hastings certainly did not look like an angel; she rather looked like a pagan goddess. Amedeo met her in 1914 and fell madly in love with her. Journalist, writer, poet, correspondent from Paris for an English newspaper, she was a woman not bound by the austere hypocrisy of the Victorian age. With her, it was a meeting of minds on equal terms. A talented person with unscrupulous charm, she was also famous for her several lovers. Her real name, which few knew, was Emily Alice Haigh, and she was five years older than the Leghorn painter. "Beautiful, refined, rich, she enjoyed showing off far-fetched English hats," the artist Foujita writes "and carrying on her arm a basket with live, quacking ducks inside."

Their tumultuous relationship lasted two years and in that time, they were inseparable. There are about ten oil portraits and countless drawings that depict her. Despite her being a writer and a journalist who told England about Paris in those years, she rarely mentioned him among the "emerging" painters.

The Great War was underway and Modigliani still wanted to be a sculptor. The meeting changed him forever. "In 1916 the relationship with Beatrice became increasingly tumultuous," Jeanne Modigliani wrote in her book *Modigliani, my father*. "In the meantime, his physical condition gets worse, in a moment of great creative and emotional tension." It is the English woman who describes Amedeo's "angry outburst" when she refused to return one of his sculptures that he had entrusted to her at the beginning of their relationship. "I was treated like an idiot; nothing human is missing from this stone, except for malice [...]. They tell me that it was incomplete, that it will never be compete, that it is not worth finishing it [...]. But I will never part with it."

Many of their friends at that time tell of their frequent quarrels, of the reciprocal violence in the apartment where he went to stay with her in rue du Montparnasse. There were many insults and theatrical gestures even in public, at the Rotonde. André Salmon recounts that when their relationship was coming to an end Modigliani, under the effect of drugs, almost destroyed the house where she had taken refuge in Montmartre, trying to get in. On another occasion, he describes her shouting from the window: "Help, murder!" accusing her lover of wanting to throw her from the window in a drunken rage. Modì was a jealous man, and she often flirted with other men, sometimes just to provoke him. As he himself would have told Lunia a few years later, Beatrice introduced him to the use of drugs.

During this relationship, Amedeo often used to meet Max Jacob, also a Jew (but converted to Catholicism); he was into the occult and astrological traditions. The Italian brushed up on his Jewish roots as he approached the study of Kabbalah and esotericism. These were his last years of sculpture. The caryatids and the primitive heads were often the products of these journeys "into the mysteries". Beatrice was well versed in these areas, so much so that between 1920 and 1925 Harry Price, a famous parapsychologist and scholar, defined her a remarkable medium.

Amedeo also started drinking during the period he was with her, perhaps to hide the worsening of his health conditions and to soothe the severe pains that afflicted him. In the life of Modigliani, Beatrice even came to represent a new way of expressing his challenge to Picasso. The excesses of a wild, essential and destructive existence would have allowed him to do battle in the amphitheatre of art, on ground the Andalusian could not reach.

She will be returning to England soon, she will be working as a newspaper editor, she will write books and she will be a politically committed woman. On October 14, 1943, she turned at the British Museum to offer all her notes, including those that would have clarified her relationship with Modigliani. But they were rejected. Shortly after, she decides to commit suicide with gas along with her pet white mouse. The corpse is found on October 31. In her home, however, there is no trace of her manuscripts.

She never officially recognised Modigliani as an artist; her interest in him was as a man. Despite this, with her lofty relationships in the intellectual world of both Paris and London, she created the basis for Amedeo to be appreciated and known. Modi's redemption would in fact have its roots in England, a few years later.

Theirs was a Bacchanalian and extreme relationship in which all the characteristics of the ancient "mysteries" appear: the alteration of their state of consciousness through wine and drugs, excesses in sexuality and relations with the afterlife. The Modigliani who returns from that "journey" has broken through his earlier limitations.

Beatrice's revolutionary, crazy, unfaithful, physical, violent and sensual passion. Lunia's presence, confidentiality, confidence, ability to listen and to be there for him. Jeanne's devotion, self-denial, sacrifice, and tolerance. Even all together, these women, with all their talents and flaws, never managed to attain the greatness and the power of the female model that Amedeo saw represented by Eugenia Garsin, his mother. Maybe it was her face that most resembled the angel in his imagination.

The uniqueness of the bond with his mother is immediately visible. He is the youngest of the four children of Eugenia and Flaminio. His birth is practically a herald of destiny: the wealth of the family vanishes at the same time as he comes into the world. The bankruptcy of his father's mining company in Sardinia plunges the Modigliani family into poverty. From that moment, it will be his mother, with her temperament, her culture and her position, who ensures the survival of the family.

Amedeo opens his eyes in the only bed left in the house in via Roma. Servants and family members had hurriedly collected all that remained of value at the bedside of the woman giving birth. The judicial officers, accompanied by law enforcement, knock at the door. But a royal law prevents the debt collectors from demanding what is kept on the bed of a woman in labour. Despite the difficulties, thanks to her and to the Garsins even the little Amedeo receives an upbringing and education worthy of his heritage.

Eugenia married her husband in 1872 after two years of engagement. She had accepted the marriage passively. She was amazed at the luxurious atmosphere that reigned in the house in via Roma. Very big, full of servants, the table always laden with opulent meals for an infinite number of relatives and friends. The Modiglianis, strictly observant Jews, appeared to Eugenia as uncultured, presumptuous and authoritarian. Flaminio was more often in Sardinia than in Leghorn, at least until the bankruptcy in 1884. The direct influence on Dedo of the head of the household was minimal and exclusively negative. In nine years the Modiglianis had four children: Emanuele, who later became a Socialist senator; Margherita, who acted as foster mother to Jeanne; Umberto, an engineer; and their last-born, Amedeo.

Eugenia passed on to her son a curiosity for the visible world, but also for the occult and superstition: on the back of a drawing of a *Nude with raised arm*, he will transcribe a prophecy of Nostradamus.

It is not difficult to identify evidence of mental disorder in all the Garsin-Modigliani family. The neurotic grandfather Isaac moved to Leghorn when his daughter was pregnant with Margherita. He and little Amedeo were inseparable companions until his death. He was a man of medium stature and elegant, with lively gestures; his physical appearance and his personality echoed in his grandson. He was a bookworm; he was particularly fond of history and philosophy. He had travelled to Belgium, he spoke fluent Italian, French, Spanish and Greek; he also spoke some English and Arabic. He used to go for long walks with Dedo; they also played chess and enjoyed pleasant conversations.

Isaac had been a banker. Upset by the death of his wife, he had become a violent man who raged frequently when his business, which stretched between London and Tunis, had failed. He had got so angry that his children, associates and relatives spoke of "madness" and they sent him to his daughter Eugenia. His delusions and his persecution complex also affected his daughter Laura and, in a milder way, his granddaughter Margherita.

Amedeo, too, probably suffered from the same disorder. He was very fond of his aunt Gabriella, who killed herself jumping from the staircase in Rome. But Eugenia had a different temperament. She faced the difficulties of life with a fighting spirit: not least, the death of Amedeo and his woman, and the consequent arrival in her home of the little orphan, Jeanne.

The mother, who spoke three foreign languages, taught until an advanced age in order to enable her child to achieve his heretical dream. She never stood in his way, believing in his talent and trusting his intelligence; on the other hand, she knew his weaknesses and she knew what difficulties he was going to face when he left Leghorn.

Amedeo Clemente returned her trust. He would never stop writing to keep her informed of how, step-by-step, he was trying to achieve his goal. Loving and confidential letters, unusual at that time, between mother and son, which she promptly noted in her precious diary. "Dear mother, thank you very much for your affectionate letter. The child is fine and so am I. I am not surprised that having been so much of a mother, you feel like a grandmother even though we are not legally married. I am sending you a picture..."

The postal order that Eugenia sent monthly to Paris enabled the young adventurer to start making his way among the French artists. During his last years, however, he wished to return to Leghorn, to the warmth of his city on the sea, to the embrace of his mother's hearth and under her loving gaze. He wanted to bring home his new family. In the last letter he wrote to her, he said: "Dear mother, I am sending you a photo. I am sorry I don't have any of the little girl. She is in the countryside with her nanny. I am thinking of a trip to Italy, maybe in the Spring. I would like to spend some time there. But I'm not sure [...]. A kiss. Dedo"

His bond with Eugenia went beyond the affection of a mother-child relationship. There was also a profound intellectual and cultural understanding between them. After all, her multilingual and progressive temperament had been passed on to each of her children, allowing them to choose their own path independently.

The mix of cultures that formed the character of the young Amedeo came from far afield. Eugenia herself had been raised by one Miss Whitfield, an English protestant governess. Later, she attended a French Catholic college. According to Jeanne Modigliani, the moral rigidity of Protestantism prevailed in her education, superseding a less formal and somewhat superficial Judaism. This was clear in the education of her descendants, including the granddaughter who, after the tragic death of her parents, was raised in Leghorn by her paternal aunt Margherita and who was to write many years later: "I was also affected by the attenuated echoes of this background and I imagine they would have been all the stronger in Modigliani's childhood."

The Disease and the drugs

Modigliani drinks; everyone knows this. They also know that he smokes a lot, including marijuana. Some say that he takes cocaine. In the misery of Montmartre, he learned to soothe the pangs of hunger and the aches of disease with absinthe, wine and cognac. His friends at his deathbed share one of the last me memories of a dying and barely conscious Amedeo, asking Jeanne for alcohol, a request that falls somewhere between pleading and anger. To the amazement of everyone, she hastens out to fill the bottle. Not out of weakness before a man consumed by drugs, but out of pity in the face of suffering that she had no other way of soothing. In fact, very severe headaches are one of the symptoms of the tubercular meningitis which doctors had diagnosed in Amedeo, and alcohol is known to reduce pressure on the brain.

Alexander Fleming would discover penicillin only eight years later, but there were other methods of treatment to contain or at least soothe the effects of infections, such as the use of morphine. We found no reference to the use of opiates in the recollections and in the testimonies of the time, but we know that precisely at that time opiates were used both as sedatives and as medical remedies against tuberculosis. The combined effects probably increased the hereditary paranoia which afflicted the Leghorn painter, but on the other hand, they may have soothed the excruciating pains he had to bear.

In the various texts we researched, there are two very different ways people remember him with respect to his vices: one for those who loved him, like Lunia and Jeanne Modigliani, and another for the art merchants, whose focus was not beauty but business and greed. There are people who describe him almost as a person who did not drink or as a moderate drinker and in any case, he does not drink while he paints; then there are people who exaggerate his vices.

He had confessed his tuberculosis to only a few people. Some of his female companions also suffered from it, for example, Lunia and Simone, and maybe he had passed it on to some of them. It was the disease of the century, but it was perceived as a shame.

For people who did not know him, Modì was just a weak and addicted artist who could be pushed to use drugs in order to produce more paintings and perhaps better ones. It is said one of his art merchants, Monsieur Guillaume, used to do this. The Chéron gallery was on rue La Boétie. They say he had made a deal with the painter: 20 francs per day plus the salary for the nude models. To force Modigliani to work, the gallery owner locked him in the basement with a model and a bottle of cognac. Then, to spend less money, he posed as a model himself, so much so that one of the few testimonies of their relationship is Modigliani's portrait of his tormentor.

According to our reconstruction, Chéron's efforts could not have yielded the desired result unless Amedeo had taken only small amounts of the alcohol provided for him. The after-effects of severe intoxication are not only mental but also physical imbalance, affecting in particular one's physical coordination. In all of Modigliani's paintings, however, we can see a geometric precision in the distribution of spaces, in addition to a clear and refined asymmetry. A mind befuddled by alcoholic excess certainly could not have produced such work.

Nina Hammet, an eccentric sculptor with whom Modigliani fell in love in 1914, offers some interesting observations that dispel the image of a violent and addicted drunkard. She writes, "A man can live quietly for months, working, scarcely getting noticed, and nobody cares. One day it happens that he gets drunk and causes a scene, as happened to Modigliani, and there it is, the single episode that spreads a negative pall over an entire period of existence ".

Modì loved life, in his own way but he loved it, otherwise how could you explain the passion that art critics tell us is clearly visible in all his works? Among the reasons for his despair, according to our reconstruction, is the pressure from the art merchants who saw his talent and probably thought they could better sell his paintings if they built around Modigliani the legend of a "damned" artist. When he was feeling better, with the TB apparently under control, he took hardly any alcohol or other substances, as many of his friends and Lunia herself would say. For example, he returned from his stay in Nice renewed in body and mind: the period at the seaside had made him stronger, and he was happy for the birth of his baby girl. He was also more productive on his return, as the dozens of paintings then produced and sold prove. Unfortunately, this lasted just a few months, until his ultimate collapse and death. A rapid series of events, which suggests that other causes may have accelerated his demise.

His last doctor, who examined him every day until he was unconscious and rushed to hospital, diagnosed a nephritis, as already mentioned. Why did the doctor not think of taking him to hospital earlier to try to save him? The outbreak of nephritis is never sudden, and there are clear symptoms that precede the most critical state. Blood in the urine, hydro saline retention and weight gain, hypertension, frequent headaches, drowsiness and nausea. All disabling symptoms that we can hardly imagine being present in those who were working as assiduously as he did, right up to the last moment. If it was nephritis, it is much more likely that the cause was due to a renal trauma: to be precise, a "closed traumatic injury". Accidents, falls or assaults produce about 90 percent of closed traumas. On the night of January 10, Modì was attacked, as already noted, and it was not the first time; on another occasion, he had even been robbed.

Amedeo was a lovable person but he was irreverent and at times violent. Probably he was also neurotic and paranoid, a hereditary trait on the Garsin side. "Acute intelligence but often disordered and sterile difficulty of social adaptation seem to me to be the predominant characteristics. The devastating violence which the Parisian environment exerted on Modigliani." His daughter Jeanne writes these words. Moreover, we also know that as well as being an artist, he was a man of his time, who lived his life with a burning intensity as if wishing to turn his entire existence into a work of art.

We are between two centuries. Young artists of the early twentieth century (perhaps like today's Millennials) perceive they can and perhaps must invent a new era. The magazine for which Beatrice Hastings writes in England is called "New Age" and she chronicles the cultural and social changes in Paris at the beginning of the century, between various genres of decadence, futurism and avant-garde. In this melting pot of ideas, seasoned with the German schools of philosophical thought that stretched from Nietzsche to Schopenhauer, there was also room for a new science: psychoanalysis. Freud carries out unscrupulous, dangerous experiments which revolutionise the way we conceive every aspect of human existence, both individual and social. A "modern" vision of socialisation tools is beginning to dissolve traditional relationships: sex and intoxicating substances are no longer taboo. Amedeo reads everything voraciously, he is like a sponge that absorbs every new trend; the revolution in social mores certainly does not escape him.

The drive towards change means that the use of cocaine in Europe, especially in artistic and cultural circles, becomes fashionable. It is easy to believe that Modigliani was captivated by it. In 1884, when Amedeo was born, Freud published a sort of eulogy of alkaloids, and recommended them as a cure-all for many ailments, including psychiatric disorders. Even the English novelist Robert Louis Stevenson, who suffered from tuberculosis just like Modi, sought the advice of the doctor with the Czech roots: as a cure, Freud prescribed him cocaine. Two years later, in 1886, apparently as an effect of his "therapy", in three nights, Stevenson wrote and later published the disturbing novel *The strange case of Dr. Jekyll and Mr. Hyde*, set in London in 1917-18, that is to say, in the same period of time of Modigliani's "perdition" in Paris.

In France the chemist Angelo Mariani, first marketed his cocaine wine, *Vin tonique Mariani à la coca du Pérou*, in 1894 - the precursor of Coca-Cola. Even two popes, Leone XIII and Pio X, soon became regular consumers of the beverage. Doctor Mariani was inspired by an essay published in 1859 by Paolo Mantegazza, an anthropologist from Monza: *On the hygienic and medicinal virtues of cocaine and on nervous foods in general*. The white powder had conquered all of Europe in those years of cultural, economic and industrial ferment; it could have hardly been missed by the Montparnasse circles.

In 1899, Freud published *The Interpretation of Dreams*, which would later become the bible of the surrealists, from Guillaume Apollinaire to Salvador Dali. The Catalan artist had tried for decades to meet the father of psychoanalysis, without success, until they met in July 1938, in London. The words that Freud himself wrote in a letter to Stefan Zweig about Dali, the day after that visit, describe how much Freudian thought has influenced the whole world of art since the beginning of the twentieth century, both in works and in social behaviour: "Until now I had considered surrealists completely senseless, though they seemed to have adopted me as a patron saint. This young Spaniard, with his candid and fanatical eyes and his undeniable technical mastery, has changed my mind".

Modì had developed his own style, but even so we cannot say that his existence, in his relationships and his art, was not influenced by fashion, and therefore also by the possible use of cocaine as a means of socialisation, as well as "therapy". Psychological and introspective analysis were also a part of Amedeo, however. In a sketchbook dated 1907 the artist writes, "What I am looking for is not the real and not even the unreal, but it is the subconscious, the mystery of the instinct of the (human) race". His friend and patron Paul Alexandre was more explicit: "Modigliani tried to express the deepest self of his models".

Critics also acknowledge the Tuscan artist's great ability to commit not so much the physical features into the portrait, but rather the psychological aspects of the characters he depicted. It is a peculiarity that also marks the way he paints and the time he spends on his paintings. He spends many hours with his models before dipping the brush into the palette, trying to understand the mood and the inner profile of those before him. Just a few glances, then he gets lost in the verses of Dante, yet he often completes the portrait in one day. His work has a physical, almost sculptural quality but it is the "soul" of the character that most draws those who admire his painting and are fascinated by it. This "soul", which his brush strokes bring to life, lifts his work beyond a mere physical depiction as it lays bare some vice, sensuality or virtue. It is the poet within him that sees the picture. He will remain the only twentieth-century painter to discover new pictorial forms exclusively through his portraits.

Amedeo slowly realises that the life of excess into which Beatrice had led him, and his metamorphosis after that relationship, brought out an artistic side that others appreciate, but with which he does not feel fully satisfied. His dream was to be a sculptor and "not being able to do so increased his discomfort and perhaps led him to take refuge in alcohol abuse," his daughter Jeanne writes. For the history of art, he will become Modì, the painter of women with long necks and empty eyes. Somewhat twisted images from another perception of reality.

Throughout his life, his only search was for a personal artistic dimension. Money was not important to him, if not for survival. But the market turned him into a perfect money-making machine; soon to grow around him, who would have predicted it, a diabolical factory of forgeries.

Second Crime Scene: Free Port of Chiasso, Switzerland
The Mystery of the Modigliani Archives

CHARACTERS

Jeanne Modigliani –daughter of Amedeo Modigliani and of the painter Jeanne Hébuterne. She was born in Nice on November 29, 1918. She was never acknowledged by her father; her birth was declared in the town hall by a nurse only three days later. She is recorded in the register as Jeanne, Jeanne Hébuterne's daughter.

Christian Parisot – art history expert. He is under investigation for forgery, receiving stolen goods, fraud and specific crimes related to violations of the rules concerning cultural heritage. In 2008, he was sentenced in France for forgery and fraud. He was arrested in Italy in 2012 for forgery and receiving stolen goods, and but in 2019 was acquitted of receiving stolen goods while the crime of forgery was dropped due to the statute of limitations. He met Jeanne Modigliani at the University of Paris in the early Seventies. From the end of the decade, he became her right hand man, later attaining the important role of archivist of the Modigliani Legal Archives.

Maria Stellina Marescalchi – Art dealer. In 2015, she acquired the property of the Legal Archives and currently owns all rights to the material.

Glenn Horowitz – among the most accredited New York booksellers-archivists. He takes part in the analysis and cataloguing of the Legal Archives.

Carlo Pepi – From Pisa, a collector of modern art and renowned expert on the work of Amedeo Modigliani. In 1983, Jeanne Modigliani and Christian Parisot brought him onto the scientific committee of the Legal Archives Association Amedeo Modigliani of Paris. He leaves the committee on September 10, 1990 in open rebellion against the other members after noticing that they had been producing certifications for fake works. For years, he has been fighting against forgeries in prosecutors' offices across Italy.

Giorgio e Guido Guastalla – Brothers, art gallery owners of Leghorn. In 1983, they became members of the Scientific Committee of the Legal Archives, together with Christian Parisot and Carlo Pepi. Since 1984, they have been publishing books and catalogues on Modigliani. They are the owners of two art galleries and they manage Modigliani House in Leghorn.

Luciano Renzi – founder of the Amedeo Modigliani Legal Archives Institute of Paris and Rome, and partner of Christian Parisot. He is currently the president of the Institute Amedeo Modigliani of Spoleto. He is under investigation for certifying forged art works on display in Palermo and in London.

Anne e Laure Modigliani Nechtschein – the daughters of Jeanne Modigliani and of Valdemar Nechtschein.

A Big Deal

Three of the Gondrand company's trucks cross the Italian-Swiss border on the morning of February 25, 2015. They had set out early, two from Cerreto d'Asti and one from Paris, arriving at the free port of Chiasso. Maria Stellina Marescalchi, an Italian-Swiss art dealer is waiting for them, anxious about their precious cargo. Like other Swiss free ports, it is a long-standing tradition for Chiasso to receives all types of merchandise and keep it safe from prying eyes of the authorities from other countries. Precious gems, fine wines and, of course, works of art: absolute discretion and tax exemption are guaranteed in reinforced rooms. It is there that Ms. Marescalchi has decided to store the mysterious documents which have just come into her possession: the Modigliani Legal Archives, which completely or perhaps only in part, had been sent to her by Christian Parisot after drawn-out and somewhat dubious negotiations.

Maria Stellina is thrilled. That entire load represents the heritage recovered over decades and no small difficulty by Jeanne Modigliani, an exercise of laborious collection and cataloguing as she tried to retrace the artistic path of her father. But what is in those archives, and why are they worth so much? Modigliani died young; he did not leave his signature on file, nor even a list with a description of the works he produced. His temper led him to paint and then often destroy his own drawings and paintings. Nobody has ever known with certainty how many, or which, works survived his changes of home and his bad moods. The Archives represent an attempt to consolidate everything that can give a clear identity to the artistic heritage left by Modì.

Whoever owns them holds the tools which can endow them with the expertise to decree if a work is true or false, or at least if a certain painting has some historical context. Often, however, they may have been used to build false chronologies or fake drafts, giving life to a veritable industry of forgeries.

The three trucks unload the dusty boxes. Inside there are documents, exhibits, papers, photocopies of drawings, original and otherwise, mementos marked by time and by neglect, often covered with foul-smelling mildew. A cultural, historical and artistic heritage of great value but poorly preserved, which arrives in the Swiss vault after years spent in the cellars of the country house of their archivist and "guardian" Christian Parisot. Maria Stellina Marescalchi has her hands on some very precious material. What does she want with it? Simply business, she will argue: being a dealer, in fact, is her only job. The goal of the whole operation is to find a buyer willing to shell out a sizeable sum. It takes time and effort to do this. Before we can put them on the market, the Archives should be analysed, purged of copies and possibly of fake documents, professionally catalogued. A critical operation, so important and delicate as to require the intervention of one of the most famous archivists in the world, the most accredited of New York booksellers, Glenn Horowitz.

Before becoming economically viable, the business must first be credible. Over the years, the archivist Parisot had built a smoke screen around the Modigliani Archives, just like a three-card trickster. First, the originals appeared, together with their scanned copies, then they disappearing to various parts of the world. Now it was time to put things in order. Glenn Horowitz is not just any book-dealer, he is the number one. He has catalogued the archives of well-known figures in the fields of history, music and literature, including Marguerite LeHand, the powerful private secretary of the President of the United States Franklin Delano Roosevelt; the musician and Nobel laureate Bob Dylan; the writer Gabriel García

Márquez; along with other characters such as Bob Woodward and Carl Bernstein, the journalists who unearthed the Watergate scandal.

With the benefit of his experience, Horowitz believes straight away that this is a good deal. He immediately sends his most trusted and expert collaborator, Lauren Miller Walsh, to Switzerland. Maria Stellina Marescalchi will host her for several days. A meticulous work of analysis and of photographic documentation of all the exhibits begins in the Chiasso vault. Once completed, Lauren flies back to her boss, who a little later decides to take on the task of restoring and cataloguing the collection. However, the Archives need to be sent to New York, preferably without them being spotted by the Italian Authorities.

Thus, the boxes leave the Swiss vault, sealed by the Swiss authorities with a duty-free bill which allows goods in transit to avoid any further checks, and return to Italy, their destination Malpensa airport. From there they will fly to the United States. After months of research, we managed to trace their route. Historical testimonies so precious for the national cultural heritage had so far escaped the careful control of qualified and respected investigative bodies around the world, such as the Specialised Unit of the Carabinieri for the Protection of Cultural Heritage, the Guardia di Finanza and the Customs Agency. Probably all this cannot be attributed to the incompetence of the investigators, but rather, as we will see, to the cunning of the parties involved and to clear regulatory failings.

It is an incredible story. Above all, there would seem to be no explanation for such neglect, such carelessness, such a lack of regard for the memory of an Italian painter who ranked among the world's most renowned. Two of his works - *Nu couché* and *Nu couché (sur le côté gauche)* - were sold, the first for 170.4 million dollars in 2015, and the second for over 157 million dollars in 2018. They are among the most expensive painting of all time, in ninth and eleventh place respectively behind the Salvador Mundi, attributed to Leonardo da Vinci, which sold for 450.3 million dollars in November 2017.[6]

---

[6] According to the most recent classifications

From the moment the boxes land in the Big Apple, Lauren will spend over a year poring over the thousands of essays, documents, postcards, photos, catalogues, drawings, notes and letters, sifting everything that is original from what is not. The approximately six thousand pieces that form the Modigliani Archives are catalogued for the first time and they acquire an official feature that is fundamental in establishing and accrediting the authentic works of the Leghorn painter, separating them from the many fakes in circulation. Of Modigliani, it is said that he produced more in death than in life. There are 337 paintings registered in the catalogue by Ambrogio Ceroni, still today the most trusted compilation of his body of work, while there are about 1200 works circulating on the market bearing his signature.

Once the research and cataloguing work is complete, Horowitz will offer the Archives for sale for 4.6 million dollars. A huge deal, considering that Maria Stellina Marescalchi likely paid less than 300,000 Euro for them in what she maintains was an off-the-books payment. The valuation offered by the famous American bookseller, therefore, may be at least fifteen times higher. The expectations of a fat profit, which prompted both Ms. Marescalchi and Horowitz to invest time and money into the reorganisation of the material, however, prove to be fruitless. To date, many potential buyers have expressed interest, but none have followed through. The reason for their reticence is almost certainly the worry of not knowing who really owns the archives. It is an issue that is yet to be settled.

The Contenders

Maria Stellina Marescalchi recalls the details of the transaction with Parisot as follows... It is Spring 2015: "After weeks, we finally schedule an appointment to sign the contract. The deal had dragged on for months, from one interminable phone call to another. In the end Parisot said he was ready." The Piedmontese archivist is in Stromboli, he is spending a short holiday in his country house with his partner. Only a few days earlier, the Archives had arrived in Chiasso for to be checked over. Marescalchi continues: "A person I had appointed joins him. At the reading of the contract, Parisot again does not seem convinced, he procrastinates for hours and he almost avoids talking about it in front of his girlfriend. At that point, the man I had appointed decides to go back. As he accompanies him to board the hydrofoil, Parisot hastily signs the document." A hurried and scrawled signature. It is impossible to believe that such hurried treatment - and of such important documents - might not give rise to legal disputes, controversies, suspicion and mistrust.

The "transfer" of ownership of the Archives dates back to March 31, 2015. The act ratifies the transfer of ownership from Christian Parisot to Maria Stellina Marescalchi. The text follows the contract with which Jeanne Modigliani, is alleged on November 12, 1982, and we emphasise the word "alleged", to have transferred the rights of control over the Legal Archives to Parisot himself. It is another document that raises many doubts, as we shall see. In both cases, the sale of such important materials, with an estimated value of over $4 million, would have been made official through a private contract. A rough, homemade deed without any legal references or notary's stamp, without witnesses who could have guaranteed its authenticity, and above all without any indication of the jurisdiction in the case of disputes.

Parisot would therefore have decided to offload the Archives, selling them on without even earning very much. He did so after many years of exhibitions, following a lawsuit filed by the lawyers of Laure Modigliani, Jeanne's daughter: a case she had set in motion to secure the moral rights[7] to the works of her grandfather. What makes him do it? "I did not want to sell them but only to lend them - he tells us - to understand if, with other initiatives such as creating a new foundation, I could have re-launched their public profile and consequently their value." The archivist, supported by one of his lawyers, denies ever having received money for the transaction

---

[7] By "moral rights", we refer to the legal right inherited by an artist's descendants needed to defend his or her honour after death. It is the tool through which an heir can and must act in order to protect the work of the relative in each judicial location. However, those who have this right do not automatically acquire the wisdom and experience to attest to the authenticity of a work. They can only do this if they have acquired specific expertise through studies, research and recognised scientific publications.

and claims that Marescalchi cheated him. Through the intermediation of the lawyer Giuseppe Miccolis of Bari, he said, she had promised to burnish the profile of the precious documents through exhibitions and events sponsored by the Puglia Region. There had been no sale. In this story, everyone tells the truth, or their own version of it.

"At the beginning I was not interested in buying," Marescalchi explains. She put much of the material on which we worked at our disposal. "Parisot called me because he knew I had useful contacts and might be able to find an interested party, a possible buyer. I had the role of guarantor because of my credibility. When a group of investors gave me the go-ahead, first I had the material checked. It was placed in boxes [of which she showed us the photos, *editor's note*], packages arrived, it was like being at the market..." According to Marescalchi, Parisot was paid €280,000, "under the table", partly in cash and partly through a balance payment made by the Swiss merchant herself to settle debts previously contracted by Parisot. The passage of money would have taken place illegally: it appears in fact that nobody issued any invoice for goods held in Italy, or for money received. "I have receipts and witnesses who can support my statements," Marescalchi says. "I paid every last cent agreed ... I was unable to make payments by wire transfer because my bank refused to send money to Parisot. I do not know what sort of mess he was in."

Statements that clash with Christian Parisot's version. "I did not sell them to Ms. Marescalchi ... There is no act of sale [although we have a copy of the alleged transaction, provided to us by the Swiss merchant, *editor's note*], there were no payments. I delivered the documents to Marescalchi because the lawyer Miccolis [who represents Marescalchi, *editor's note*] offered to review and examine the Archives to see if there was any chance of establishing a foundation that could promote Modigliani's work professionally. The lawyer had contacted my lawyer Rocco [Parisot's consultant, *editor's note*] proposing some cultural events to be organised in the Apulian capital to promote the figure of the artist." The lawyer Rocco confirms Parisot's version. "Jeanne, too, would have wanted the project focused on the Archives to be a serious one," the archivist continues. "With this in mind, I sent the most outstanding materials: manuscripts, old and new catalogues ... all contained in three trucks which arrived in Chiasso from Cerreto d'Asti and from Paris. But she took unwarranted possession of them, and sent them abroad via Malpensa. Upon delivery of the documents, I received an insurance policy from Marescalchi of two million Euros as a guarantee. The policy turned out to be false. So I reported it to the French customs officials, who understood the scam and the illegal export of the material, and launched an investigation."

Maria Stellina Marescalchi does not want to be branded a thief. "I did not misappropriate anything," she replies to Parisot's accusations. "I have had the Modigliani Legal Archives for four years. I was even summoned to show the documents to the Swiss customs authorities. In addition, if that is true, why did Parisot never report me for misappropriation or theft? There was a transfer of property - Marescalchi continues - against payment; I have proof of money withdrawals and delivery. Moreover - she insists - it is absolutely not true that the insurance policy was fake."

Parisot claims that Glenn Horowitz had known since January 2018 that he was claiming ownership of the Archives, having informed him by email of the alleged misappropriation. Maria Stellina Marescalchi, in turn, claims to have evidence that Parisot sent letters to the American bookseller intimidating him with fake logos and fake embassy seals. At the end of October 2018 the archivist wrote to us announcing that soon a delegation of his lawyers would visit Horowitz in New York to have the material returned. Otherwise, he would immediately report him to the American authorities for embezzlement.

They planned to carry out this supposed mission after the bank holidays in early November of the same year. After that deadline, we again contacted Parisot, who said he was satisfied with the outcome of the operation, assuring us that soon we would be able to view the Archives exclusively in Italy. We then wrote to Horowitz, who assured us, via a hastily sent email signed by his assistant Lauren, that no Italian lawyers had been in touch with him.

In our opinion, Parisot's credibility has always been questionable. His web site, www.modigliani -amedeo.com, appears to be a hoax. The website touts the possibility of viewing the Legal Archives at the Paris headquarters. But when we reserved a viewing, it was cancelled. A female voice, in Italian, had invited us to fill in a form and put our names on the waiting list. We never had a reply. Rather than getting discouraged, we went the old building at number 13 of rue Portefoin. No nameplate, not even an intercom.

A new Claimant

Parisot however is not the only fox in the hen house.

Rome, Viale Giulio Cesare. It is the morning of November 22, 2018. Lawyers arrive sporadically. They walk the corridors of the 17th section of the civil court. We try to mingle with the many magistrates who enter and leave the various rooms where a variety of hearings take place. This is the room we were looking for. Nobody notices when we sit down to listen. While the judge peruses confidential matters of a civil nature, the lawyers talk among themselves and discuss other topics. Parisot told us about the hearing a few days before: "I sued them, I took them to court, Luciano Renzi and his friends, who now claim they have become the most important experts in Modigliani; so much so that they even make appraisals and get paid, though they have no relevant skills. There will be a court trial and we will see if they still have the right to call themselves the Modigliani Institute".

We arrive at the court trial. In the courtroom, however we learn things are the other way around. The Modigliani Institute has sued the archivist. None of the parties is present, leaving the floor to three young professionals standing in for the main lawyers. They stand before the presiding judge. The dispute in question, according to the defenders of the Modigliani Institute, does not concern moral right, which is the judge's sphere of competence, but is rather about establishing whether the archivist is in breach of contract. In practice, the issue is that Parisot is alleged to have passed custody and control of the Archives to the Institute, through an agreement which was then broken.

The lawyers are therefore asking the judge to decline the hearing. The case concerning the legacy left by the artist and laboriously collated by his daughter Jeanne is not a matter of "moral right". It is about Parisot not complying with an agreement he himself signed, saying the ownership of the Archives would be passed to the Institute. If that was true, perhaps the archivist was no longer the legitimate owner of the Archives by the time he began negotiating with Marescalchi.

Like some production in the theatre of the absurd, everything and the opposite of everything happens in the name of Amedeo Modigliani. This is a fertile ground for frausdsters and forgers. The extraordinary beauty of Modì's art is trafficked in murky deals typical of the underworld.

The Paris/Rome-based Legal Archives of the Amedeo Modigliani Institute were created in 2005 from an agreement between Parisot and Luciano Renzi, a self-styled journalist and no relation to the former Italian premier. Parisot had thought his association with Renzi to be useful because the latter was well connected to the political circles that mattered in Rome. The right person in the right place. With him, you could go forward, get access to the powerful people in the capital. "At the time, Renzi was president of Adnkronos ...," Parisot tells us. Too bad, then, that as of today Renzi's name does not appear on the list of any official organisation or union of journalists.[8]

Parisot and Renzi work in tandem for several years, two inseparable partners. Theirs is a perfect understanding. The goal of both is to make the history and art of Modì even more relevant in Italy, organising high profile exhibitions and projects. The two associates present themselves at institutions with a very ambitious project: to take Rome by storm with a series of large international events. The first one will be the exhibition at the Vittoriano complex, from February to June 2006, with over one hundred art works on display. A few months later, on November 14 of the

---

[8] As far as we know, Renzi has never been listed in the order of journalists, the industry body in Italy. Yet, he introduces himself as a journalist when he appears in the election campaigns of the 1996 political elections interviewing the politician and former journalist Walter Veltroni at the Adnkronos room in a meeting with the members of the Rome's electoral college; the interview was recorded and then broadcast by Radio Radicale. The same happened in 2004, when he moderated a meeting of the provincial leaders of the Margherita political party in Frascati with Arturo Parisi as chairperson. His acquaintances perhaps open doors for him in the Municipality of Rome, making the introduction to Mayor Veltroni, but also in the Cultural Heritage ministry with its Minister Rutelli, when he makes the media-grabbing but spurious donation of the Modigliani Archives to Italy's State Archives.

same year, the big announcement finally comes: the Modigliani Legal Archives will be transferred from Paris to Rome. A ceremony in great pomp is set up at the cloister of Sant'Ivo alla Sapienza, the headquarters of the State Archives, with the involvement of the highest institutional offices: from the Presidency of the Republic to the Ministry of Cultural Heritage and the Municipality of Rome. The cloister is adjacent to and part of Palazzo Madama, home of the Italian Senate. To mark the occasion Laure Modigliani Nechtschein, together with Christian Parisot, delivers to Italy a bronze statue more than two meters high, a monumental replica of the original *Tête de caryatide,* produced in 1909. The imposing sculpture, "unveiled" by the undersecretary Danielle Gattegno Mazzonis, will be placed in Sant'Ivo, but only for a few days. The two partners, Parisot and Renzi, are overjoyed; on the eve of the ceremony, they are aware that the then President of the Republic Giorgio Napolitano will be among the cheering spectators as they make their proud announcement to the audience crowded into the cloister. Renzi is the master of ceremonies on the day. Like a conquering hero, he declaims in stentorian tones:

> *Doctor Christian Parisot, president - doctor Luciano Renzi, secretary general - the Modigliani Institute of Legal Archives of Paris and Rome... The great bronze sculpture Tête de caryatide by Amedeo Modigliani at the Palazzo della Sapienza symbolically greets the arrival in the Italian capital of the Legal Archives of Modigliani. The presence in Rome of this prestigious documentary heritage of the great artist and the concurrent arrangement of the activities of the Modigliani Institute of Paris-Rome underline and enhance the close cultural exchange that has always distinguished the cities of Rome and Paris, and which finds in this day further important testimony. It is significant that these events of importance for our artistic and cultural life take place in the name and under the sign of Amedeo Modigliani. A Tuscan artist from Leghorn born from a French mother; he more than anyone, through his life and his works, lived and embodied the partnership, the indissoluble interweaving of history and civilisation that links Italian and French culture. In this spirit, it is fitting that the President of the Republic should be present at the ceremony to deliver in person his welcome to the president and the secretary general of the Modigliani Institute, Minister Rutelli, the authorities and all those present – a cordial greeting to which I add my own.*

Thus is celebrated the supposed transfer to Rome of the six thousand historical documents and exhibits from the archives: in reality very little will land in the Italian capital.

On the day of the event, the director general of the State Archives, Maurizio Fallace, declares, "The ceremony marks a turning point in the institutional mission of the archival administration. Efforts to protect our history have reached beyond the borders of our country to collect the documents of a master of twentieth century painting, and bring them home." Parisot and Laure are awarded the State Archives' silver medal, an acknowledgment of the cultural value of their work.

The overall objective was to create a "Modigliani House" in the capital. Parisot and Renzi take about two years to start the project. In the meantime, they weave their dense network of relationships: meeting the then mayor Walter Veltroni and arousing an unexpectedly enthusiastic response from the Minister of Cultural Heritage, Francesco Rutelli. Too bad that the police in Paris had already put the archivist under investigation for forgery and fraud. Parisot, who had held in his safekeeping for a while some original drawings by Jeanne Hébuterne, had made reproductions of them that he had passed off as originals in an exhibition in Spain. Luc Prunet, the rightful owner and a cousin of Jeanne Modigliani, noticed it and reported Parisot for forging the seventy works on display. Hence, the search conducted in September 2006 and the discovery that the premises at the Montparnasse museum where Parisot said he kept, among other things, the Modigliani Archives, were actually empty. In Italy, however nobody knew anything about the ongoing investigation. Nobody even bothered to find out.[9]

At the State Archives there is no trace of the materials attributed to Amedeo Modigliani, they do not seem to have even been logged, said the

---

[9] In 2008 Parisot was sentenced by the Paris Court to two years of imprisonment, suspended for sixteen months, and fined 8000 euros. The plan to create a Modigliani house in Rome takes place under the patronage of the Presidency of the Council of Ministers, of the Ministry of Cultural Heritage, UNESCO and Enit (the National Agency of tourism). Even the highest office of the state is involved in this farce. The situation becomes even more serious when nobody has the foresight to advise President Napolitano that he is endorsing a person who had been previously investigated by the Paris police for forgery, specifically in the context of his activity as guardian of Modigliani's image.

director Paolo Buonora who carried out an internal investigation for us. In short, a scam: only a small part of that documentation, so precious to the national artistic heritage, will come to Rome. It will not pass through the State Archives, but will go to Palazzo Taverna under the supervision of the Superintendence for the archaeological and cultural heritage of the Lazio region. Years later, as we have seen, it will be "sold" for cash and shipped overseas. The huge *Tête de caryatide* will remain only a few days in the centre of the courtyard, at the cloister of the church of Sant'Ivo, and then it will be placed under the porticoes. After a few months, because of its size, it will be brought to the Forlanini gardens in remembrance of Modigliani's stay in the Roman hospital.[10] We too have seen it there; for years it was surrounded by overgrown weeds in the middle of the neglected flowerbeds of the dilapidated Roman hospital, which would be closed in 2015 after eighty years of history.

With the closure of the hospital, the *Caryatide* would eventually be transported to Cosenza, where today it enriches the Bilotti open-air museum located on Corso Mazzini, the main street of the city. Who removed it from Borromini's colonnade in Rome? Why and how did it end up in Calabria? A mystery within a mystery. The *Caryatide* was the only trace left of that "glorious" day in which Parisot, Renzi and Laure Modigliani supposedly "delivered" the Legal Archives to a rather distracted Italy.

It is therefore likely that even then, all the material that today is worth several million dollars was decaying in the cellars of Parisot's paternal home in Cerreto d'Asti. The then Minister Rutelli, who had shown so much enthusiasm for the return of the Archives to Italy, refused to comment to

---

[10] The young Modì, seriously ill with tuberculosis (a disease that he keeps secret until his death from all except his closest relatives), was, in the winter of 1901, sent to the South by his mother Eugenia Garsin to recover his strength and health. He leaves Leghorn, reaching Naples and then Capri, where he stays for a few weeks before moving to Rome, remaining there for several months. He is also hospitalised in the Forlanini sanatorium. The charm of the city and the therapies restore him, even if at that time he seems to grow aware that he has not long to live, and almost seems resigned to the sad fate that awaits him. "I am in the grip of the ebbs and flows of very powerful forces," he will write to his painter friend Oscar Ghiglia.

the reporters of "ArtNews" when he learned of the Police raid at the Montparnasse museum. Still today, he prefers to keep his peace. Even his party colleague and former mayor of Rome Veltroni prefers not to answer our questions about what prompted him to give Parisot so much credit, despite his problems with the French authorities. If it is true, as Fallace was quick to affirm, that the Archives were donated to Italy, why then there is no evidence of them being passed to the State Archives? Furthermore, how was it possible for a national cultural heritage to be shipped abroad without any authorisation, and in an apparently fraudulent way?

For years, the Modigliani Archives will only be a "hologram" that haunts the capital. A virtual reality of enormous real value, which moves from one part of the city to the other, from one institution to another, but never in physical form. The Casa Modigliani project, which embodied the goal of moving the Archives to Rome, is alleged to have received public funding of 1.7 million euro, according to the newspapers at the time. The funding was provided by various bodies involved in the project, and was intended to finance the digitalisation of all the exhibits. The aim would have been to organise a series of highly technological events to attract enthusiasts and school groups. After nine years, when we asked Parisot about the funding, he replied in plainly unsettled tones: "It would have been a dream, 1.7 million ... but I never got any of it ... who might have taken it? You have to understand who took it!" During the same period, Renzi opens a company called Chapter 75 Srl, which is little more than a branch of Renzi & Partners Srl.

The various exhibitions scheduled following the government-sponsored inauguration and the alleged award of such a considerable sum should have driven a combination of public and private efforts to give lustre to an Italian artist hitherto almost forgotten by the cultural institutions of his country of origin. Over time, however, the project amounted to little more than an itinerant and grotesque projection of photographs without any artistic value. An opportunity for many associations to gain the maximum profit with the minimum of effort, giving visitors the illusion that they could admire the beauty and charm of Modi's artworks without seeing them in tangible form.

Modigliani: a ghost at Palazzo Taverna

The national press will again focus on the Modigliani Legal Archives on July 5, 2007 to report their alleged transfer to the new headquarters of Palazzo Taverna. An apartment of six hundred square metres in the delightful area of via di Monte Giordano, a palace built on the ruins of Giordano Orsini's fortress and recalled by Dante in the XVIII canto of *Inferno*. The terms of the transfer also provided for a permanent exhibition open to the public, perhaps heralding an artistic heritage of great value. Instead, the exhibition ended in 2012, first with the seizure of the building by the police, then with eviction for rent arrears. Today the residence, which once belonged to cardinals and ambassadors, is home to the University of Arkansas Rome Center.

The journalist Adele Cambria, colleague of Camilla Cederna and friend of the murdered film director Pier Paolo Pasolini and the famed Italian author Dacia Maraini, well remembers those rooms.

In the autumn of 2008, Monsieur Parisot kindly led me through the solemn rooms of Palazzo Taverna to view a series of drawings by one of the most mesmerising and ill-starred Italian artists, Amedeo Modigliani. The drawings were reproduced on the computer – my Cicero admitted - to safeguard the originals which were kept, he said, in the famous Modigliani Legal Archives, whose headquarters were in Rome and Paris. My visit to Palazzo Taverna was over. What was my impression? I was not an art critic, but I did not like those spotty drawings on the screen, nor even those few African heads, abandoned as they were in the corners of the dusty salons[11].

The Piedmontese archivist has received a guest of acute intelligence and strong moral values. Doubts lead the influential journalist to return to Palazzo Taverna the next day, accompanied by a young but talented art critic, Sandro Barbagallo, who is today the curator of the Historical Collections department in the Vatican Museums and of the Lateran Treasure Museum, as well as an expert witness for the Civil Court in

---

[11] Adele Cambria, *Monsieur Parisot, the gentle swindler who peddles the Modìs*, "Il Venerdì di Repubblica", January 18 2013.

Rome. "His expertise on the subject allowed Sandro to politely challenge Monsieur Parisot; our doubts deepened."[12]

Adele Cambria (who died in 2015) would not tell this story for several years, because she had been "invited" by her editorial staff – as she herself writes - to leave Parisot alone, a man who served as a consultant for the Carabinieri of the Heritage Protection Unit"[13]. As Carlo Pepi, an expert collector of Modigliani's artwork says, "They allowed the fox to guard the hen house." Sandro Barbagallo, who shortly after will become an art critic for "L'Osservatore Romano", does not forget the exhibition and continues to follow the activities of the archivist from afar. Their paths cross once again and probably from that moment, Parisot's decline begins.

In December 2010, an exhibition dedicated to Modigliani opens at Castello Ursino in Catania. The exhibition consists of twenty-five drawings, four oils on canvas, five sculptures, and seven selected drawings among those owned by Sicilian collectors, which had been produced in Paris between 1909 and 1919. In addition, there are many historical exhibits from the Modigliani Archives: photos, notebooks, letters, postcards and even Amedeo's school report card.

Most of the same works had been in the exhibition organised by the Amedeo Modigliani Institute of Legal Archives Paris-Rome only a few months earlier, in Palestrina, in the province of Rome. In Sicily, though the exhibition has a greater impact, mainly thanks to the support of the Ministry of Cultural Heritage and the Municipality of Catania. Claudio Strinati is the coordinator of the scientific committee. He is already superintendent of the museum complex of Rome and he celebrates Modigliani's exhibition in Sicily describing the "works" in triumphant tones: "Modigliani's stroke, handwriting and painting are of an extreme, introverted, introspective quality, dedicated to portrait painting." There as a lot of press coverage, a glowing review on the beauty and importance of the exhibition for the island, but not just that. The mayor Raffaele Stancanelli and the Culture Commissioner Marella Ferrera were very enthusiastic about

---

[12] *Ibid*

[13] *Ibid*

the exhibition. Perhaps they too, like the other thirty thousand visitors to the exhibition, had not realised: none of the exhibited works was original. They were high definition photocopies, some of them touched up with colour to make them look more realistic.

Not only that: there were even photocopies of paintings and drawings which were themselves fake, that is to say, replicas of subjects never painted by Modigliani. *Simone Thiroux* and *La Donna dagli occhi blu*, for example. As Pepi says, "Fakes squared". An extensive catalogue has been made of all the works on display, but nowhere was it stated that copies had been used in the exhibition.

The inauguration was preceded by a controversy raised by the newspaper of the Holy See concerning a drawing attributed to Modì, *Ritratto di Agatae*, sketched on the back of a letter from the bishop of Noto, dated 1879 – that is to say, five years before the birth of the Leghorn artist, who in any case had never been to Sicily. The drawing, owned by an Italian-English collector, disappears immediately after the inauguration. Nothing more will be heard of it. A photograph of Vittorio Sgarbi, a celebrity art critic who had endorsed the event, right under Saint Agatha's effigy, is one of the few signs that will remain of that exhibition.

According to what the Carabinieri told us, the discussions on Catania only mention works of art, never reproductions. Material promoting the event is still visible on the Catania Municipality website, but there is no reference to the fact that the exhibits were reproductions. Amongst the scheduled events, there were guided tours with art historians, seminars on the work and life of Modigliani led by teachers from the academy and Catania University. Were they aware they were dealing with mere photocopies? Moreover, why so did many distinguished professors lavish praise and produce lengthy, erudite articles for an exhibition that did not display original works? The fact that they were reproductions emerges only during a court case. Some years later, we would have found Parisot in the dock, accused of forgery and receiving stolen goods. The archivist was acquitted thanks to a small pamphlet produced by a defence lawyer, in which it was explained that the works were replicas. But the Carabinieri had never found that pamphlet during their searches in Catania and Palestrina.

The works and materials of the Archives had passed through the regional import office to get to Sicily. After the exhibition, it does not appears that they were ever returned to the original galleries. Instead, paintings, drawings and other items were loaded onto a van and taken to Palazzo Taverna in Rome. Here, after about a year, the Carabinieri would seize everything and arrest Christian Parisot.

The understanding between Parisot and Renzi continues until 2012, when the archivist ends up under house arrest on charges of counterfeiting artworks. An unexpected turn of events that upends their relationship. But what happened? Parisot is accused of "introducing into legitimate channels of the contemporary art market, forged works of art by Amedeo Modigliani, after fraudulently issuing the necessary certificates of authenticity". An earthquake for the Modigliani Institute and for its scientific committee, which includes authoritative and influential art historians such as Claudio Strinati.

The Squad Car and the Scales

The Carabinieri squad car moves fast in the slalom of false trails laid by the counterfeiters. The scales of justice, ever precariously balanced between good and evil, move slowly, often too slowly for fear of error. But this lengthens the time it needs to reach the finish line, and it quickly loses the ground gained by the charge of the squad car. As we said at the start; ours is a cry of indignation. Furthermore, we will state our findings clearly, without fear or hesitation. We will use neither slander, nor defamation; we have reported and will report only documented facts. The reader will judge. The fragments that reflect the light of an extraordinary artist are likely to dissolve among the grey hues of the crimes committed mainly to his detriment.

The body of his work was severely tarnished as early as the first half of the twentieth century, when expert counterfeiters such as the Hungarian Elmyr de Hory set his sights on him and other contemporary artists. However, it was Christian Parisot who ultimately dealt the near-fatal blow. We interviewed him dozens of times during our research for this book, without ever getting the same version of events. We always gave him a hearing, but in the meantime, we checked every detail he offered. What the archivist had certified, the works he had exhibited, what he said since he took the role in the early eighties, all of it can be considered unreliable, to say the least. In some cases it was clearly false.

Parisot may have muddied Modigliani's cultural heritage for years. Anyone who owns a painting, drawing or sculpture that was certified by Parisot would do well to check the exact origin of the artwork. For many years, the Piedmontese was the undisputed voice of truth. All the authorities turned to him, including the excellent investigators of the Carabinieri unit for the protection of cultural heritage. There was no one else in the world with the same authority on Modì. Parisot had been the right hand man, the factotum, the companion of Jeanne Modigliani. His self-confidence in his role induced him to unscrupulous acts such as, for example, the unauthorized use of seals and symbols of the state (Embassy, Prime Minister, Regions, Municipalities, UNESCO, Ministry of Cultural Heritage). He also deceived the public over many years with exhibitions almost always composed of fake works or reproductions passed off as originals.

As the Carabinieri of the Unit for the protection of the cultural heritage explained:

> *There are various types of forgery perpetrated by Parisot:*
> *a) Drawings he produced, or someone produced for him; found on the market and restored, authenticated by himself and then sold;*
> *b) High definition photocopies of his forged drawings, often retouched, sometimes with colour, so as to give the impression of a textured painting; framed and under a glass plate, they look like originals;*
> *c) Paintings commissioned to counterfeiters of his acquaintance.*

The Law Enforcement officers, who until 2010 considered Parisot as a reliable person and took his certifications as sacrosanct, are incredulous as they see him for the first time in the role of a suspected forger of the works exhibited at the Archaeological Museum in Palestrina, *Modigliani: from classicism to cubism*, which opened on June 23 of that year. On shaky, unprotected stands under direct sunlight there is a bedraggled exhibition of dozens of hastily assembled bronze sculptures, drawings and oil paintings. The director of the museum, Sandra Gatti organised it all. She is also a senior official at the Ministry of Cultural Heritage, where she manages the Export Office of antiques and art objects. She has jurisdiction over the circulation of international cultural heritage, and her office issues the necessary authorisations when artworks enter and leave the country definitively or temporarily.

Twenty-nine pieces attributed to Modì arrive in Palestrina, but this time fate does not smile upon the archivist. While Parisot strives to set up the exhibition, thus adding a new catalogue to his collection, the Carabinieri begin their investigations and make a covert inspection. In the same period, they arrest Maurizio Calorì, a citizen of Bari with numerous convictions who specialises in receiving and marketing forged works. During a house search, law enforcement agencies find documentation that ties the activities of Calorì to the Modigliani Legal Archives. The investigations continue and lead to Matteo Vignapiano, an art dealer already investigated in Bari for the possession of three drawings and a bronze sculpture signed by Modigliani and considered to be of "dubious authenticity". Vignapiano had sold the works to Sandra Vellani, who had bought them on behalf her daughter, the well-known designer Frida Giannini, who was at the time the creative director of the Gucci fashion house. The Modigliani Legal Archives had certified the fake artworks. According to the police report, Parisot is alleged to have "outsourced" the issuance of archive certificates and the opportunity to "sign them in his place" to his co-defendant.

The system

Other convicted criminals and chancers - Rome's counterfeiting elite - frequent the circles of Parisot and Vignapiano. A machine that, once in motion, brings into play a foul-smelling network of complicity with the local crime underworld. One can understand how unscrupulous they were by simply reading the wiretaps, but the negligence and lack of organisation by the relevant institutions is also clear.

Thanks to his contacts, Parisot obtained export permits for the Archives[14] while maintaining constant contact with the archival Superintendence of

---

[14] As we have been able to document, the Archives contain reproductions of fake art works as well as copies of authentic paintings.

Lazio, in particular with Donato Tamblé, and with Luciano Scala, *pro tempore* general manager of the Ministerial Archives. Probably thanks to these relationships, by using his usual strategy of providing the ministry with scant details on the temporary exhibition of pieces contained in the Archives, Parisot may have been able to ship the forgeries from Italy and organise exhibitions in Taiwan, Seoul, Prague, Moscow and Sao Paulo in Brazil. To grant these permissions, the Ministry officials are satisfied with a couple of lines of explanation which do not even state which artefacts are entering or leaving the country. This is the transcript of one recorded conversation between the archivist and his secretary:

> *Secretary: "... but without a frame ... (softly) I don't know ... do you remember what they look like...?"*
> *Parisot: "... eh ... of course!"*
> *S .: "Well I don't know if we should ..."*
> *P .: "Well I know, but you can imagine ... sending a box back ..."*
> *S .: "Well I don't know, if then they then open it and see ... no? ..."*
> *P .: "So what? ... but no, they won't open it ... as if customs would open it.."*
> *S .: "No, not the customs ... if ... if when they remove the frame ...".*
> *P .: "Eh.. but no one removes the frame, don't worry, they don't have the right ... no ...no..."*
> *S.: "Well who would remove the frame them ... you said have them sent them without a frame?"*
> *P.: "Nooo, I was saying ... ehm ... ehm".*
> *S.: "Someone will have to open them?"*
> *P .: "But I don't know ... aaah over there yes, over there, there is ... the thing ... you can say, here they are, they have arrived ... but who would check them, sorry ... if they did not check them on the way out how can they check them on the way back?"*
> *S .: "And in fact ... I ... in fact I wouldn't know."*
> *P .: "That's exactly ... and then where should they be sent? ... to which customs? ... 'here, that's what not' ... 'who did ... who did this... the exporter did it ... him ... our friend did it, thingy over there didn't do it, what's his name, him over there,..."*
> *S .: "Look, I don't know ... because basically a request was made and they said okay, a request to Tamblé ..."*

In this business carousel, no one is paying attention, not even those with an interest Ito do so, such as the company that issued the insurance policies. Progress Fine Art insured The Modigliani Archives with a supposed value of several million dollars, for €18,200 on their transoceanic travels. A no brainer, if you think that for the exhibition organised by the French art critic Marc Restellini in St. Petersburg in 2017 the insured value of twenty paintings was half a billion Euro.

"A tissue of lies shrouds the traffic of painting reproductions, bad-faith export requests to the Superintendence and false statements to collectors as well as to museums such as the Pushkin Museum," the Carabinieri report attests. Parisot did not therefore limit himself to selling fake drawings and sculptures after authenticating them. Before passing them on, he would make high definition digital copies, then create yet more copies to use in exhibitions in different parts of the world, where they were beyond any authenticating checks.

Vignapiano had also foisted a bronze head on the designer Giannini - produced in a historic foundry in Trastevere, Rome, for the price of 2,500 euros - he paid 30,000 euros for it, along with an authentication on the headed paper of the Modigliani Institute, with Parisot's signature falsified by Vignapiano, as established by the sentence. In an effort to reassure Giannini, an invitation was extended to her for a gala evening at Palazzo Taverna, where the Modigliani Legal Archives were supposed to be kept. The buyer, an unsuspecting victim, would cooperate with the Carabinieri by handing over the forgeries, which were impounded. Arrest warrants are issued for Parisot and Vignapiano. The investigations in Palestrina allow the mapping of the "criminal dynamics engaged by the Amedeo Modigliani Legal Archives".

Parisot's undoing is thanks to his clients, often smarter and more honest than he imagined. This is also the case with Annamaria Guerra, an Italian citizen who had for many years lived in Paris, where she met the archivist. Parisot sells her a drawing which turned out to be a forgery. The victim receives compensation after taking legal action in France, but she does not stop there. She tells the Carabinieri involved in the investigation in Palestrina that during the sale, at the free port of Chiasso where Parisot keeps his "goods", she had discovered other drawings kept in boxes.

The investigators ask for and obtain, through the public prosecutor Pierluigi Cipolla, an international request for judicial assistance. They conduct a search at the duty-free depot, where they seize eleven drawings attributed to Modigliani, of the same type as those found at Palazzo

Taverna and in Palestrina. "The same hand, which appears to work with a template," Cipolla explains. Many other exhibitions are set up across the peninsula using the same materials, as emerges from the Carabinieri report. At the Ursino Castle in Catania; at the legal office of the state in Rome, where a portrait of Simone Thiroux, complete with a dedicated catalogue, is exhibited and later confiscated by the Carabinieri; in Gallarate, at the Biennale of Venice, in Ascoli Piceno, in Cagliari, Caserta, Domodossola, Riccione, Arezzo, Pisa, Forlì, Prague, San Paulo in Brazil. It appears that countless exhibitions displayed the works put in circulation by Parisot. It is possible that a simple collection of high definition photocopies could have travelled the world? The insurance policies taken out for the works could be misleading. In Palestrina, for example, a reproduction of the painting, a forgery depicting Simone Thiroux, had been insured for 400,000 Euro. The entire collection of "papers" and bronze casts never produced by the artist had been insured for over 2.5 million Euro.

According to the Carabinieri report, even people steeped in culture and well-known art experts presented Christian Parisot's projects and vouched for them before a number of Italian and foreign institutions. Among these, the following names stand out: Claudio Strinati, for some years a member of the scientific committee of the Legal Archives alongside with Maurizio Fallace, general manager of the Ministry of Cultural Heritage; Italo Zannier, art historian and teacher at Ca 'Foscari in Venice; Marisol Monica Rossetti, restorer; Gilberto Ganzer, director of the Pordenone Civic Art Museum. "Strinati's support allowed Parisot to overcome any resistance or doubt from people appointed to authorise cultural initiatives proposed by the Amedeo Modigliani Legal Archives," the investigators write. "Strinati collaborated actively with Parisot in staging and refining exhibitions and events, and received a considerable fee."

Strinati's collaboration includes the compilation of official documents, drawn up and signed in his capacity as superintendent of the Roman museum complex. With these, he certifies the value and relevance of the Amedeo Modigliani Legal Archives upon the request of Parisot, who will use these documents to validate the authenticity and importance of the documentary and artistic material of the Archives to various clients. Although Strinati was never listed in the register of people under investigation, the Carabinieri specialists censure the professor's behaviour for "both omission and commission".

The famed art historian, author of the great documentary on Caravaggio recently shown in cinemas, is stunned. When the Carabinieri show him a now confiscated painting by Modigliani, which is nothing more than a high-definition print the has been retouched and aged, he shamefully admits that it is actually an obvious forgery, but claims it has nothing to do with him. Then he talks of the embarrassing episode during the exhibition in San Paolo for the opening of the Casa Modigliani in Brazil; it had caused much indignation and embarrassment to his Brazilian counterparts, who got very angry when they discovered that the body of work sent to South America consisted solely of "photocopies."

When we call him for his opinion on the events of Genoa, after he had affirmed that in his opinion, the works seized at the Doge's Palace in July 2017 were not forgeries, Strinati tries to dissuade us from continuing our investigation: "Be careful, anyone who deals with Modigliani falls under the curse." But we are not superstitious.

A very profitable job

The Piedmontese archivist does not have any scruples in conducting his business. He is certainly not afraid of curses, either. Angelo Crespi, advisor to the then Minister of Cultural Heritage Sandro Bondi, is among Parisot's "institutional friends". Crespi was also president of the Museum of Gallarate, which exhibited several paintings that were later - in Palestrina - identified as reproductions.

It is Parisot himself who admits that they were only photocopies. But this is not enough for the archivist, who asks third parties to intervene. "Through his institutional acquaintances, Parisot tries influence the commander of the Counterfeiting and Contemporary Art Section, captain Corrado Catesi, asking Dr. Angelo Crespi to get involved." This is exactly what the Carabinieri in the unit for the protection of cultural heritage write in their reports.

We could say that the work of Christian Parisot, through so many years of activity, was painstaking, meticulous, and almost scientific in the pursuit of his own interests. Much did he gain, earning large amounts of money whose path took it beyond the view of the Italian tax authorities. As the Carabinieri wrote, "he has never officially done any other professional activity apart from that as President of the Legal Archives". Certainly a very profitable job. "You just need to sell one painting, make it look authentic, and you are set up for life, you and your descendants. When in your life can you honestly earn 43 million?" Carlo Pepi asks with typical Tuscan irony.[15]

It is history that passes a negative moral judgement on Parisot, not a court decision. We deduce it from the details of the investigations that have come into our possession: complete, precise, full of evidentiary detail, interceptions, checks, expert reports, tailing suspects. The best you could hope for: a judicial police that is competent, prudent, not vindictive, expertly directed by colonel Nicola Candido, Captain Fabio Castagna and lieutenant Andrea Dentale. A public prosecutor, Pierluigi Cipolla, passionate, meticulous, intelligent, who spends the vast majority of his time in those rooms on the second floor of building C of Piazzale Clodio in Rome. None of them looks like a hanging judge, a sadistic stickler for the law. The precautionary measure applied to Parisot and to his co-defendant, Matteo Vignapiano, was the mildest possible: house arrest. Parisot spends part of this time in Ginostra, a kind of earthly paradise on the island of Stromboli, not behind bars. From there, relatively free, he probably continued to weave his network of relationships.[16]

---

[15] Pepi is probably referring to the painting of Simone Theroux seized by the Carabinieri.

[16] The proceeding against Parisot ended in a preliminary judgement on February 28, 2019. The Piedmontese archivist was absolved of the charge of receiving stolen goods, while the charge of forgery had fallen into prescription. Vignapiano was sentenced to eighteen months in prison for receiving stolen goods. The judgment that acquitted Parisot for the crime of receiving stolen goods is, as it turns out, based on a fundamental issue: the subjective element of the crime was missing. Having included the word "copies" in the brochure, a brochure that the Carabinieri never found during the investigation and which appears only during the hearings, the archivist supposedly did not intend to defraud the public. Indeed, the code of cultural heritage, in article 179, provides for cases of not taking action: when the

We ask ourselves how many fake painting have magically become authentic via spurious certifications. How much is a business of this kind worth in total? A fortune. Who knows if one day someone will balance the books with a detailed tax investigation? One of our contacts passed us a certification dated 1974 signed by Jeanne Modigliani, for a drawing by her father. We can now say that this "expert appraisal" has a fake date and a forged signature. There are presumably hundreds of fake certificates in circulation, worth millions of euros. In this matter, the chart produced by www.secretmodigliani.com, is interesting and it says a lot. Then vertical axis shows the value, in millions of American dollars, of the "Modigliani market", while the horizontal axis shows its evolution over the years.

■

---

exhibiting curator expressly declares that the material is not authentic, by written annotation on the work or object. In the case of the exhibitions in Palestrina and in Catania, according to what the Carabinieri tell us, not only was it possible to indicate the inauthenticity of the works on display, but under each painting there was a written caption, for example: "Modigliani 1911". The visitor, who was never informed through the media of the non-originality of the exhibited material, did not have the necessary information to be aware that these were not original works, given the clear and express indication of the author and of the year of production. That is, unless they had carefully read the small guide allegedly distributed at the exhibition entrance but never discovered by the Carabinieri during the investigation. It seems to us that the law contradicts the judgement: "The provisions of article 178 do not apply to those who reproduce, store, offer for sale or otherwise circulate copies of works of painting, sculpture or drawings, or copies or imitations of objects of antiquity or historical or archaeological interest, expressly declared not to be authentic at the time of display or sale, by means of a written annotation on the work or object or, when this is not possible due to the nature or size of the copy or imitation, by declaration issued at the time of display or sale. [...]"

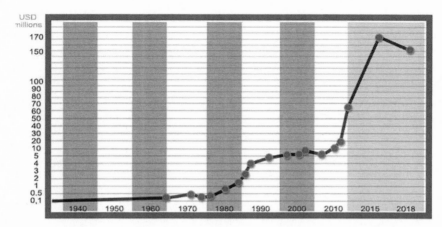

Parisot enters the market forcefully in 1982. Did his skills send the value of the "Modigliani market" soaring? In effect, the average price for the works of Modì in circulation remained almost constant at between 500,000 dollars and $1 million, until the early 1980s.

As can be seen from the chart, after Jeanne Modigliani's death, the prices for a painting or a drawing begin their sharp rise. Prices begin to soar when the archivist pushes on the accelerator: in eight years, starting in 2000, he increases the pace of the assembly line of forgeries. He manages to be greeted with great pomp by the country's cultural authorities when he arrives with the most precious artistic heritage in the world and voilà, it is done, everything is ready. Buying a Modigliani, or any other work of art, even a forgery, is a guarantee if it is certified. Many of those who need to invest money earned illegally can easily launder it by buying an overpriced painting; no matter if it is counterfeit, from now on the artwork can be used as a credit guarantee equal to its cost.

In light of all this, in our opinion, in the excellent work of the Carabinieri there is one gaping hole: not including wealth discrepancies as part of the investigation. It was a tax investigation conducted by federal agents from the department of the US Treasury that enabled the capture and imprisonment of Al Capone. Therein lies the key to all investigations involving large, illegal cash flows. Giovanni Falcone understood it when, while tracking an avalanche of post-dated promissory notes and cheques, he set up the "maxi-trial" that dealt a decisive blow to "Cosa Nostra".[17]

If there had been closer coordination of the various excellent investigative skills that Italy has available, we are confident that the system designed and implemented by Parisot and his "partners" would not have lasted for decades. The Guastalla brothers told of a tax audit in their art gallery that lasted two years. Carlo Pepi had Finance Police officials at his home for a year. Why did specialised financial investigators never set foot in Cerreto D'Asti, Palazzo Taverna, in Spoleto, in Ginostra, where Parisot and his associates ran their businesses? Nor do we know if they ever visited the offices or houses belonging to the company that registered the Modigliani brand, the aforementioned Chapter 75 Srl. Before going bankrupt, it would move its assets to Malta, after first moving from London. Behind Chapter 75, it might be possible to find Luciano Renzi and his London -based company, Housing Management 2013. The company paid up 60,000 Euro of share capital, but it has never filed accounts in England.

When, in 2012, the archivist Parisot ends up under house arrest, Luciano Renzi tries to distance himself. The partner continues to work with the name of the Institute and moves the headquarters from Rome to Spoleto. The litigation between the two concerning the custody of the Archives starts in 2012. According to Renzi, supported by his lawyers, the non-profit association that had taken the name of Istituto Modigliani obtained the precious Archives as a legacy. The defenders of Parisot, on the other hand, claim that there has never been any property transfer; the Archives belong to their client who had temporarily made them available to the Institute without ceding ownership. Today we know for sure that the material flown to Horowitz in New York had never been moved to the Institute's premises, nor had it ever arrived in Rome. Again, the controversy surrounding the materials poses many questions about the real ownership of the Archives.

---

[17] Judgment written by President Pietro Grasso who also oversaw the epilogue to this book.

The Forgery Hunter

Crespina. A group of houses in the Tuscan hinterland, in the hills that separate Pisa and Leghorn. A villa from another era. The austere charm of the country residences of the late nineteenth century. The shards of terracotta in the courtyard, tall pines shaped by the wind from the sea that blows through the hills. On the column of the old, wrought iron, gate, a travertine plaque with the words "Villa Modigliani". A strange twist of fate. This is indeed the family home and now "museum" of Carlo Pepi, collector of over twenty thousand avant-garde works, starting with the Macchiaioli, of which he owns six hundred paintings. For his long participation in the battle against forgeries, Pepi is considered one of Modigliani's greatest connoisseurs. The summer residence of a part of the Leghorn painter's family is now his "treasure chest".

"It's been a lifelong obsession," he tells us. "I lived as a bachelor, all I earned, and also what I did not earn - I took out loans - I spent it all on paintings. Always artists that I like, whom I thought were great and whom maybe I supported and took care of: I believe I have the world record of the least expense for the most artistic quality." Immersed, spiritually and physically, in his works of art - some of them are piled up in the villa's bathrooms - Pepi has been visiting every exhibition dedicated to the Leghorn artist for the last fifty years, both in Italy and, when possible, in Europe. He keeps catalogues, newspaper clippings, photos, comments on each exhibition. Years of study, collecting materials, all arranged in a chaotic order where, among the thousands of pieces gathered over a lifetime, he and only he is capable of finding, in a just few minutes, a drawing, a catalogue, a letter.

Thanks to his ability to spot fakes, he was in the past contacted by James Beck, a famous historian of Italian art at Columbia University, known for its battles fought in the name of beauty against forgers and dubious masterpiece restorations. Beck invited him to join ArtWatch International Inc., an association that deals with the protection of works of art around the world which are threatened by private and institutional interests: for the "competence and courage shown in the field", Pepi will be appointed director of the fake and counterfeiting section.

Nevertheless, precisely because *"a prophet is not without honour, except... in his own home"*, it is only now, after decades of tireless activism, that the complaints and reports he has lodged begin to be taken seriously. He is often called as a consultant by prosecutors' offices throughout Italy: the most recent is in Forlì, where the Tuscan collector is an expert witness for the prosecution in a forgery trial. However, he notes that "between 1991 and 2002 I could not get the attention of General Roberto Conforti of the Unit for the protection of cultural heritage. Instead, Parisot was summoned to carry out expert reports. It was like calling a poacher to guard the game."

After forty years of non-stop work, Modì's daughter becomes aware of the need to organise the large amount of material discovered. We are on the eve of the centenary of Modigliani's birth and Leghorn is preparing for celebrations. Jeanne decides to enlist four afficionados of Amedeo's art to look after and manage the Archives: Christian Parisot, to whom she has been linked for several years; Carlo Pepi; and Giorgio and Guido Guastalla, brothers and art gallery owners from Leghorn (the last three are all from Tuscany). Through Jeanne's efforts, the Modigliani Legal Archives were born in 1983: an association that was meant to be a fulcrum for research and studies which would guarantee, protect, preserve and extend knowledge of her father's work. Leghorn itself, birthplace of the great Amedeo, would be their home. This at least was the initial plan. For some time the headquarters had been established at the Modigliani Birthplace Foundation, created by Pepi, who had taken on the task of renting the premises at his own expense. Jeanne would die a year later, on July 27, 1984, right in the middle of the centenary celebrations. The circumstances of her death were never fully clarified. The association born through her efforts, which bears the name of the Legal Archives Institute, continues its activity at full speed until 1990, when all hell breaks loose within the board. Pepi continues:

> *In 1990 Parisot, together with the Guastallas, presented an expensive catalogue financed by the Leghorn Savings Bank which included many paintings and drawings that I considered forgeries. I did not want my name to appear in the catalogue, but they put it in anyway. I was still a member of the board of the legal archives and so, to avoid being complicit, I sent them a formal notice by telegram, officially expressing my chagrin and my suspicions. I refused to*

participate in the presentation of the catalogue and of Jeanne's book [when she had been dead for years, ed] published by the Guastalla publishing house, and said publicly that they had shamelessly included several fakes, undermining the credibility of the whole operation. If the truth be told, Parisot had always tried to include supporting documentation for forgeries in the Archives, but they were small things and he did it sparingly, attempting to go unnoticed.

I was threatened with lawsuits. They had important friends. I was always in a minority when voting on options: three against one. Therefore, I decided to leave. On September 10, 1990, I went to the notary to leave officially. I felt discriminated against even by the state. Despite this, I have always continued to report the fakes that I identified at various exhibitions. They organised exhibitions in the Far East, Japan, Taiwan, then in Europe, in capital cities like Prague and then Belgrade.

Pepi is a passionate man; he gets excited when telling of the various disputes in which he has been involved:

I went to exhibitions for as long as I could. My mere presence annoyed them. In Viterbo, I sat in the audience during the inauguration of the exhibition in the presence of Vittorio Sgarbi. I stood up pointing one by one to all the forgeries on display and I invited him to denounce that charade, not to promote it. The professor did not reply - he well knows that he is a great expert of sixteenth and seventeenth century art, but he does not understand anything about modern art, particularly Modigliani.

September 1991. Carabinieri officers from the unit for the protection of cultural heritage go to Viterbo, to the Palazzo dei Papi. The exhibition dedicated to Modì had started a few days earlier. The police raid, after a complaint by the Modigliani Archives, is followed by the seizure of seventy-nine drawings attributed to a very young Modì, works which nobody knew existed. In this case, everything arises from a general catalogue dedicated to the Leghorn painter by two critics and scholars,

Osvaldo Patani and Alberindo Grimani, who presented the paintings in question.[18]

Vittorio Sgarbi, with his habitual irony, will tell the media: "Let's face it, for the organisers of the exhibition it is great advertising. Everyone will flock to Viterbo, a town that is usually outside the great circuit [of art exhibitions, *ed*]. They should pay those chaps from the Archives [who lodged the complaint, *ed*]!" In fact, the crowds do come. The Carabinieri raid is characterised by a clear incongruity. The drawings are "sequestered" but they are not removed from Palazzo dei Papi: they will remain there on display, entrusted to the judicial protection of the curator himself, Renato Di Martino, until further developments take place. The Deputy Prosecutor Franco Pacifici does not order the building to be sealed, so the queue of onlookers at the entrance gets longer, to the increasing satisfaction of the curator himself as he continues to sell tickets.

Something similar happened more recently at the exhibition at Palazzo Bonocore, in Palermo, in 2018-19. On this occasion, too, the Carabinieri arrived for paintings on display that had been denounced as fake by Carlo Pepi, but this "has only served to increase the number of spectators", according to the organiser, Salvatore Lacagnina. "So much so, that in the first fifteen days of the exhibition we recorded ten thousand visitors." Perhaps what Sgarbi says is true: "For curious tourists who enter these exhibitions, it is not important that the works they are seeing are authentic."

A lively man, a rebellious and playful spirit, Pepi was also an aficionado of the nightlife of Leghorn, as well as its cultural and intellectual clubs. It was also he who, thanks to a photo, discovered that Roberto Simoncini, a vendor at the Nuova Venezia Market near the workshop of the painter, was none other than the subject depicted in Modì's famous 1909 painting which critics dubbed *Il Mendicante di Livorno* [*the Beggar of Leghorn,* ed].

A life spent in the struggle against forgeries and counterfeiters. However, while Pepi claims to be a "fake hunter", there are others who accuse him of owning some of those forgeries in his impressive collection in Crespina.

---

[18] From the information that we managed to gather, the case appears to have been dismissed.

But that is to misinterpret the word "forgery". While some of works that Pepi has collected are in the style of certain great masters, they are neither signed in false names, nor has he ever sought to pass as originals or have them authenticated erroneously, and certainly not to sell them for astronomical sums.

This story dates back to 1998. The Guardia di Finanza of Leghorn enters the art gallery of the Guastalla brothers for an inspection. The investigation continues for eighteen months. According to the art experts, Carlo Pepi was behind the raid. The Guardia di Finanza in turn collect a report from the gallery owners, according to which Pepi himself owns fakes.

Over the years, the Modigliani-inspired racket has shattered friendships and relationships, causing bitterness and disagreements that have never healed. The officers of the Guardia di Finanza also visit Villa Modigliani, seat of Pepi's house-museum, and search the premises of an exhibition organised by the collector in the summer months in Follonica. Completing the checks and collecting all the necessary feedback will take months. Before leaving, the officers will affix seals to one of the rooms of the house in Crespina that contains about seventy works erroneously deemed "forgeries".

In the few metres that separate Amedeo Modigliani's birthplace from Giorgio Guastalla's elegant Leghorn gallery in via Roma, just as Giorgio is passing on these details, we by chance run into the Marshal of the Guardia di Finanza who had led both investigations: "Pepi, Pepi, yes, he was acquitted. But go and read the judge's rationale in the sentence". "What did the judge write?" we then ask the Marshal. "I can't tell you ... Go and read ... However he wasn't considered a critic, an expert, someone who could make judgments. Then he had all those fakes! They were returned to him because he kept them for personal use; he did not sell them or speculate on them. "

Carlo Pepi was tried by the court for trade in forged works and was acquitted. Seventy of his paintings were adjudged to be inauthentic - but as noted above, he had never claimed any of them were originals, or tried to pass them off as such.

Friends and enemies alike acknowledge the great courage of the collector who has always gone against the flow; he fought his battles to the end, taking full responsibility for them. Enemies and friends, however, also point to his narcissism, his impression of being infallible, enlightened, the one and only custodian of truth. For him, the last letter received from Jeanne Modigliani before her death still represents a spiritual testament, a passing of the baton in the name of legality.

In Search of a Lost Family

But what is in the famous Legal Archives that could convince certain people to take such outlandish risks to own them? Drawings, letters, stamps, notes, palettes, photos, postcards, manuscripts, old catalogues, family documents, materials that are, as we have seen, fundamental in demonstrating the authenticity of the works. A collection that was born in the early fifties, from the burning wish of his daughter Jeanne to give public testimony of the personality and talent of "Modigliani", as she herself calls him, trying to break down the character's bohemian and reckless stereotype, the unruly genius, as others would have history recall him. "To me he is always a young boy, how could I have seen him as my father?" Jeanne spoke thus in 1981, during a television interview, on the sidelines of the most important exhibition ever dedicated to the work of Modigliani, which she herself had organised in Paris between March and June of that year.

What does it mean to love a father you have never met, who you only know from the stories told by others? Jeanne spends her tormented life trying to fashion a man and a father out of that brilliant but unruly young man with whom she had shared such a short time and who she didn't remember at all. She was just over a year old when she was there, at his bedside, with her mother Jeanne Hébuterne, pregnant again; when Modigliani was brought to the Hôpital de la Charité where he would die after two days of suffering. No memories, but perhaps an anguish which left its imprint on her mind and her soul.

That little girl who hardly knew her parents spent a lifetime hearing stories of them told by others, first it was mostly her grandmother Eugenia, and later, other relatives and friends. In her book *Modigliani, mio padre*, she tells how she slowly got closer to her father figure. Jeanne grew up in the house in Leghorn which was also home to the young Amedeo. The daily ritual of shining their shoes before going to school is one of the few memories that bind them. Every morning the meeting with the father she had never known lasted a few minutes: it was all down to a piece of brown velvet. A flap of the famous ribbed jacket, increasingly worn, which the painter is has on in nearly all the pictures portraying him. It was all for her, just to remind her whose daughter she was. Her aunt, while polishing her shoes, always repeated the same phrase: "This piece of cloth belonged to your father."

From a very young age, Jeanne begins a meticulous search which continues until her death, to reconstruct, by unearthing thousands of fragments, a relatively complete puzzle that helps understand the life of the artist in all its richness and complexity. Two important events intervene to interrupt and trouble her research: the rise of anti-Semitic fascism and the Second World War which, with their destructive power, erase most of the documentary evidence of the life and works of the Jewish artist. From Leghorn, "A complete and documented biography of Modigliani does not and will never exist. The elements essential for this work are missing," Jeanne will say in an interview.

At the end of the 1970s, after the death of Joseph Lanthemann, the old archivist who helped her collect and manage the material belonging to her father, Jeanne entrusts the task to Parisot. The two, as we shall see, had met a few years earlier at the Sorbonne. Parisot subsequently assumed the role of President of the Institute Modigliani Legal Archives, with Pepi and the Guastalla brothers joining him on the board. "Mom collected testimonies and documents which she compared, methodically analysed and critiqued," says Laure Modigliani Nechtschein, Jeanne's daughter, in one of her rare interviews. "She paid dearly for her work. At times she also paid dearly for her freedom of expression and for the originality of her positions. Because she soon ran into resistance, obstacles, and she attracted much hostility. As if she were breaking some sort of taboo as she deconstructed myths, one after the other ,about her father. These had become an integral part of the collective memory of the time, in accordance with the romantic clichés held dear by some and with the commercial interests of others."[19]

Modì's life and work had to be reconstructed through the documents that could be pieced together if they were not to be swept aside by facile storylines and in particular, by those same interests in search of fat profits that began to emerge just a few days after the artist's death.

This work was indispensable "to defend herself legally from a constant flurry of so-called experts who try by all means to take control of her father's work," Laure says again in the interview. In short, Jeanne was well aware of the business that moved around her father's work. We collected Carlo Pepi's testimony on those years, which may have finally marked a turning point for the public perception of Modì and his works. "I met Jeanne Modigliani in the early eighties; I had the chance to earn her esteem. Her last letter was to me, and it was sent to me on the day of her death. For a few years, there was a lot of harmony between those of us who managed the association called Institute Amedeo Modigliani Legal Archives, with headquarters in Modigliani's childhood home. We exchanged opinions, appraisals and experiences. I was proud to be part of the Archives."

However the catalogue published in 1990 by the Graphis-Arte publishing house, owned by the Guastalla brothers as already mentioned, triggered a war on the very same board; a war made of complaints and posturing which would culminate on September 10, 1990 with the notary deed by which Carlo Pepi officially left the association, in open conflict with everyone else. Pepi had for two years been denouncing the insertion of false documents in the catalogue and in the archive certifications.

I kept the documents that Jeanne collected for years, I read them all, and I studied them. I left the association because they always outvoted me. I went to the notary, I predicted that there could be problems with those forgeries and I wanted my position and my estrangement from the actions of the association to be clear from that moment on. I went to many institutions to explain that I was sure there were several forged drawings and paintings. I also had some idea of who had made or certified them. Nobody listened to me. I

---

[19] Laura Larcan, *I segreti di Modì*, "la Repubblica", February 20 2006

waited thirty years to be proved right, but not all the work is done
yet. Just a few months ago, I received a phone call telling me that the
Archives were on sale, that I could have joined a consortium to buy
them. I would have liked to, but my condition was that there should
be a clean-up. It could greatly help to eliminate the hundreds of
fakes around the world. As I always say, Modigliani produced more
in death than in life.

After Jeanne's death in 1984, the Archives, at least part of them, were transferred from Paris to Leghorn for a short time. They would remain at Modigliani's birthplace, in via Roma, until 1990. Then they take the road that leads to Cerreto d'Asti, where they will remain in Christian Parisot's cellar for decades. Maybe ... because from 1990 the history of the Archives is full of darkness and mystery. With Pepi gone from the board of the Institute Legal Archives, the Guastalla brothers buy the apartment, which still belongs to them today. For at least ten years, according to Pepi, they rent it to local professionals, voiding it of any historical value. We have visited the building and we can say that today it is once again a cultural reference point, the only tribute of his city to the painter. A highly engaging place of remembrance, that exists only through the efforts of Giorgio Guastalla and his daughter Laura. Amedeo Modigliani's birthplace is open to visiting schoolchildren, but it does not look like a museum.

Since the 1990s, some documents have been lost without trace. Like a three-card trickster, Parisot confuses his observers. In 2005, he gets the chance to pull the Archives from his top hat thanks to the Marciana National Library in Venice, with which he organises an exhibition of historical artefacts. As it emerges from subsequent Carabinieri report, the Piedmontese archivist uses a sleight-of-hand, knowing he can count on the director of the export office at the Ministry of Cultural Heritage. Sandra Gatti is head of that office; she is the same person with whom some time later he will organise the exhibition at the Archaeological Museum of Palestrina.

Parisot simply needs a short and generic list of some documents he says he wants to bring temporarily to Italy. The department in charge immediately grants the authorisation without even carrying out any checks. From then on, it is downhill all the way. When the authorisation expires, he simply needs to send a fax of the already authorised list in order for not just the modest materials listed but also a much fuller collection of photocopies to wing their way around the world. Along the way, between exhibitions in, for example, Taiwan and Sao Paulo, something is sold on the spot and no longer returns to Italy. Keeping up with the technology of the times, Parisot and his new partner Luciano Renzi build a virtual library of the material in a few short years. Then the Archives begin to travel the world, until they arrive in New York, as we have told.

If some institution had listened to Carlo Pepi's voice in the wilderness and immediately intervened, the Archives would have remained in Italy, becoming a cultural heritage of our country, and above all, independent experts could have assessed their consistency, authority and value.

The seal of the judges

There hundreds paintings and drawings by Amedeo Modigliani seized by prosecutors throughout Italy and certified as authentic by: Christian Parisot, Luciano Renzi, the art historian Alberto D'Atanasio, Jeanne Modigliani's husband Victor Leduc, Joseph Lanthemann, a 1970's archivist and colleague of Modi' s daughter; by Klaus Perls, an American gallery owner and collector, by Ambrogio Ceroni's wife, Angela (her husband's catalogue is still today considered the most credible), and even Jeanne Modigliani, who without meaning to, may have contributed to extending the list of authentications of fake works.

However, how did Parisot secure a right of possession of the Archives as debatable as it was precarious, along with "moral right" to the works by Modigliani? In Italy, the latter right is accorded only to the descendants of the artist and cannot be transferred to third parties. Emanuele Modigliani, brother of Amedeo, lawyer and senator of the Kingdom of Italy, as well as one of the founders of the Socialist Party, had the prophetic vision of protecting the heirs. He in fact fought so that Jeanne, born illegitimate, could have Amedeo's paternity and his moral legacy. Emanuele took care to safeguard the future copyright. However, after Jeanne's tragic death in July 1984, the Piedmontese archivist only had to quell the legitimate claims of those who could claim this moral legacy as their birthright.

At stake, let us remember, is the right to authenticate and certify the works by Modì. A business worth millions. A project of a criminal kind could easily fit in here. The evidence we collected during our investigation raises the suspicion that there has been a strategy since the early 1980s to deceive Jeanne, who was in precarious psychophysical conditions linked to her addiction to alcohol, as her ex-husband Valdemar Nechtschein, aka Victor Leduc has acknowledged.

The plan, perhaps, involved a "pincer movement" ate ensnare the last descendants, Jeanne's daughters, with the probable aim of conquering and maintaining possession of the precious Archives. One of Jeanne's two daughters, Anne, had been out of the game since early in her life, affected by a cerebral haemorrhage when still an infant. Physically and mentally, handicapped, when her parents died she had been entrusted to the care of a family friend and lived in a crowded neighbourhood in Paris. The younger daughter, Laure, equally fragile and timid, was instead rendered harmless after a dispute that lasted years, made up of agreements, exchanges of letters and sudden estrangements. A dispute brought to court in 2010, to reclaim that moral right on Modigliani's artistic legacy that tempts so many. Jeanne's daughter has been asking Parisot to return the Archives since the early nineties, even though he claims he wants to respect her mother's wishes, summed up in two documents: the alleged act of donation of the Archives dated September 23, 1974 and the similarly dubious contract of November 12 1982. Laure is not so interested in the custody and promotion of the work of Amedeo Modigliani all over the world, what she claims for herself is the possession of the Archives, basing the claim on her moral right, as Jeanne's daughter.

On March 22, 2005, Parisot assured Laure in a special letter addressed to her that he kept the Archives only as a "mere holder": the Modigliani family owned the property. In a letter dated October 2, 2005, Laure recognised the role that her mother had allegedly granted the archivist and on September 19, 2006, she signed a contract with him. Probably all of these steps are attributable to an economic agreement between Parisot and Laure, an agreement that the Piedmontese archivist told us had resolved the issue until 2010. Laure, in short, for years would have been "satisfied" with an "annuity", renouncing the exercise of her moral right on the work of her grandfather. [20]

However, from 2010 Laure changes strategy. Maybe the "salary" no longer seems sufficient, or she realises the enormous potential of gain that could derive from the exploitation of her inheritance. On May 14, 2010 Parisot and the Legal Archives Institute Paris-Rome receive an injunction from the Court of Rome. Laure asks for the court to order the Institute and its pro tempore representative to return the historical material. [21]

Parisot obviously opposes it. The court rejects the request and orders Laure to pay the court costs. At the same time the Institute, represented by its lawyer, sues Laure before the IX Section of the Civil Court of Rome, to settle the financial controversy that has arisen between the parties. The "annuity" accorded to Laure would be the object of the dispute in this case; it had not been due at least since 2006, according to the letter of September 19 of that year and produced at trial. If Laure indeed had signed a contract, in which she recognised Parisot's role, why would the latter have to pay her?

Intimidated by the sentence to refund the money received as an "annuity", a total of about 90,000 Euro inclusive of legal fees, Laure accepts the advice of her lawyer, Fabrizio Lemme. To waive the appeal. To even waive any possible claim from her heirs against Parisot.

The final act of the dispute is staged at the Court of Rome, in the last months of 2013. The lawyer, well known for cases related to works of art, Fabrizio Lemme, loses against Parisot and his crowd of lawyers. An unfavourable judicial epilogue for a prince of the forum accustomed to

---

[20] Our doubts are mirrored in the letter dated November 7, 1989 and sent from Parisot to Carlo Pepi as a "warning", from which we quote verbatim: "Everything must be under control and I am responsible for it, and I must answer for it in front of Laure who has taken matters into her own hands and rightly controls everything ...". Now, if it had been true that Jeanne had given all the rights to him in 1974, why did he have to respond to Laure if she had been improperly empowered by her mother?

[21] At this point, some legitimate considerations arise. Why does Laure resort to an Italian judge instead of asserting her rights in France? The jurisdiction, if we consider the presented documents as valid, should have been Paris. Not only were the Archives, however, at stake: the moral rights were the core of the dispute.

fighting and winning in the halls of justice. Laure eventually gives up, relying completely on her attorney's advice and accepting the verdict without appeal. It could have been possible to appeal the sentence and seek a forensic evaluation of the handwriting on the transfer documents of the Archives allegedly signed by Jeanne. Instead, Laure signs a waiver covering herself and her offspring. "She didn't have the money for the evaluation," Lemme told us. This verdict is covered in two sentences, published respectively on October 7 and December 12, 2013.

We asked Lavinia Savini, a lawyer specialised in intellectual property and art law, to comment on the dispute between Laure and the Modigliani Institute. "Given only partial knowledge of the documents relating to the legal actions mentioned, we can only offer some reflections. Of course, some questions arise spontaneously. In the transaction you submitted Laure, as mentioned, not only commits to giving up the appeal against the original sentence. She also commits to "eschew all other claims, shares and / or rights deriving from all relations with the parties," which are issues that had nothing to do with the nature of the lost lawsuits.

"Once again we go back to the moral rights of the author. When you read the transaction, you could consider, in fact, that Laure has disposed of the moral right to the ownership of the Master's work. It would follow, paradoxically, that the transaction would be void for the same legal principle for which Laure lost the cases in the Court of Rome: the moral rights of the author are not available in Italy and so the acts of settlement concerning it are void. In the case of unavailable rights, the power of settlement related to them is limited *ex lege*. Consequently, the subject who owns them can exercise them, but they cannot make them the object of business, free of charge or against payment, which implies transfer, relinquishment (direct or indirect) or insertion in settlement agreements.

"It is confirmed that the present case is an act of settlement under the law also by the economic exploitation of the moral right to the authorship of the work that Laure puts in place with her conduct. The *a posteriori* recognition of the lawfulness of the reproductions, and implicitly of their authenticity, in favour of the Modigliani Archives Institute is used, in fact, as a bargaining chip in a settlement to pay off the debt on which it is encumbered. The economic exploitation of the moral right is not permitted by the nature of the right in question because it is considered as an act of settlement of the same (as, moreover, expressly declared by the Court of Rome in the sentence that Laure lost against the same Institute). The same civil code in regulating transactions expressly provides for the nullity of settlement transactions in the event that the rights covered by them, "by nature or by express provision of the law, are not available to the parties."

"But there is more. Doubts arise about the legitimacy of the settlement made by Laure, through the transaction, if it is considered as established doctrine and jurisprudence that the persons indicated by Article 23 of the Italian copyright law acquire the right on the author's death, allowing them to defend the author's social esteem and image against possible acts which harm his works and could damage his name and reputation. In the present case, since the reproduction of the works and sculptures made by the Institute aimed above all at the economic interest of the same, any purpose of protecting the Master's reputation would seem to be completely absent. On the contrary, since as you reported some of the same *d' après* bronze sculptures would even been seized because of doubts about their authenticity, you could identify harm to the reputation of the artist."

However, what is Laure's truth? It is surprisingly different. In a report given to the judicial police concerning the case against Parisot for the events at Palazzo Taverna, in the presence of her attorney Lemme, on January 21, 2013 (ten months before the civil courts ruled against her), Amedeo Modigliani's granddaughter gave a version of the facts that could have reversed the subsequent verdict.

Here are some extracts from that report.

> *Carabinieri: "In your view, is the private contract dated October 30, 1982 and signed by your mother on the transfer of the Archive and the duties "for life" as an archivist in favour of Professor Parisot authentic or could they ever have been spontaneously desired by your mother?"*
> *Laure Modigliani Nechtschein: "The handwriting is certainly not my mother's, as it had a completely different shape, while on the signature I am not sure whether it is false or authentic [...]. I can't say my mother wrote this declaration willingly, or other letters or declarations like it, because in the last years of her life she was unstable in terms of her character and mental health".*
> *Carabinieri: "Do you confirm the signature on the private contract in French between you and Parisot, dated November 12, 1982?"*

Laure Modigliani Nechtschein: "I do not remember ever signing the contract shown to me and I can confirm with certainty that my acronym L.N. is false. Among other things, with respect to its content, which defines professor Parisot as a "lifelong archivist" of the Modigliani Archive, I would have never agreed to sign and confirm such a statement."

Lawyer Lemme's choice is striking. Having witnessed the questioning and being now aware of a version of events that is completely at odds with the version hitherto given to the magistrates – why does he not take steps to protect his client? Why doesn't he go to the magistrates to say what Laure Modigliani Nechtschein has stated before the judicial police? In the following months, everything proceeds as if nothing had happened.

With Christian Parisot's Roman experience having ended in house arrest, the Archives reappear in the small village of Cerreto d'Asti. Here the incredulous villagers say that for months, paintings, drawings and various materials belonging to Modigliani have been kept, or rather abandoned, on the premises of the small municipal kindergarten, at that time unattended during the school holidays. On the reopening of the school, they were taken to the cellars of some farmhouse in the Langhe and Monferrato, to allow time to pass, and investigations and complaints to be forgotten for a while.

Therefore, we come to the auction for the Modigliani Legal Archives, which are offered around the world in a few short months. As we have noted, Maria Stellina Marescalchi manages the sale; she is the woman who today claims the ownership rights, affirming that she bought them directly from Parisot.

Third Crime Scene: 55 Boulevard Saint-Michel, Paris
The mystery of the donations

CHARACTERS

Joseph Lanthemann - archivist and Jeanne Modigliani's long-time helper.

Serge Gérald Thiroux-Villette - Jeanne Modigliani's half-brother, Amedeo Modigliani's never-acknowledged son.

Emanuele Modigliani - Amedeo's older brother, lawyer, Senator of the Kingdom of Italy, one of the founders of the Italian Socialist Party.

Luc Prunet - Jeanne Hébuterne's nephew.

And again: Jeanne Modigliani, Christian Parisot, Carlo Pepi, Giorgio and Guido Guastalla, Luciano Renzi and Laure Modigliani Nechtschein.

Liaisons amoureuses

Paris, September 23, 1974. This story starts with a previously unpublished document. A yellowed letter of only fifteen lines, typed and with many details added in pen, takes us to 55 boulevard Saint-Michel, one of the last residences of Amedeo Modigliani's daughter, a stone's throw from Notre-Dame. In fact, there various pens and different handwriting styles have been used. Numerous messed up corrections, some erasures. At the top right, written by hand, you can read *"acte de donation"*, but nobody can say for sure where this document was written, who would have signed it or when. It is only the first of a series of incomprehensible anomalies that have as their objective the ownership and legitimate use of the Modigliani Legal Archives.

acte de donation
J. Modigliani
23.09.74
N.B. envoyer chez Notre J.L. Nitot, le ... 89
~4 pages~ J. Modigliani

Jeanne Modigliani
55, Bld. Saint-Michel
Paris

à christian Parisot,

Suite à nos accords précédents avec les éditions Graphis-Arts
à ce jour la donation de mes documents personnels : *A. Modigliani*.
Photographies, lettres manuscrites et autres témoignages
d'époque concernant ses amis, est faite par moi-même à
Monsieur Christian Parisot, résidant à Paris,
84 Bld Rochechouart - Paris
en le chargeant de les reproduire,et éventuellement de les
céder en totalité, ou partie pour l'aider dans la suite de
ses recherches pour le Catalogue.
Pour ma part, je conserve la photocopie de tous les documents
remis ce jour à monsieur Christian Parisot.

Je me réserve également le droit légal de percevoir les droits
de reproduction et de signer les "bons à tirer".
en qualité d'unique ayant-droit d'Amedeo Modigliani
Fait à Paris le 23.09 . 1974

Jeanne Modigliani

Fait à Paris le 23.09. 1974

Fait à Paris —
J. Modigliani, fait à Paris le 10/12/1980 — N.B. copie conforme J.L. Nitot

Donation deed, September 23, 1974

The document allows Christian Parisot to declare himself owner of the Archives. The archivist presented it in court in 2011, along with other materials, in order to rebut the complaint of Laure, Jeanne Modigliani's daughter and the last heir of the great painter from Leghorn.

Nevertheless, let us start from the beginning. What happened in that faraway year 1974? A penniless Piedmontese student of art history had recently moved to Paris from Cerreto d'Asti. His father was an artist, but he has never really made it. He dreams of opening his way and affirming himself in the golden world of collectors. He wants to be part of the circles that matter, mingling with the right people. His name is Christian and he is enrolled at the most prestigious university in the French capital.

At the Sorbonne, he meets an older, much tormented woman, Jeanne Modigliani, who in those years was a teacher of Italian language and literature. The two like each other, they begin to see each other assiduously. The young student becomes Jeanne's shadow, he follows her everywhere, and he almost venerates her. He arrived in the city of artists and fate, or perhaps an out of the ordinary will, brought him before the heir of one of the most exceptional Italian painters of the twentieth century. A person who has been trying for years to give a complete and coherent form to the production of her father's art, collecting materials of all kinds, work tools, letters, documents. The collection will later be named Modigliani Legal Archives.

In those years, Jeanne has a right hand man called Joseph Lanthemann. He helps her with the meticulous collection and cataloguing. He is the archivist and he will retain this role until the end of his days. A scholar of art history as well as an expert in Modigliani's work, Lanthemann will also contribute to the university training of the young Piedmontese student who had arrived in Paris full of ambition.

Throughout the second half of the seventies, the Modigliani-Parisot couple proceeds in harmony. Jeanne is busy collecting materials in various parts of the world; Parisot, thanks to his closeness with the painter's daughter becomes a reference point for Amedeo Modigliani's fans.

Christian is twenty-five when he meets Jeanne; she is fifty-five. At that time, Modì's daughter spent her life between the Sorbonne and the Jardin du Luxembourg, the park where the father used to walk around in pleasant conversation with one of his favourite friends and models, Lunia Czechowska. It remains inexplicable how and why, ten years later, she could have ended her days away from that bohemian scene in a public housing block.

The rumours in the small village of Cerreto, in the hills near Asti, say that a *liaison amoureuse* might have begun between Christian and Jeanne. A close bond, but very reserved. It looks like the usual village gossip, yet there must be a hint of truth if even Carlo Pepi and Maria Stellina Marescalchi confirm those reports, which tell of an important relationship between that young art lover and the heir of the great Italian painter. At the recurring allusions, Parisot himself replies that Jeanne had been a great friend of his mother. Too bad the two women, albeit peers, had never met. We cannot say for sure what kind of relationship it was. What is certain and documented, however, is that Jeanne indulged in a number of excesses at that time, drinking and *ménages à trois*[22]. Her daughter Anne says that, returning home one evening, she found her mother naked, drunk and in company of two young men.

Jeanne was a free-living woman; she had conceived two daughters with Valdemar Nechtschein, aka Victor Leduc, a German Jew of Russian origin, a philosopher, communist and partisan who, being already married, had not been able to acknowledge his daughters until the 1990s.

We can presume that the spark between the young student and the mature intellectual became irrepressible. Parisot's "charm" may have enthralled the impressionable Jeanne, enough to induce her, just a year after their first meeting, to hand him control over the whole artistic heritage of the father. A fatal attraction cannot be otherwise. Or else why would Modì's daughter ever give Parisot the only valuable thing that she owned, one which ensured her financial freedom and allowed her to lead a dignified life?

Is it believable? Did Jeanne really want, through that document, to give Parisot all her assets, a treasure put together with dedication and overriding passion, thus depriving her two daughters as well as the man she had acknowledged as a brother only two years earlier (in 1972)?

---

[22] Meryle Secrest, *Modigliani, l'uomo e il mito*, Mondadori, Milan 2012.

The "awful mess" of 1974

What is this *acte de donation*? We are going to explore it thoroughly. We collected several elements that allow us to see the shadows, the curiosities, the contradictions surrounding this fundamental document. To begin with, you get lost among the dates. Jeanne's donation, apparently, dates back to 1974. Another date, however, appears written in pen on the document. It is not very clear; it seems to be 1988, or 1983. A last minute correction, by someone who perhaps realised they had made a thoughtless mistake. In fact, in 1988 Jeanne had already been dead for four years, so she couldn't have sent anything to the notary, unless she spoke from the afterlife. It would be better to correct it to a more realistic 1983. A true *pastis*, as they say in Turin, Parisot's hometown. Typed dates and handwritten notes. Corrections and attempts to hide them.

This is the translation:

> *Today, following our previous agreements with Graphis-Arte editions, I, the undersigned, hereby donate my personal documents - photographs, handwritten letters and other historical evidence [of Amedeo Modigliani, ed.] regarding his friends - to Mr Christian Parisot, resident in Paris, 84 boulevard Rochechouart, with the task of reproducing them or possibly selling them, in whole or in part, to help him continue his research for the Catalogue. For my part, I will keep the photocopies of all the documents given today to Mr Christian Parisot. I also reserve the legal right to collect the reproduction rights and to sign the permission to print as the sole owner of the rights of Amedeo Modigliani.*

There are many considerations to be made. The first concerns the language. According to Sylvie Pipari, a French teacher in the faculty of Economics at the University of Turin, the typed part, that is the body of the letter, is very correct, in the legal language typical of notary acts. At the top right, a handwritten annotation clearly contains an error. «Jeanne Modigliani donation deed you send [or "to send", infinitive - ed.] to the notary», in French "*envoyer [o envoyez] chez le notaire*", December 10 1983 (or 1988, it is not clear). It should have read «Sent to the notary», «*envoyé*», not «*envoyer / envoyez*». In other words, the person who wrote it confused the infinitive (or imperative) with the past participle, an error made by those who do not know the language well. In fact, the action is presented as already completed, given that it is followed by the date. However, for those who are not familiar with the written language this distinction is difficult, because the three words (*envoyer / envoyez / envoyé*) are pronounced in the same way.

Jeanne was a Parisian, a graduate, educated, a refined intellectual, a teacher of Italian language and literature at the Sorbonne. She would never have made such a trivial grammatical error. Why would she have to sign such a sloppy sheet? Is it possible that no one ever questioned its authenticity? We also know that no French notary ever registered it; otherwise, the notary documents would have been attached to those of the Italian colleague Paolo Fenoaltea, who would certify the copy, but only in 2011, that is when the document is first presented in the legal proceedings brought by Laure Modigliani.

It does not end there. The 1974 donation in fact contains more than one false statement. The first: "*en qualité d'unique ayant-droit d 'Amedeo Modigliani*", as the sole owner of the rights of Amedeo Modigliani." Jeanne, however, was not the only heir to that heritage; she was not the painter's only daughter. Everyone knew about the existence of the Parisian priest, Gérald Thiroux-Villette, Amedeo and Simone Thiroux's son, even though he was not acknowledged. The act therefore would not be valid.

Jeanne could not give what was not hers alone. She, Modì's daughter, helped the investigative journalist François Mattei to track down her half-brother. Gérald became a priest and practised his ministry in the parish of Boutigny-sur-Essonne, a village fifty kilometres from Paris. His story, in 1972, was published in a beautiful report in the magazine *Epoca*. Jeanne cried when, in May of that the same year, she welcomed Gérald to her home. The two exchanged anecdotes, memories, life stories, and then she took a picture of Amedeo from the wallet: the resemblance of the father to the brother she had just met was incredible. They had never seen each other before, two different fates that at some point might have even merged, if in 1920 the senator Emanuele Modigliani, brother of the painter, had not chosen only one of the two grandchildren, deciding to bring Jeanne to Italy and leaving Gérald in the care of some friends of his mother, who took him in after Simone's death. Later Gérald would later move to the orphanage, where he would remain until 1931, when he was given to a family in adoption.

I was adopted by the Carlinot couple. My father [adoptive, ed] had a very bad temper. He was a colonial administrator in Indochina; on his return he bought a paper mill in Paris. After a while there he sold it and stopped working. Since he no longer had the workers on whom to vent his bad temper, his wife paid the expenses of his angry outbursts. The situation soon deteriorated until the completely broke down. There was a divorce and he [the father, ed] took me with him to Algeria. I was thirteen and I couldn't stand a nomadic life: when I managed to, I ran away, jumped on a ship and went back to my mother.[23]

The priest told his sister what the adoptive mother had told him, describing his father as she saw him: handsome and charming, totally in love with Jeanne Hébuterne, Jeanne's mother, who committed suicide the day after burying her beloved artist. Simone Thiroux was a young and beautiful girl. She arrived in Paris intending to study medicine at the Sorbonne; however, she came across the artists of Montparnasse. There she met the handsome Italian. She insistently courted him, but he repeatedly rebuffed her. He already had his muse, with whom he would conceive Jeanne and another child, though the latter would never be born.

It is known, however, that Modì was very attracted to women, especially if they were interesting and resourceful. Simone was like that. Therefore, he succumbed to the young woman. On September 15, 1917, Gérald was born, to the total disinterest of his natural father. In the meantime, his mother had fallen ill with phthisis, probably because of her contact with the artist, who was infected by the bacterium for years. A few months later, in March 1918, Jeanne Hébuterne also became pregnant and Jeanne was born on November 29. On the same day, quite a coincidence, her stepbrother Gérald was baptised.

At the time of the alleged signature of the donation deed, therefore, Jeanne Modigliani had not only known for at least two years that her father had had a son, but she had actually spent her money to track him down and she had even met him. The priest died on October 30, 2004. But on the date when the agreements were signed, Gerald, too, owned all moral rights to

[23] «Epoca», May 1972

the works and documents belonging to Amedeo Modigliani supposedly passed from Jeanne to her archivist.

That is not all. The hereditary rights, theoretically, would belong also to Laure and her older sister, Anne. The same judges in Rome, issuing an injunction in 2010 against Parisot and the Modigliani Institute, had recognised that Laure was entitled the moral right and that this right was non-transferable. In short, the document dated September 23, 1974 does not pass muster: it is muddled, hasty, inaccurate and probably devoid of any legal value. In addition, even if Jeanne had signed the donation herself, the strong suspicion remains that in the late seventies and early eighties she had fallen into a state of alcoholism. Her husband Valdemar said "it had made her mad." Is it all a fraud, then? What is certain is that the Court of Rome failed to carefully analyse this document. And with control of the Archives, anyone can rewrite the history of works attributed to Amedeo Modigliani.

An outrageous historical forgery

While writing this book, we contacted the president of the Court of Rome. We wanted to see clearly by first reading the entire procedural file relating to the dispute between Laure and Parisot; but we did not get authorisation and we had to be satisfied with the verdict[24]. The court issued a judgment favourable to Christian Parisot, recognising his right of property of the Archives and therefore also of expressing an opinion on the authenticity of the works of Modigliani.

All this happened after Parisot himself had already been arrested in France and convicted of falsifying seventy paintings signed by Jeanne Hébuterne. The final judgment will not take into account the profile of the person involved and will take as authentic deeds that would later be adjudged forgeries by an expert graphologist.

If further investigation had been made, a clear anomaly would have been spotted in the timeline of the letter. «*Suite à nos accords précédents avec*

---

[24] Issued on December 30, 2013, VIII civil section of the Court of Rome, filed on January 4, 2014 as no. 51/2014, which became final in 2015.

les éditions Graphis-Arte» is seen in the first line. What is Graphis-Arte and what relationship does Jeanne have with this publishing house? On the first page of the book *Jeanne Modigliani racconta Modigliani* there is a copy of the letter that the painter's daughter sent to the brothers Giorgio and Guido Guastalla on headed paper of the Amedeo Modigliani Legal Archives: «Rome, June 2, 1984 [...]. "Dear friends, I will send you the final text of *Modigliani racconta Modigliani* as soon as possible." The Guastallas, well-known Jewish art dealers from Leghorn, had been Amedeo Modigliani's neighbours. Their mother had been a pupil of Dedo's mother.

In truth, they do not have a real publishing house, but a printing house for graphic works. The real publishers were the maternal uncles, the Belmontes, who for centuries had published in Leghorn, mainly texts of Jewish culture and tradition. Both brothers, separately, repeatedly confirmed that the relations with Jeanne and with the Parisot, who had been introduced by Modì's daughter, began towards the end of 1983, a few months before they received the June assignment relating to the publication by Graphis-Arte of Jeanne's book. "We were working on the preparations for the centenary of the birth [July 1984, *ed.*] and we wrote to Jeanne," Giorgio says. "She put us in touch with Parisot as her trusted man who would help us. First Parisot came to meet us in Leghorn. Then we all met with Jeanne, in Naples, where there was an exhibition on Modigliani. Carlo Pepi was with us, too. Later we met together in Rome, and finally in Leghorn."

The first edition of Jeanne's book, *Modigliani racconta Modigliani*, was published posthumously. So far, nothing strange, if not for the fact that in 1974 Jeanne Modigliani didn't even know of the existence of the Guastalla brothers, much less that in Leghorn there was a publishing house called Graphis-Arte, whose business we moreover are sure of: it was connected to the art gallery that from the end of the sixties produced lithographs. Guido Guastalla confirmed this.

The alleged act of donation of 1974 refers specifically to a catalogue of Modì's works and not to the publication of the book *Modigliani racconta Modigliani*. But that catalogue, which is even mentioned in the court ruling on the dispute with Laure, was only printed in 1990.

"I remember well that day in Naples in late 1983. The Guastalla brothers and I had long wanted to meet Jeanne Modigliani," Carlo Pepi says. "We had founded the Casa Modigliani in the small building in via Roma where the painter was born and where little Jeanne had lived," Giorgio Guastalla says. "The initiative aimed at remembering and enriching the figure of the great artist, then as today little present among the cultural events of his city. Finally, Parisot managed to bring Jeanne back to Leghorn. She entrusted us with the publication of her book and I reached her myself a few months later in Turin, to deliver cash."

A detail confirmed by Christian Parisot himself, who remembers perfectly the year and the circumstance in which they became acquainted: "I convinced Jeanne to return to Leghorn. Moving on from the Naples exhibition, I introduced her to the Guastallas and Carlo Pepi on that occasion." In 1984, according to what the archivist told us, falling into obvious contradiction with the content of the deed, "Jeanne signed an agreement with Graphis-Arte for the publication of her book on her father that would be put on market the following year." Before the Eighties, therefore, Jeanne knows nothing of Graphis-Arte; how is it possible then that the publishing house appears in the act of donation dated 1974? More and more doubts about the dates and authenticity of the document arise.

In 2010, Parisot is taken to court by Jeanne's daughter, Laure, and is preparing to embark on a legal battle. The act of donation officially comes out only then. To oppose the injunction obtained by Laure, which would have obliged him to deliver the Legal Archives to the legitimate heirs, the archivist considers it appropriate to submit a copy of the act of donation to the Court of Rome conforming to the original, complete with notary seal, but only dated 2011. The document arrives at the studio of his lawyer, Francesca Perri, and the notary Paolo Fenoaltea signed it. The latter, contacted by us after some effort, politely and professionally told us he didn't remember the episode at all. However, "consulting his agenda", he noted that, in respect of the prerogatives that the law assigns to a public official, he had limited himself, "on December 1 2011, to certifying the copy of the original of the act of donation."

The paper presented to the notary, which we have seen, is dotted with smudges, with obvious erasures, overlapping dates, annotations in the margin, which might indicate the date as December 10, 1988, that is when Jeanne was deceased.

When we remind him of Parisot, the professional remains unperturbed and claims not to remember him. Yet the archivist of one of the most valued painters in the world certainly cannot go unnoticed, he is not an ordinary man who turns to the notary for an entailment, nor is Modigliani such a common name. It's not a trivial story, we are talking about an act of donation of precious and rare historical documents.

Jeanne Modigliani's hand doesn't seem to have written the document, but that of someone else. Is this someone named Parisot? What we do know is that it benefited only him. That Christian, initially Cristian without the "h", as his fellow villagers remind us, who, leaving Cerreto d'Asti, managed to entered the life of the great painter's daughter, first as some sort of factotum, then as her archivist, and finally laying claim to the right to authenticate Modì's works.

An almost perfect forger

For the talented and penniless young Piedmontese, Paris was the dream of a suffered redemption. Having arrived in France with few belongings and with the ambition to break through where perhaps his father had failed, he settled in the city of artists after growing up in Cerreto d'Asti, a tiny village. The only place in the world where the memory of his father remains; the painter Adriano Parisot, one of the artists and intellectuals close to Athanasio Soldati who founded the Mac (Movement for concrete art). Jeanne Modigliani is Cristian's opportunity of a lifetime. From that moment on, his name will become Christian. From their first casual encounter in 1973 at the Sorbonne, Parisot begins the plan that will bring him to an unimaginable goal from his room on the hills of Monferrato. On November 12, 1982, the archivist holds the queen in check. After years of working with Joseph Lanthemann, upon the latter's death he finally can free his creative genius and imagine the future of the Legal Archives. For some time Jeanne has not been in control of her frailties. Pain and disorder debilitated a cultured and sensitive woman, who struggled to manage with difficulty her daily existence.

It would seem that in 1982 Parisot had no problem in getting Jeanne to sign another document: the contract of sale of the moral rights from

Modigliani's daughter dated November 12. It further confirms the contents of the 1974 act of donation, but even this document leaves us the same doubts and the same perplexities. The paper that we publish here for the first time also bears an unclear header, with contradictory signatures and dates. The content is a melange and above all, once again it was signed far from the sight of witnesses or family members.

In 1982 Jeanne was sixty-four. She is slightly shabby, but she has no conditions that would cause her to think that death approaches. With this "will and testament", however, she seems to give up everything in exchange for nothing.

How does she plan on living? Why would she wish to cut out her daughters, one of whom, Anne, is very ill as the result of a cerebral haemorrhage that partially paralysed her at just sixteen months, and who definitely needs care and assistance? According to the law on *droit moral*, Jeanne held control over her father's work. But apart from criticism of the legislation, which is not our job, we find it strange, paradoxical, even senseless than having for years built the Archives as though they were a trench to defend the creations and talent of the father figure, suddenly, just a year and a half before Amedeo Modigliani's birth centenary, his daughter decides to sell everything to Parisot. Even committing a crime in the alleged assignment deed: that is, by making a false declaration.

In fact, in 1982 the archives did not exist yet. Although collected over half a century, it was only in 1983 that Jeanne decided to formalise their creation through a specific statute, which will give legal significance to her dream of a lifetime. But it is possible to grant a third party an asset that does not exist yet? Parisot is claiming this, nothing less. The association Legal Archives Amedeo Modigliani was born with a declaration at the Prefecture of Paris on June 16, 1983. According to the archivist, Jeanne signed the donation of the same a year earlier. A prophetic act.

ARCHIVES
LEGALES
AMEDEO
MODIGLIANI

In data odierna I2/II/I982,dichiaro di delegare i miei poteri
legali, civili e penali, secondo la legge e per rappresentarh
e rappresentarmi presso i tribunali internazionali riconosciuti
dalla convenzione di Berna, per tutelare e proteggere l'immagine
e l'opera di Amedeo Modigliani,essendo la figlia unica del l'artista.
Conformemente alle mie intenzioni, il Signor Christian Parisot,
nato a Torino il I4/2/48, e residente a Parigi ,84 Bl. Rochechouart
I8° Parigi,sarà il rappresentatnte unico da me delegato, avente
funzioni di Archivista,avente diritto morale, al fine di far
rispettare attraverso la sua persona e quella degli eredi, il
rispetto dell'operato di Amedeo Modigliani in tutte le sue
forme, ed in tutte le manifestazioni pubbliche.
I documenti,manoscritti,e fotografici sono a partire dalla dau
odierna ,di sua proprietà,e con essi tutti i documenti dello
Archivio Amedeo Modigliani da me raccolto e custodito.
I timbri contrassegnati dalla firma di MODIGLIANI, che rappresentano
l'autorizzazione ad autenticare le opere,e contrassegnarle
in caso di produzione di oggetti derivati (Litografie,multipli,
e vari oggetti) sono, a partire dalla data odierna , di proprietà
di Christian Parisot. (3 in totale).
I) Timbro della firma dell'artista in gomma rappresentante la firma:

2) Timbro degli Archives Légales Amedeo Modigliani,che rappresenta
la futura Associazione, che riunirà gli archivi da me raccolti
e che serve e servirà come contrassegno per le autentiche.

ARCHIVES
LEGALES
AMEDEO
MODIGLIANI

3) Timbro a secco in rilievo portante l'iscrizione in caratteri
ebraici al centro,e l'indicazione Archives Légales Amedeo Modigliani
che serve e servirà per contrassegnare le opere derivate su carta
ed a contraddistinguere tutti i documenti emananti da e per gli
Archives Légales Amedeo Modigliani,

Contract between Jeanne Modigliani and Christian Parisot November 12 1982.

2

I benefici derivanti dai servizi resi, o dalle prestazioni professionali, saranno decisi di comune accordo, e sempre rispettando le leggi in vigore.

Ciascuno di questi documenti potrà essere venduto o separato dall'insieme del materiale riunito; al fine di creare una futura istituzione, o fondazione, con lo scopo di rappresentare e divulgare l'immagine e l'opera di Amedeo Modigliani.

La pubblicazione del Catalogo Ragionato dell'opera completa di Amedeo Modigliani è affidato alla competenza di Christian Parisot, che ne curerà l'edizione, la divulgazione e l'aggiornamento seguendo le regole scientifiche ed estetiche.

Nessuna deroga o derogazione è possibile, in materia di competenza, che resta unica e solidaria con l'attuale Archivista avente diritto, e dovere di fronte alla legge.

Le opere derivate dovranno rispettare: in primo luogo la specificità dell'operato, l'attinenza e le qualità d'esecuzione che deve essere adattata e realizzata da persone competenti, con risultati confermati dalla persona responsabile, dall'attuale Archivista, che ne curerà la diffusione.

Questo documento non mi vincola nelle eventuali iniziative, ma solidaria alla Associazione, futura fondazione, nella ricerca di enti privati e pubblici per la realizzazione e concretizzazione di un Centro di Ricerche che porterà il nome di Amedeo Modigliani.

Le persone private porteranno la responsabilità in caso di contestazioni, o violazioni della legge, alle quali faranno ricorso alle persone competenti e nei tribunali.

Questo documento ha validità immediata ed è firmato da Christian Parisot, avente diritto, e dall'attuale erede e figlia riconosciuta Jeanne Modigliani. Questo documento privato ha valore legale.

Fatto a Parigi 12/III/ 1982

Christian Parisot

Jeanne Modigliani

ARCHIVES LÉGALES AMEDEO MODIGLIANI

(2)

12/11/1982

Paris le 12. 11/ 1982

J. Modigliani
205 Bd Vincent Auriol Paris 13°

"Jeanne was our reference point right up to her tragic death," Carlo Pepi recalls. "It was she who signed everything. Parisot yes, he was important, much more than me, I was nothing, but it was her, Jeanne, who represented us; Christian had to report to her." Jeanne wished to give the Archives to the city of Leghorn after the establishment of an authoritative scientific committee.

Her efforts to protect the image of her father seem to be reflected in the last letter that she supposedly wrote to Pepi a few hours before dying. A document that shows her anxious for what is happening in the city: overwhelmed by the uninformed collective euphoria for the discovery of the "heads" in the "Fosso Reale"[25], Jeanne would have been ready to leave Paris to assert her influence and bring everyone back to their senses. So on the date of July 26, 1984, a few hours before her death, Jeanne would have still felt able to autonomously manage, under her own weight, the Archives and all the related rights. The suspicion, then, becomes more concrete. Parisot himself unconsciously confirms this in an interview with "Panorama" on September 17, 1984: "Jeanne wanted to donate all the archives, handwritten letters and documentation concerning her father to the Municipality of Leghorn".

Yet according to Christian Parisot in court, Jeanne had already given him full power over them. The Piedmontese archivist is careful not to tell his colleagues at Casa Modigliani that he has become the *deus ex machina* of everything that gravitates around the artist, this at least until the demise of the association's president. In addition, if it was so, if in 1974, and with a wider power since 1982, he had already had control of all the material collected and archived, why did he always feel obliged to seek Jeanne's consent? Why did he have he to answer for his choices? Why did he make sure she was always there to sign personally, or certify with her seal, the authenticity of sometimes forged works, if he could freely and independently dispose of the stamps and rights based on an authority recognised since 1982? "In Naples, during the 1983 exhibition, a forged drawing was on display, a horrible thing. Parisot asked Jeanne to stand in

---

[25] It will be the stage of the fourth crime scene in this book.

front of it, to be photographed together," Pepi says remembering the first days he met Dedo's daughter in person.

Today, November 12, 1982, I declare that I delegate my powers, legal, civil and criminal, according to the law, to represent it and represent me at the international courts recognised by the Bern Convention, to preserve and protect the image and work of Amedeo Modigliani, being the artist's only daughter.

Thus begins the act through which Jeanne would renew the act of donation signed in 1974. In the first part, the document is similar to the power of attorney, via which Jeanne attributes to Parisot mere powers of representation before authority, abstractly quoting the Bern agreement. Later, however, with a disarming simplicity, the woman surrenders all moral rights to the archivist, depriving its legitimate heirs. Again, the questions are many, too many. It is not conceivable that a mentally sane person would give up her rights and of those of her heirs to transfer them to someone who is outside of the family. What influence did the Piedmontese have on poor Jeanne? At some point, the act of 1982 suddenly turns into a definitive assignment. Not before underlining, however, that "the benefits deriving from the rendered services, or the professional services will be decided by mutual agreement". What a mess. What benefits did Jeanne refer to? Probably to the economic ones deriving from the authentications, and we know from Pepi that forgeries may often have been authenticated. Then, what sense does it make to declare that Parisot would become the sole owner from that moment? Why don't we find the same doubts, the same perplexity, in the various legal sentences?

In the document, Parisot committed not to sell or to yield, even if only in part, anything Modigliani's daughter had given to him. However, the materials are immediately sent abroad to unknown collectors; Parisot moves frantically between the Far East, China and Japan, as far as South America, where he will try to organise an exhibition in Sao Paulo, without success. Then the Archives are given to Luciano Renzi's Modigliani Institute; in the end they would be sold definitively to the art dealer Maria Stellina Marescalchi, via a change of ownership transaction identical to the one signed by him and Jeanne, and with off the books payments.

Not bad for someone who over a few decades of activity as the highest expert, repository and custodian of Amedeo Modigliani's image was taken to court several times: in Rome in 2011 (hearings ended on February 28, 2019 with prescription for the crime of forgery and acquittal for receiving stolen goods); in 2013, 2014 and 2017, again in Rome; in 2011 another investigation in Venice; identical fate in Padua in 2014 and in Arezzo in 2015. The alleged offences: forgery, fraud and receiving stolen goods. Then the confiscations: in Rome and Arezzo. Twice arrested, first in France then in Italy, and definitively sentenced as a forger in Paris.

Parisot's first known troubles date back to 2000. Taking advantage of his acquaintance with the family of the painter Jeanne Hébuterne, Jeanne Modigliani's mother, as well as the authority that derived from being Modì's archivist, Parisot borrowed around seventy drawings and watercolours by the Leghorn painter's last companion for an exhibition in Venice. After the exhibition closes, controversy breaks out because of the inclusion of some paintings that do not convince Luc Prunet, Jeanne Hébuterne's nephew and custodian of her works. Prunet asks for the return of all the material. After a few months, he becomes aware of a new exhibition of his aunt's drawings in Spain. At least this is what the press says; in reality, those works are fakes that imitate the style of the painter. Parisot is charged. The trial is held only three years later, in 2003. The owners of some of the drawings falsely attributed to Hébuterne are present at the hearing and denounce the Piedmontese archivist for the certifications he granted, against a huge payment: certificates of false artworks. The sentence in the first instance is two years in prison, suspended for sixteen months. On appeal, however, the Paris courts changed the sentence to two years, with a conditional suspension and payment of a fine of 50,000 euros, in addition to compensation for another 50,000 to Luc Prunet.

They say that crime does not pay. The statement doesn't hold water, at least considering the profits that the archivist had made since he started his plotting. After Jeanne's death, her daughter, Laure, appears immortalised with Parisot while, with a lost gaze, she leans against a giant copy of a caryatid. Then comes the turn of the alleged granddaughter. "Parisot introduced us to a pretty and shy girl," the reporter Adele Cambria writes, recounting her visit to the exhibition at Palazzo Taverna, where the archivist acted as her guide. "He called her *"fille de Jeanne"*. However, the girl, who vanished from view after a few minutes, could not be Modigliani's granddaughter, but, if anything, his great-granddaughter.

Without any regard his the guest, Monsieur Parisot justified the apparition-disappearance ray saying that she was undergoing therapy for depression. Today I wonder if it wasn't an authentic abuse to carry that defenceless creature around the world, to legitimise his hidden trafficking ..."[26]

The trial for the events of Palazzo Taverna, where investigations began in 2010, ended on February 28, 2019 after reaching the statute of limitations. So nobody will pay for those crimes, nobody will compensate the people defrauded by Parisot and his co-defendant Vignapiano; the latter was sentenced, only for receiving stolen goods, while Parisot, acquitted for the latter crime, benefitted from the prescription of forgery charges. In the ruling in this case, the judge orders the destruction of the works except for those purchased by Sandra Vellani, but only after affixing an indelible stamp: "This is a false work, as declared by the judicial authority."

---

[26] Adele Cambria, *Monsieur Parisot, the gentle swindler who peddles Modì*, «Il Venerdi' di Repubblica ", January 18 2013.

Fourth Crime Scene: New Venice district, Leghorn
The case of Modi's heads

CHARACTERS

Dario Durbé – superintendent of the National Gallery of Modern Art of Rome, expert of the Macchiaioli and, from a young age, a political activist in the ranks of the Leghorn PCI political party.

Vera Durbé – Dario's twin sister, director of the progressive contemporary art museum of Leghorn and conservator of the civic museums of the city. She is also a member of the Communist Party having previously been among the partisans.

Michele Caturegli – engineer at the Municipality of Leghorn, construction manager of dredging of the "Fosso Reale" in 1984. Eyewitness of almost everything that happened in those months around the recovery project of the legendary heads of Modigliani.

Claudio Frontera – councillor for culture in Leghorn. He will promote the recovery of the heads in an effort to relaunch the image of the city.

Pietro Luridiana, Pierfrancesco Ferrucci, Michele Ghelarducci, Michele Genovesi – students. They are the creators of the head named Modi 2, found in the "Fosso Reale".

Angelo Froglia – young Dadaist painter-sculptor; in 1974 he took part in the Quadrennial of Rome, in 1977, he entered the armed struggle becoming a militant of the far left with Azione Rivoluzionaria and ending up in prison until 1981. He is the creator of the heads known as Modi 1 and Modi 3.

Piero Vaccari – Leghorn sculptor, creator of a head for Carlo Pepi.

Massimino Filippelli – framer, his shop in the heart of the market district in the seventies and eighties became a breeding ground for young talents and a meeting place for those who want to measure their artistic knowledge and skill.

Alessandro Bulgini – artist, painter, friend of Angelo Froglia. He is the author of the portrait of Modigliani in the hallway of the Leghorn railway station.

Massimo Seghetti – employee at the Municipality of Leghorn, at the Department of Culture where he carries out activities related to audio-visual recordings. Angelo Froglia's friend and accomplice.

Lido Bellandi – employee at the Municipality of Leghorn, Angelo Froglia's friend and accomplice, owner of the boat used to throw the heads in the ditch.

Elisabetta De Paz – employee at the Municipality of Leghorn, deputy of Vera Durbé, Massimo Seghetti's partner, Angelo Froglia's friend and accomplice.

Antonino Filastò – Florentine lawyer, defender of Angelo Froglia and Carlo Pepi.

Carla Panicali – noblewoman and gallery owner from Rome, member of the scientific committee of the exhibition at Villa Maria for the centenary of Modigliani's birth, sales manager of the exhibition, friend of Klaus Perls and Dario Durbé.

Klaus Perls – New York gallery owner, some of his works will be exhibited at Villa Maria.

Joseph Laposata – commander of the American military base at Camp Darby stationed in Pisa.

And again: Jeanne Modigliani, Christian Parisot, Carlo Pepi, Giorgio e Guido Guastalla.

"Fosso Reale", Royal Ditch[27] *June 1, 1984 (one month before the beginning of the drama), 17.45 hours*

Italy is glued to the TV. The final stage of the European football championship is being played in Nantes. The Italians have already been eliminated but Michel Platini is on the pitch, a Juventus champion of Piedmontese origin, a genius of the ball and, as such, revered beyond the barriers of national partisanship. The expectations for a show will be rewarded; with class and elegance he will score three of the five goals with which France defeats Belgium. After half an hour of the first time, the score is already two-nil. There is not a soul around. As if the game weren't enough to dissuade the people of Leghorn from taking a walk, the summer heat, which at that time is twenty-nine degrees with almost 80 percent of humidity, does the rest.

It is the right time, everything is going according to plan. A long, dark car approaches the edge of the "Fosso Reale", near the food market. Five people, men and women, get out. Three of them are in uniform. One of sturdy build, medals on his chest and many stars on his epaulettes, has the bearing of one used to observing and issuing commands. The two women are also in uniform, but their demeanour is gentle rather than martial. In the city, people would immediately know that they are American officials from the nearby base of Camp Darby.

The last two in the group are Tuscan: one is small, skinny, with quick movements. The older one laughs as he opens the trunk and looks inside. Then he closes it again, shaking his head. The other Italian seems relieved. The Americans, however, look disappointed. Everyone gets back in the car and leaves.

Carlo Pepi is driving. The officer at his side is the commander Joseph Laposata, head of the most important American strategic base in the Mediterranean. Today he is no longer among us, he died at the age of

---

[27] It is the name of the largest Medici canal of the river system designed by Leonardo da Vinci to integrate the city with the port, making them one. It represents one of the most fascinating aspects of Leghorn.

eighty on December 3, 2018 in Florida, where, as a three-star general, he had retired after an illustrious career during which he had commanded companies of soldiers in all major war theatres, from Iraq to Afghanistan. Behind sits the sculptor Piero Vaccari, creator of the stone head "Alla Modigliani", along with the two women, Mary and Katherine.

The idea seemed to have sprung from the irreverent Leghorn spirit. An ironic lampoon, but one that could deal a mortal blow to the already shaky credibility of the municipal administration in Leghorn, and perhaps above all to pompous head of the progressive Museum of contemporary art, Vera Durbé, who also has the role of conservator of the Leghorn civic museums. Some time before, Mary had approached Carlo, an accountant from Pisa and a renowned art connoisseur. She had introduced herself as head of the logistics at the base, looking for apartments to rent for her colleagues. It was the beginning of an unusual acquaintance.

"Fosso Reale", July 14, 1984, 22.00 hours

The canal is partially occupied by the dredger platform[28] which, in a few days, will begin to rummage among the stones on the canal bed. The city waste will be hauled out: bicycles, guns, toilets and bidets, old carts and a load of rocks. The moorings on the banks are all free. The evening is warm and bright. At the oars of a small boat, Massimo Seghetti, an employee of the Municipality of Leghorn, approaches the platform as close as possible. Lido Bellandi is with him; fishing is his hobby and knows the place like the back of his hand. He enjoys the trip in comfort; all he has to do is indicate a specific place. When he thinks he is there, he gestures to the comrade to stop the boat. He indicates a place where the arm of the dredger should begin its search. They move carefully to avoid ending up in the water because of the backwash: the contents of the bundle they have to lift is heavy. Here, they drop the two stones one after the other. They disappear with a splash that resounds loudly in the silence of the night and makes them wince.

---

[28] A floating platform fitted with a machine for underwater excavation.

Angelo Froglia had given them those sculpted stones. He is an artist not yet thirty years old, who spends his time between his artistic work with brushes and chisels, his job at the port and his revolutionary activities (a few years previously he had taken part to an attack for which he was sentenced to more than three years in prison). They are deliberately rough works, which differ from Modigliani's style and appear rather coarsely inspired by Picasso's "primitive" works. For Froglia, this is also, in its way, an attack: he intends to demolish the sacred cow represented by the world of art critics, who, in his opinion, "don't understand fuck all" about art. Like Modigliani, his illustrious fellow citizen, he is a "fighting" man. He wants to lay open to ridicule the "experts" of his time, to mortify the presumptuous leaders among these self-styled connoisseurs. For this purpose, he throws the heads of discord into "Fosso Reale", rough and ugly works that in his opinion, Amedeo would never have made. He throws this poisoned bait for the world of admirers, great experts of Modì, self-important characters who had said they were all but certain of finding, in the canal, the masterpieces abandoned by the artist. Here are some worthless rocks: go ahead and binge on them. Use the canal dredger to glorify your incompetence.

Later they would say that it probably wasn't his idea; he had climbed aboard without knowing where he was going.

"Fosso Reale", July 23 1984, 23.00 hours

At sunrise, the bucket will sink again into the mud of the canal. A group of students stops on the bridge. First, they had passed by their favourite bar to meet friends. They had joked about what they were going to do, some people thought they were bluffing so they go along to see if these others dare to carry out their plans. They laugh, but without making too much noise. They carry a heavy package, which they now open. It contains a large flat stone with a long engraved nose. They throw it into the water.

They really had wanted to emulate Modigliani. A few hours earlier, they had still been in the backyard, armed with an electric drill and chisels to attack that boulder to destroy, with a few blows, the reputation of the city's so-called connoisseurs.

As the would-be sculpture falls into the water, someone is watching them from afar. Franco Rigoni had been standing at his open bedroom window because of the heat: the following morning he would recount what he had seen to Michele Caturegli, an engineer and head of the Municipality's technical office, who was coordinating the dredging operations under Vera Durbé's direction.

Rigoni clearly saw six young men; later they would find out that two of them were just onlookers who had come to take pictures of the event. Rigoni had had a good view of the stone, he would recognise it immediately when it was recovered, but nobody would want to believe him. Those youngsters who had thrown it right next to the dredging platform were Pietro Luridiana, Pierfrancesco Ferrucci, Michele Ghelarducci and Michele Genovesi. Four names that all Leghorn would know very soon.

"Fosso Reale", a sultry night in July 1909

Amedeo Modigliani and his drinking buddy wander around chatting in the narrow streets of the Market district. One an artist, the other a framer in via Gherardi del Testa, an alley close to the wall that runs alongside the "Fosso Reale" and flanks the market. For a few weeks, the two have shared a small courtyard between their workplaces.

At the beginning of the summer, Modigliani had returned from Paris to recover from a bad relapse of tuberculosis and he hopes to regain his strength so that he can depart once again. They walk, and between a Pernod and a white Elba wine they discuss politics and art. They proceed slowly, pushing a cart loaded with heavy granite stones, each one very different from the other. They recovered them, as always, at the port, from the residues left by cargo ships. Modì had worked them. In those days, he thought that his artistic future would be as a sculptor, but his delicate health would stand in the way. Now he has to find a place, a safe home for those sculptures of his: he certainly cannot take them to France. He has two alternatives: throw them away, or leave them with someone who can look after them until his return. Maybe that night-time walk would help him decide what to do.

Modigliani was very fond of sculpture: stone was better than "mud", he said. Some people deny Amedeo took a subsequent trip to Leghorn in 1913. But thanks to the irrefutable documentation provided by Giorgio Guastalla, we can say that in July of that year Modigliani wrote postcards from Carrara addressed to his friend Paul Alexandre. "Pictures from Carrara and from Lucca, and also from Leghorn. Possibly, like other sculptors, he had a shop in Carrara, the city of marble," the Leghorn gallery owner says. "He may have had it there earlier, in 1909. There is no trace of the shop in via Gherardi del Testa now, there are just rumours."

Different voices that tell contradictory stories, but they pass from bar to bar, from ear to ear, until they become common heritage, an urban legend. When Modigliani becomes famous, so too does the story according to which, one day during one of his returns from Paris, he may have thrown away one or more of his sculpted works.

The thought becomes reality, legend becomes truth.

On January 2, 1984, the curator of Leghorn civic museums Vera Durbé announces far and wide, with the assuredness of an ancient soothsayer, that the famous heads of Modigliani now lie in the waters of his hometown. She asks the Municipality to dredge the Royal Ditch. Together with her brother Dario (superintendent of the National Gallery of Modern Art in Rome summoned by the Region of Tuscany to Leghorn to promote the image of Amedeo Modigliani and of the Macchiaioli), she is the curator of the exhibition dedicated to the artist on the centenary of his birth. It will open on July 1 and will continue all summer, until September: what better time?

The assumption of the official is apparently based on the story by Constantin Brâncusi, a friend of Amedeo, a Romanian sculptor who moved in the same bohemian circles and was repeatedly taken into psychiatric hospital. The culture councillor, Claudio Frontera, quotes the book by the Romanian writer Peter Neagoë entitled *The Saint of Montparnasse*,[29] in

---

[29] Peter Neagoe, *The Saint of Montparnasse. A Novel Based on the Life of Constantin Brancusi*, Chilton Books, Philadelphia 1965.

which the Parisian memories of Brâncuşi are recalled. Durbé's belief is based on similar written reports, as well as on "old pub stories" handed down by indirect Tuscan "witnesses", by hearsay. Yet the director of the museum, against all logic, has managed to convince the whole municipal administration, which on March 13 approved the budget to dredge that part of the canal.

The recent history of Leghorn, however, is something Durbé should know well. The Tuscan port-city suffered bombings during the Second World War. The setting of this somewhat absurd pantomime, the district of New Venice, he had been fairly torn apart, so much so that one of the two bridges between which the dredging is carried out had been completely destroyed, and was only rebuilt many years after the end of the conflict. Which administration does not provide for the removal of war ordinance after the end of hostilities?

Leghorn, which for decades had been - and still is - a model of good governance, often dredged its "noble" Medici channels, both with the specific purpose of clearing its navigation waters from rubble and unexploded devices, and periodically, to free the riverbed from debris and malodorous slime. How likely is it that a dredger will find recover a weighty object thrown into the water a hundred years ago? In addition, over the years the free flowing water, aided by a series of floods and storms, would have swept away much of the debris, large and small, in a swirl of fresh water rushing down to the sea. Vera Durbé brushes these questions aside when she insists on pointing the workers dredging to the exact spot where they might find the heads. Because they can be found only in that place. It is not down to intuition, or the culmination of extensive historical research, but because the heads had just been thrown there, for a hidden but precise purpose.

The widely acclaimed triumph will breathe life into the as yet rather insipid celebrations for the centenary of Modigliani's birth. The event has great media appeal, bringing the world's attention to the city of Leghorn along with a large influx of tourists and media. "If there is one person responsible for everything that happened that year at the ditch it is me." The engineer Michele Caturegli, after thirty-five years, expresses his *mea culpa*. He was better known in Leghorn, and everywhere at that time, as "the bucket man".

"They were convincing. I do not understand art, but when I saw the others so moved, I convinced myself that they were authentic. 'It shows the resurrection,' they said ... then maybe it's true, I thought. Durbé paid no attention to Jeanne Modigliani's research. 'What can she know about it, she is just his daughter,' she said. The Municipality listened to her because they couldn't take it anymore - she was very stubborn - but mainly because I had found an inexpensive way to explore the ditch."

Jeanne Modigliani, in fact, had raised her voice from Paris to Leghorn, saying there was no way her father would have ever thrown the works into a canal. However, the Durbé siblings had managed to bamboozle everyone, even people like the educated, calm and rational engineer.

He tells us about Caturegli, recalling the memories and emotions of those days lived at unbearable speed, especially for those accustomed to a quiet provincial life.

As if by magic, these stone heads began to pop out like fireworks that catch a spark and explode, partly by chance, partly according to a sequence, cleverly choreographed like a giant pyrotechnic display coming to a crescendo. One might easily believe it was Vera Durbé's imagination that triggered everything ... but I feel obliged to say that I materially triggered the first firework. I didn't put the project forward, but I found the way to make it possible. Without my work, those fireworks could not have been ignited. My plan only cost 10 percent of the entire exhibition budget. A poor exhibition to which the dredging project, which no one seemed to believe in, could contribute by increasing the advertising hype. However, nobody really believed the sculptures would be found.

I started to think. I felt that a platform with a bulldozer on board could perform the required job. The Superintendence rejected the proposal because the bucket teeth could ruin any discoveries. I set to work and, together with a technician from the Pacini Company that had the contract for some of the works, we designed tailor made teeth that allowed the jaws of the bulldozer to be tightened without damaging the extracted material. Soft, rubber coated teeth, wide enough to drain debris. We spent a few days experimenting with vases made of increasingly fragile material. It passed the test. The Superintendence approved. The Municipality allocated 40 million Lire to perform the job.

The work was due to begin on May 21. It was not so. Durbé did not come and the work did not start, because there was no testing. Everything was finally ready on July 16, but work was again held up.

On July 19, the dredger finally begins to explore the "Fosso Reale". The digger searches the bottom without results for five days. *We found sod all!* was the sardonic headline in the *Vernacoliere*. Just when many people had begun to mock the administration, the money allocated to the operation was running out and the attention of the media began to wane, on 24 July at 9 am the Municipality of Leghorn's dredger brought to the surface the first head that would be attributed to Modigliani (Modì 1). Only a few hours will pass and at 5 pm on the same day, a second sculpture (Modì 2) would see the light once more.

"I was there when the first head was found among the stones, and I was still there in the afternoon when the second one appeared from under the water," Caturegli remembers today. He shows us his snapshots. We see him as a young man, with a thick blond forelock. As the work progresses he spends the day with the workers and Ms Durbé on the embankment. Photography is his passion, and his snapshots, the only proof, accompany the headlines of all the world's newspapers. Even today he remains proud of those photographs.

Modì 1 is found right near the floating platform, it may have bounced on one of the anchor cables before reaching the canal bed.

When I showed the head to the councillor [Claudio Frontera, Leghorn's councillor of Culture, ed] his first words were: "And they thought we were a joke." Vera, on the other hand, is moved, she hugs it saying: "Like a son who was lost and is now found". Dario Durbé arrives the next day.

It was decided to take it to the upper floor of the exhibition in Villa Maria. Modì 2 was also brought there. However, when we load it up on a car with a Pisan number plate to take it from the ditch to the Museum, people run after us shouting that "the Pisans are taking Modigliani's sculpture" and try to stop us.

Meanwhile, in Paris, Jeanne dies in those same days. It is July 28 when the news arrives in Leghorn. At least two weeks will pass between then and the day Carlo Pepi receives a letter from Jeanne dated July 26, 1984, and sent the following day from Paris.

Giorgio Guastalla gave the official statement on behalf of the Legal Archives. However, that morning Parisot calls Carlo Pepi first. The latter also sends a note to the Ansa Agency and passes on the Paris number of the archivist for further explanations by telephone. Parisot is immediately reached and makes some initial statements and gives an account of the events, which he will later deny.

Guido Guastalla told us about Jeanne's most recent intentions, when she was incredulous at how everything had happened so quickly: "Jeanne absolutely wanted to bring forward her departure for Leghorn, scheduled for September. We had spoken over the phone and she had seemed determined to get to the city as soon as possible to put a halt to the events."

The woman's untimely death causes quite a commotion. It occurs in circumstances and in a way that could cause one to think it was no accident. In those difficult days, the newspapers explore many hypotheses. In the meantime, the Leghorn authorities try to play down the drama, so much so that I comments: "once again those promoting the exhibition and those in charge of the event show a lack of sensitivity."

In the meantime, a whole phalanx of Leghorn's townspeople has gravitated to the embankments of the Fossi; the media circus, including dozens of television and radio stations, newspapers and correspondents from all over the world flock between the canal and the town hall. Towards the end of July, the city is overwhelmed by rumours that the heads are a grotesque farce; despite this, the Municipality, which had suspended the dredging on July 30, gave orders to resume the work to recover any other sculptures, shortly after noon on August 6. On 9 August at 9.30, the bucket again sinks its teeth into the mud to bring to light the third head (Modì 3). However, it was not Lady Luck who caused the treasure to appear magically from the ditches: as one of the main players in this story will tell us, someone had spent a lot of effort to make the scene credible, and knew very well that there were two sculptures to be found, both made by the same hand.

The story will go down in history not as a lucky find, but as the hoax of the century, even if that is not quite accurate. "We wasted a unique opportunity," Caturegli says with regret looking back on the enthusiasm of the city in those days. "An opportunity for Leghorn to feel pride and a rare sense of cohesion. Instead, we went down in history as a city of jokers, even though it's not true. In Leghorn, we are irreverent, sarcastic, but we are not clowns. In fact, it was no joke, not even then."

The "Mud" of the Leghorn ditches

Let's start at the beginning. The Leghorn municipal administration charges the director of the progressive museum of contemporary art with organising artistic and cultural events for the upcoming commemoration of the centenary of Amedeo Modigliani's birth. It is June 20, 1984, a few days before the opening of the exhibition at Villa Maria,[30] when Modì's daughter takes pen and paper and writes to the Municipality and to the board of the Museum, complaining that she had been deliberately left out of the project despite offering her complete cooperation. She had even offered some of the documents she had collected for the Archives to Leghorn, offering to make the donations to expand the exhibition. But the refusal of "Richelieu", Dario Durbé, was stark, especially considering that Parisot had asked for every work presented at Villa Maria to be accompanied by the stamp of the Legal Archives. The superintendent, however, remained the only person authorised to guarantee the authenticity of the material exhibited.

Vera, the official curator of the events for the centenary celebrations of Amedeo Modigliani's birth, grew up in the shadow of her grandfather, the playwright Dario Niccodemi. Her ancestry is somehow the fundamental pillar of her brief curriculum - her studies were also brief, ending after middle school - but she is supported by partisan political activists. For this reason, too, she is not well-loved in her office; other people put up with her and for some, she has become a symbol that needs to be brought down.

Her brother, who was named after his grandfather, is an influential character of culture. His career as a critic, almost entirely focused on the Macchiaioli, brought him respect and an enviable position, but he is also a political party man (PCI) and a prize-hunter.

---

[30] The exhibition at Villa Maria goes from July 1 to September 9 1984.

From 19 to 24 July, when the excavations in "Fosso Reale" begin, Vera rarely leaves her position near the barge. She directs the operations, guiding the technicians where she says she is convinced that Modigliani threw his sculptures. In the TV pictures that travel around the world you can always see her there, like an old captain at the helm of the ship. She reaches out from the pier, pointing her finger and insisting: "they are here ... dig here."

When the dredger brings the first head to the surface, Vera and Dario Durbé are moved. After the second, they break out into "love" declarations for the stones. They even say that Dario is "in physical contact" with Modigliani.

"A few words to describe an episode and the emotions that would have required the space of an entire book," writes the superintendent in his catalogue *Due pietre ritrovate di Amedeo Modigliani.*[31]

"I felt close to Modigliani, as if that stone had the power to put us in physical contact and cancel seventy-five years that separated his bitter gesture from the glory of our discovery."

Other illustrious self-proclaimed art history gurus also share their enthusiasm; they seem enchanted. As if they had all been bewitched, they say they are certain of the authenticity of the "sculptures". Cesare Brandi, art historian, writes on the pages of the *Corriere della Sera* newspaper, where he is a columnist, "They are made by Modigliani. They have an inner light [...]. In those two rough stones there is an announcement, there is a presence." For Giulio Carlo Argan, one of the most renowned, if not the greatest art critic of the twentieth century: "Subject to careful analysis of the findings, I trust the thesis of the authenticity of the sculptures, even if they are not masterpieces". And Ludovico Ragghianti, a politician, art critic and historian: "They are fundamental for Modigliani and for modern sculpture". Sculptors like Pietro Cascella and Lorenzo Guerrini find in them "the hand of an artist who has not yet mastered the appropriate use of his tools". Rino Giannini, of the Carrara Academy of Fine Arts, while

---

[31] Dario Durbe' (edited byi), *Due pietre ritrovate di Amedeo Modigliani*, Books & Company, Leghorn 1984.

speaking of "marks made by unusually large chisels", supports the idea that "the executive process appears to be typical of Modi".

"Be circumspect, don't be credulous, did you see the heads?" Guido Guastalla tells us about the conversation he had then with Professor Enzo Carli, art historian. "No, I haven't seen them - the latter is said to have replied - but why should I doubt the word a friend, a colleague like Dario Durbé?" The gallery owner, secretary of the Modigliani Legal Archives repeats to the academic, who had invited Jeanne Modigliani to his degree presentation. "Listen to me; be careful, look at them first, they are really ugly."

Superintendent Durbé had put a lot of pressure on the experts he had contacted. To win them over, he had sent a car service to escort them one by one, he had wined and dined them, he had practically rolled out the red carpet for them.

Meanwhile, Marco Franzini, Professor of Mineralogy in Pisa who analysed the stones, declares, "Nothing emerges to refute the hypothesis that they have been lying on the canal bed since 1909". Later, scientists find microalgae embedded in the rock that they believe to have been "deposited over decades".

They also carry out coring on the bottom of the ditch, in order to take older mud and to evaluate its consistency and compare it with the microorganisms present on the recovered "artefacts". Surprisingly it seems that this also fits the hypothesis. Actually the analyses were entrusted to a Leghorn laboratory, devoid of any specific experience, while the necessary tests for reliability would require much more time and expertise. Even the laboratory admits it; they express themselves with caution and tell Dario Durbé that further in-depth analysis would be needed. Nevertheless, the superintendent decides that in the meantime the analyses performed are enough, even if not conclusive, and hurries to announce the news, closing the door on any further type of investigation.

The chief restorer of the Modern Art Gallery in Rome, Enzo Pagliani, who conducted the initial cleaning of the heads, says he is convinced. "I have no doubt about the authenticity of the sculptures; the examination of the mud deposited between the interstices of the stone proves that the heads were thrown into the ditch many years ago."[32] Perhaps some outside influence had interfered with the analysis of the mud, as well as the professionalism and experience of the scientists involved.

On Sunday, September 2, 1984 at the progressive museum of contemporary art in Leghorn everything is ready for the exhibition of the "find" and the presentation of the book by Dario Durbé, *Due pietre ritrovate di Amedeo Modigliani*. In less than two weeks since the recovery of the second head, Dario Durbé - the superintendent of Rome's gallery of modern art, the "mystic" brother of the Leghorn exhibition's curator, has managed to write a treatise on the sculptures, had them photographed and published his book. But in the meantime there were now three stones, not two, as published in Durbé's "work". What does this mean? There is only one explanation: the superintendent must have sent his precious tome to be printed before the discovery of the third find, therefore before August 9. He did not expect to find the third head, and this would confirm our hypothesis: those who threw in the third work knew about the other two.

However, not everything turns out as it should. While the Durbé siblings and the municipal administrators are about to enjoy the fruits of their labours with the global recognition of the discovery, the party is ruined by a news flash. The agency Ansa AP reports a shocking story: in a blow to the cherished national culture, three students have given a detailed interview to the magazine "Panorama" which covers the whole of Leghorn in ignominy.

On the evening of September 1, Pierfrancesco Ferrucci, with Dario Durbé's catalogue under his arm, calls at Vera's house. He introduces himself on behalf of all "friends of Modigliani" and asks her to autograph the book. Flattered and pleased, the manager of the museum signs with the inscription: "To Modigliani's friends. Vera Durbe'". A few days are left before the exhibition at Villa Maria closes. Only a few hours later, the weekly magazine's scoop makes news across the world. The three students say it was they who carved one of those heads; indeed, they produced it with a Black & Decker drill. The town hall building trembles. Nobody

---

[32] Daniela Pasti, *La testa della discordia*, «la Repubblica», 5 settembre 1984.

believes or wants to believe it. Vera Durbé tries to fight back, still arguing the unsustainable and making a passionate speech in defence of the historical authenticity of the "caryatids".

On the afternoon of September 7, the bailiff affixes the seals on the Modì 2 sculpture, which two days later is transferred to a vault in the Bank of Italy. Terrible days will follow! Vera, however, does not give up even in face of the evidence, taking every opportunity to stress her belief. Eventually, a nervous breakdown leaves her hospitalised and under sedatives. Meanwhile, on September 9, as scheduled, the exhibition at Villa Maria for the centenary of Modigliani's birth closes amid recriminations and controversy. There had been fifty thousand visitors, a success in spite of everything.

Discharged from the clinic on September 11, Vera insists: "I am fully convinced that all three heads recovered from the ditch are Modigliani's. I await the final results of the chemical analyses which I'm sure will confirm the authenticity of the three sculptures". As if by magic, those results will arrive, but they will soon be proven wrong again and they will cause the same shame previously experienced by those self-styled experts who were "certain" about the sculptures.

On September 12, the Amedeo Modigliani Legal Archives from Paris and from Leghorn launch an appeal "to the authors of the other two sculptures attributed to Modì", in the name of the "ethical-legal responsibility of the Archives."[33] They invite any of those responsible to get in contact with them immediately, something that had already happened a few weeks earlier. On July 19, in fact, the Legal Archives had received an anonymous letter claiming the existence of other forgers. The letter contained a drawing that clearly referenced to Modì 1, but the head had not been found yet. The Archives guaranteed absolute confidentiality to those willing to

---

[33] Ansa AP, September 12 1984.

come forward and offered to provide "legal assistance in civil and criminal matters".[34]

On September 13 comes a new twist. The message sent out the day before by Giorgio Guastalla is promptly received by the young Angelo Froglia, who calls the secretary of the Legal Archives. He is the author of the others two heads, and before coming forward he wants confirmation of the promises of assistance made by the gallery owner, including, if needed, legal assistance. "Once we received Foglia's self-declaration, we called the Carabinieri Unit for the protection of artistic heritage, who wanted to interview the boy before the press conference". Giorgio Guastalla himself gives us these details. However, things are in motion and shortly after, the meeting with journalists is convened at the studio of the famous criminal lawyer Arrigo Melani. The Guastallas are present, too. Pepi tells us that the lawyer was a friend of his and of the two gallery owners, and had represented Froglia when he was sentenced to serve three months in prison for a drugs conviction. At that point, the lawyer tells Ansa that he had already received Angelo's confession the previous Monday, September 10, as soon as the exhibition had closed.

Froglia says he carved three heads: Modì 1, Modì 3 and a third one which he had not thrown into the ditch. He worked on them with a traditional sculptor's tools between June and July; he "cooked" them with a substance made of industrial detergent and muriatic acid, so that anyone who checked could see that it was not material that was in use seventy-five years earlier. Froglia explains he did not want this to be a "hoax", but a cultural operation similar to that of the "happening" in the preceding years at the Venice Biennale. That is to say, a performance in the form of an event, where the sculptures did not have anything to do with Amedeo Modigliani's work, but rather they were exactly the opposite of the great artist's style. The lawyer and his client then show the head that was not thrown into the ditch,

---

[34] Giorgio Guastalla wrote the press release. His and his brother's presence needs to be seen in this perspective when the author of the heads convenes the press conference in his lawyer's studio.

as proof that they had been worked in an identical manner as those that emerged from the mud.

"My acts, my sculptures - Froglia explains in a press conference - are nothing more than works containing signs and messages within them that denounce their apocryphal nature. For example, there is bitumen in Modì 3 and there are some "squared-off edges" that are the complete opposite of Modigliani's elasticity." Outside of his lawyer's studio, Angelo Froglia finds the Carabinieri from the Unit for the protection of cultural heritage waiting for him and they take him to their station in Leghorn. They question him for hours; they can do so because he is on probation. They show him the anonymous letter addressed to the Archives and withdrawn by Christian Parisot.

He feels betrayed. However, he still keeps back the whole truth. Rather, as we shall see, he keeps secret something that, right from the start, had shown him that he was being used. He will reveal it only nine years later.

In the meantime, we should wonder why Angelo Froglia had waited for the exhibition to close. Was he waiting for a signal? Was he waiting for someone to authorise him to speak? Moreover, why does he then protect those who betrayed him or used him? Two days later, Froglia decides to show everyone the footage that attests to his version of the events. In a pizzeria of the Ardenza district, he projects the entire film of his performance, professionally shot and edited. The whole system of cultural heritage management is shaken by this umpteenth revelation.

The Durbé siblings pay the highest price. In October of the same year, Dario is dismissed from the Superintendence of the National Gallery of Modern Art, albeit the official justification has no connection with the series of events that recently put him under such an unflattering spotlight. And in February 1985, the city council orders the precautionary transfer of Vera Durbé, conservator of the civic museums of Leghorn, to another role following the announcement of a criminal investigation by the Public Prosecutor's Office. Her brother Dario, and Angelo Titonel, who had managed the photography for the catalogue *Due pietre ritrovate di Amedeo Modigliani*, are also put on notice. In 1991, the court will decide that the accused had acted in good faith.

"*The law is equal for everyone* is a nice expression that cheers up the poor, when they see it written above the heads of the judges on the back of courtroom walls. But when they realise that they need wealth that they don't have in order to invoke the equality of the law in their defence, then that claim seems to them to make a mockery of their misery." The quotation, by the illustrious jurist Piero Calamandrei, fits perfectly. It would have been reasonable at least to call those responsible to answer for the serious financial damage caused.

Of course, at the time the facts were not yet as clear as they would become nine years later, when Froglia decided to give another version of the story and to tell "almost the whole truth" in an exclusive interview to Paolo Brosio in a 1993 national news transmission. But in our opinion, what Froglia told the news programme about the heads still skipped some details:

> *I was not on that boat. Massimo Seghetti, an employee of the Municipality of Leghorn, and Lido Bellandi, the owner of the boat, threw the two sculptures overboard. When I handed over the two heads, Seghetti was with his fiancée, Elisabetta De Paz [Durbé's deputy, ed]. I did not speak to the Carabinieri about it because it was important for me to cover for them. At the time, I thought they were acting solely out of friendship with me. However, the night of my interrogation, which lasted from 9pm to 2am, the Carabinieri asked me if I really had acted alone and I confirmed it once again. A Marshall eventually showed me the photocopy of the anonymous letter sent to Jeanne Modigliani. In that letter, sent before the dredger started digging, it was written that two heads would be found in the "Fosso Reale". It stated the measures, the weight and the material of one of the heads. I was deeply saddened; I thought there was something that didn't make sense. I realised I had to be on my guard: the only people who had had the head when I was not there, and who therefore could have weighed and measured it, were Massimo Seghetti and his girlfriend.*
>
> *Even so, that's not the only strange circumstance. The excavation work began in a very precise point. Then they stopped after the second head was found. However, the widely published stories never said how many heads Modigliani was supposed to have thrown into the ditch. But the excavators were satisfied because they were sure that there were two. I am forced to imagine that those people who were close to me were not simply friends. There are strange*

> *circumstances that make me assume a plot: and interests at stake*
> *which so far I have not been able to understand.*[35]

Angelo Froglia's later statements provide information that is irrefutable and verifiable, so much so that the judicial officials then opened an investigation into the anonymous letters. However they lack the most important detail, the one in which Froglia, playing the part of a Dadaist artist, also appears in the role of an addict constantly looking for money. Many times Angelo has said that someone had promised him exhibitions in New York and great international success. But who had really convinced him to take part in that drama, and how, and why? The facts and names that had so far come out were not sufficient to explain what had happened. Even more so because the facts emerged sporadically, in slow motion.

Everybody deserves a Black & Decker drill and a camera

Thirty-five years later, we wanted to check on that old wound. We went to Leghorn; we followed the story in reverse by going to the places where the events had taken place, again giving voice to the principal actors of the time. Today they have grown old and grey, and have and a different view of the "hoax". Everyone told us their own version and we decided to review the story frame by frame. We analysed everything written or said, looking for the most detached and neutral recollections to form our own opinions and tell the story as it has never been told before.

Carlo Pepi, Pietro Luridiana, Pierfrancesco Ferrucci, Michele Ghelarducci, Michele Genovesi and Angelo Froglia. Are they the main actors, or bit players in this tangled story?

We began with the assumption that it is highly unlikely, or rather, impossible, that different people, all from the same small city (except for one, the oldest, who is also from the region), had the same idea at the same time and implemented it in the same way. Not only that: each of them felt the need to document what they were doing, even then thinking they would

---

[35] «Il Tirreno», April 26 1993; «Panorama», May 2 1993.

have to prove one day the truth of their own statements. It is illogical to believe it a coincidence.

Then, we looked through the available documents, before turning to one of the parties directly involved: Carlo Pepi. Here is his version of events:

Somehow, I had to show everyone that the people rushing to the "Fosso Reale" to spend 40 million lire of public money understood nothing about Modigliani. I had the idea of getting help from two of my artist friends, Sandro Sodini, who made a couple of small bronze sculptures, and Piero Vaccari, who helped me to produce the sculpture that I still have in my garden. We then made some heads in Modigliani's style. For some days, I strolled the streets of the New Venice district near the Municipality and around the ditches, with a butterfly net on my shoulders in which there was a small bronze caryatid. Then I had another idea. I talked about it with the brothers Guido and Giorgio Guastalla and with Parisot. We were all members of the board of Modigliani House. The Municipality had left us out of the preparations for the centenary of Amedeo's birth, favouring others such as the Durbés. So I said: "we'll take them and throw them in the Royal Ditch ... In the morning the dredger finds them and we see if they fall for it. Then we come out and tell the truth." The Guastallas liked the project very much; they seemed enthusiastic. The idea came to me after reading an interview with Vera Durbé that indicated the precise point where she would have dredged the river. I organised everything, even the international witnesses who would ensure the news went far and wide. I also talked about it with the painters of the Baracchina Rossa and the Casini dell'Ardenza. When Sandro Sodini, Piero Vaccari and I decided to create false works by Modì, we did it in public at the Casini dell'Ardenza, where many Leghorn artists used to go. It was a taunt, which I immediately explained to my colleagues in the Legal Archives. Parisot, I am sure, told Jeanne about it and later I learned that she had also told others. My friend Joseph Laposata, commander of the American base at Camp Darby, had sent me two female soldiers, two officers with the rank of captain. The sculptor Vaccari had worked for a few days and with an amateur camera, we decided to film all the phases in the preparation of the fake Modì head. The idea was to throw it in on the afternoon of June 16, while they were broadcasting an international football game, but the work had begun a couple of months earlier."

It is a strange coincidence: the four students who played their own prank also hung out at the Baracchina Rossa like Pepi. They also talked about it in loud voices at the bar. Pietro Luridiana proposed embarking on the adventure on July 17. "Let's give them those blessed heads ourselves! We'll make them, throw them in the ditch and let them find them." Faced with the question of how to carry out the plan and how many works to prepare, Pietro replies: "Bah. Two?" Minimum. They talk about many heads. They take the original ones seen at the exhibition as models.[36]

After preparing their rather rough work, they go to their usual bar. On July 23, they do not go to the "Fosso Reale" alone; some friends tag along to witness the last phase of the joke.

In late August, the four authors of the hoax give *Panorama* the details. To the second question, why they had done it, there is a ready answer; it's simply a well-known and marked feature of the Leghorn character. It is a way of distinguishing themselves, only the Neapolitans come close to the irreverent and iconoclastic people of Leghorn.

Those four spoofers had got the idea when they saw how much apparently unmotivated enthusiasm the organisers of that farcical dredging were showing, especially Durbé. Modigliani and the legend of the statues in the canal, okay, but aren't they being a little too presumptuous, while blithely spending everyone's money?

At that point, after about one week during which the channel had yielded only sludge and waste, they got to work. They took chisel and drill, they recovered a stone paving slab and they sketched the features, copying them from the photograph of a sculpture in the exhibition catalogue at Villa Maria. Then, four blows from the chisel and there you have an image on the stone.

The weekly magazine *Panorama* plays an important role in this strange tableau. The young men who produced Modì 2 signed a national and international exclusive with the magazine. It would be interesting to know exactly when. Gianni Farneti from Leghorn was the deputy editor of the

---

[36] Daniele Cerrai, *Grigio Modì. Storia di tre teste ritrovate*, Round Robin Editrice, Roma 2014.

magazine but at that stage he was also acting director. He is also the uncle of one of the four students, and it is he who writes the articles. He himself later admitted the kinship, but even so, sources in Leghorn say that in July he was present there and, like a good journalist, he was closely following the work of the dredger.

In his September 17 article, Farneti is hesitant about confessing his links with the city. According to his article, the curtain rose on the comedy of Leghorn at the gates of Milan; to be precise, in Segrate, home to Palazzo Mondadori, on the afternoon of Tuesday, August 28. According to Farneti, a woman called the newspaper: "I have a strange story to tell ..." At three in the afternoon, the main players in the story are already at the journalist's desk. It is a big scoop for the weekly magazine, which only a year earlier had lost a lot of credibility by splashing on its front cover the world scoop on the discovery of Hitler's diaries, later revealed as a massive hoax.

After more than three decades, we know things didn't happen quite like that. The young men did not just play a mere joke; they did not immediately reveal the truth once everyone had fallen for their trick, as normal pranksters might have done. Instead, they waited patiently for the right moment to reveal themselves to the world, and they did it on August 28, knowing that the Durbés had announced that their catalogue would be presented on September 2. On the morning of Sunday, September 2, with astute journalistic timing, Ansa gives a preview of the weekly magazine that has the exclusive news, but which is not issued on Sundays. The following morning *Panorama* sells out immediately, as do all subsequent editions of photographic reports and articles with the statements of three of the four tricksters. Was it their intention to steal the limelight from the Durbés? Consider that, a few hours before the buffet presentation of a book by the director of the most important modern art gallery in Italy, one of the students had made further fun of Vera Durbé by getting her to autograph a copy of the book. Everything appears to have been stage managed, with perfect theatrical timing.

Gianni Farneti, in a September 16, 2016 interview with Costanza Baldini from the online newspaper Intoscana.it, recalls after decades a rumour which had echoed loudly among the canals and streets of the city-port. Born in Leghorn in January 21, 1921, Farneti knew the local stories and customs thoroughly. He explains that from the early hours of that

September 2, his fellow citizens had thought it might be a political plot against the Communist Party, which had run the city practically forever. According to his telling, some people thought it might have been an effort by the magazine, which was anything but left-leaning - with the complicity of the city's wealthy class - to score points against the Communists. In fact, all four of the young men involved in the hoax lived in the Ardenza district which, with its Art Nouveau buildings overlooking the sea, far from the port and its proletarian districts, is mainly inhabited by wealthy professionals and their families. The political conspiracy theory also gained support because of the parliamentary and municipal consultations proposed by Altero Matteoli, member of the right wing Italian Social Movement, a Member of Parliament and an opposition city councillor in Leghorn. Even so, the consultations he proposed were widely considered to be well-grounded civic projects.

There were two consultations: the first one to the Municipality, in which the deputy asked the mayor Ali Nannipieri and his council to resign. The second one concerned the Minister of Cultural Heritage Antonino Gullotti.

Matteoli rightly asked for the resignation of the mayor and of the whole Livorno council. In effect, the actions of the administration seem to stretch even the most generous definition of "good faith". Although it never unequivocally showed favouritism towards private interests, the Municipality certainly facilitated the plans of Dario and Vera Durbé.

The conspiracy of Villa Maria

Let's take a step back in time. Out of twenty-eight sculptures attributed to Modigliani around the world, four are exhibited in Leghorn for the 1984 centenary. One comes from London's Tate Modern, one from the Centre Pompidou in Paris, while the other two belong to private American collections; one, in particular, belongs to the gallery owner Klaus Perls, a member of the scientific committee of the exhibition.

Jeanne Modigliani expressed serious doubts about these last two sculptures. It is not by chance that Dario Durbé, replying to Modigliani's daughter, said he believed both could be authentic on June 27, during the opening of the exhibition, stating: "We'll have to investigate further, but already today we believe it possible that the two heads are those made in Leghorn by the artist, who might not have thrown them into the ditch, as legend has it, but instead taken them to Paris". An obvious contradiction in terms. Of the two one: either they were actually thrown into the water, or the dredger his sister wanted to engage was completely useless. Or perhaps there was another objective?

Even so, the young men know nothing about this, and begin working with their drill. Before completing their lampoon, they consult with the lawyer Cyrano Luridiana, Pietro's father. The latter, who as a fierce Livornese can only be proud of the idea conceived by his son and his friends, excludes the possibility of criminal charges, but not civil actions for damages, however improbable. However, in the minds of the four boys, unlike the other actors in this affair, there is no sign that they know they may be committing a crime, or are willing to do so.

Angelo Froglia is the most enigmatic character among them. He never wanted to be considered a joker: he prefers to be seen as a provocateur throwing down a "political" challenge. He has few real friends. Many took advantage of his artistic inclinations and his life as a drifter. Alessandro Bulgini, another accomplished painter and Massimino Filippelli, the dean of the Leghorn frame makers, with whom for a few years Froglia shared his passion are among the few people who really liked him. "Not very tall, with an intense and challenging look, long black hair which was always untidy, an attractive physique and a level of cultural preparation which was out of the ordinary": this is how Bulgini remembers him. A fragile man, a drug addict but capable of dominating the effect through his creative flair. A "damned" artist, but not named Modigliani. He felt as though he had been deliberately sentenced to oblivion as an artist, almost as if others wanted to erase the truth. With that controversial act, the most sensational of his life (throwing the heads into the ditch), he would shake the world of the art critics, demolish the monuments of State culture. Because of his outrageous act, we never talk about Angelo Froglia; his works have almost completely disappeared from the market, ending up in some private collection in Rimini.

A mystery wrapped in an enigma, we find the third head that Angelo had carved in July 1984 among Bettino Craxi's[37] souvenirs in his Hammamet compound in Tunisia. It is not clear how it ended up among the mementos of the socialist leader. In fact, the sculpture was seized by the judicial authority in 1997 and passed to the Superintendence of Pisa along with the others. Angelo is a street boy, a Pasolinian character, a son of the people who politically flanked the terrorism of those violent years; he served in prison with "political prisoners." Then, when out of jail angrier than ever, he ended up at the port of Leghorn among the stevedores, for whom he sculpted and painted. Irony of fate, those wheeler-dealers and those institutions that he so fiercely opposed probably just used him. Two characters whom at the time he considered friends, Massimo Seghetti, a municipal employee close to the councillor Frontera, and his partner, Elisabetta De Paz, encourage him to make the heads. He shares some evenings drinking with them, and gets whatever else was needed to keep their role in the story secret until 1993.

Froglia takes two stones. One was made of granite, which Modigliani never used, considering it too hard; the other one was sandstone, more malleable and often used by Modì. The latter is recovered from a pavement near the Vannucci barracks in Leghorn: "It smelled of naphtha, oil and fat and was impregnated with gasoline".[38]

He works on it for a few days, careful not to imitate Modigliani; rather, he takes inspiration from "primitive" sculptures. He uses chisels, and acids mixed with pumice powders to age them. He puts the stones in a heated oven. Seghetti films him throughout his performance, in which he recounts what his controversial actions mean for him.

Froglia will then explain:

> *I wasn't interested in playing a mere joke, the hoax of the three students was a crazy variable that got very much in my way. My intent was to highlight how through, a process of collective*

[37] A former Italian prime minister and leader of the Socialist party who fled the country in the early 1990s when threatened with arrest for corruption

[38] Alice Barontini, *Alla ricerca di Modì. Angelo Froglia e la performance che mise in crisi la critica*, Polistampa, Firenze 2010, p. 133.

persuasion, through national television, newspapers, small talk between people, you can condition people's beliefs. In addition, I am an artist, I move through the channels of art, I wanted to spark a debate on ways of art and I fully achieved this. Mine was a conceptual operation, if you like; in a certain sense it was also a work of art, like Christo and his packing monuments...

His video story would later become a film, *Peitho and Apate ... della persuasione e dell' inganno (Cherchez Modi)*, presented at the Turin Film Festival and critically acclaimed. Angelo will not know where the "heads" were thrown: Massimo Seghetti and Lido Bellandi bring them to the ditch by boat. They, conversely, know well where Durbé will go looking for them.

"This part of the story is the least romantic. Even today I prefer to think that Angelo did it for an artistic purpose". The framer-restorer Massimino Filippelli utters these words when we remind him that Angelo Froglia had put his trust in the three municipal employees to conclude his "Dadaist" action. However, what sort of iconoclasm is it, when the representatives of public institutions and commercial and economic interests are involved?

Froglia had started out wanting to tarnish the ideas of the critics, but in the end he probably just tarnished himself. "It was a beautiful, clear-cut, clean project," the framer continues. "One day he speaks to me of a Dadaist idea: 'I know there is a plan to dredge the ditches and I want to prepare a plan to help them find the heads they seek: if I succeed, I will go down in history'. All this happened a month before the find. I was thrilled too.

"Then a couple of weeks before they threw the works in the ditch we all gathered at his dad's house. The film that our friend had prepared was shown. A childish little thing, we might say ... I'm going to keep my peace, but there were six or seven of us friends and if one of them speaks out, everything is ruined, the word gets around. At that time," - Filippelli continues - "I had lost sight of Froglia because some customers had complained that I was hosting a drug addict and they were afraid he would steal something." Other witnesses agree there was a "dark period", about fifteen days, in which Froglia avoids company, from just after the glorious evening of the film preview until after the heads are in the water.

In this short time frame, Angelo's plan changes, taking on a different form from the original one. "I never understood why he didn't throw the heads in himself... We even experimented with his scuba-diver brother to check the depths and the places where he could throw them in. His dad was a docker, what would it need for him to get a boat? The brother had also already prepared an underwater video to give lustre to the project. We had thought about not revealing the truth until four or five years had passed. It would have been a sensational gesture," the framer concludes. "Something happened, I don't know what. Angelo changed his plan and entrusts the heads to the three municipal employees."

Apparently Pepi's provocative idea takes hold all over Leghorn, almost subliminally. He inspires many jokes and tricks. With those who want to imitate the "heads" hoax, there are also those who sardonically ride the carnival wave pervading the city at that time.

One of Froglia's friends who had also been afflicted by drug addiction and who worked at the Museum with Ms Durbé, made a large stone phallus and throws it into the ditch. This "cock" he tells a television interviewer, was inscribed with the words "'N culo ai Durbé" or "Fuck the Durbés". But it will never be found.

Mario Camici and Ivo Cozzi, who work in the shipyards under the supervision of the workshop manager Alfredo Morganti, transport a large slab of granite inside with a crane. It is over a meter long. They work on it for days with difficulty, imitating Modì's style. An oblong head with two nice big round balls carved at the base of what would be the neck, like a bow tie. It is obvious which head they are referring to...

The celebrations have turned into an unmitigated farce. The name of the Durbés and the Municipality of Leghorn flood the media, they are mocked in news stories around world. After the discovery of the heads and the almost immediate collapse in credibility of those who had staked their academic titles and reputations to vouch for the authenticity of these fakes, the matter is resolved with suspicious haste, adding to the success of the hoax.

Leghorn's famed irreverence becomes the leitmotiv of the summer in advertisements, newspaper headlines and television shows throughout Italy and for some time throughout Europe. The four students from Leghorn, united a month later with another young man, Angelo Froglia, will remain the most prominent actors in a "hoax" designed to mock power and art criticism, along with their rites and shrines.

This is the message that establishes itself in the collective memory. Almost as if the world were content with simply seeing pride punished and the arrogance with which cultural elites sometimes express themselves laid low; but no thoughts on the part played by the criminal underworld. It is rather strange.

Over the years, there have been other investigations, unpublished confessions and new lines of investigation that revealed the gravity of those events. Nobody remembers now. We examined those investigations to get a better idea of what might have really happened in that summer of 1984, where, on the banks of the royal ditch, institutional powers and art dealers met and clashed. Where a hoax played by four young adults was nothing more than a chance variable, an unexpected trick of fate that accidentally threw light on what appears to be a criminal racket.

The "young bucks" of Baracchina Rossa

Leghorn is not a big city. The main players in the events of 1984 mostly knew each other and moved more or less in the same circles: all except the students. They frequented the same environments, and we can say that some of those places were the true melting pots of the events that followed. The story of those frenetic months takes place in the space of a kilometre between the large market and the Baracchina Rossa.

1. *The Baracchina Rossa*. It has ever been a meeting place for Leghorn's whimsical artists. Here Carlo Pepi, between laughs, shows off his "brilliant idea for a lampoon". He talks about it to all the artists and to the "young Turks" who hang out there. The day after the dredging began, Pietro Luridiana, Pierfrancesco Ferrucci, Michele Ghelarducci and Michele Genovesi, thought up their own little spoof at the tables of this same bar. We are sure they were not involved in any other plots; we wonder, though if they were not influenced by the rumours going around the bar. Might the acquaintance of the boys' families, all of them living in the chic Ardenza district, have played a role in the development of their plan?

2. *The Guastalla art gallery*. Here the framer Massimino Filippelli meets with Angelo Froglia, Christian Parisot, Jeanne Modigliani and, last but not least, Carlo Pepi. In his rooms, the latter expands on his potential spoof, exciting the enthusiasm of his colleagues from the Modigliani Legal Archives.

3. *Massimino Filippelli's workshop*. Here Angelo Froglia, Massimo Seghetti, Elisabetta De Paz, the Guastalla brothers, Carlo Pepi and perhaps also the commissioner Claudio Frontera meet regularly.

4. *The port.* Here Angelo Froglia works on his heads while other dockers try make their own efforts towards the success of the Livornese "carnival".

5. *The museum and the municipal offices.* Here the employees like Seghetti, De Paz, Bellandi, Councillor Frontera, the brother and sister Dario and Vera Durbé and the scientific committee (of which the American gallery owner Klaus Perls is a member), come and go. Perls himself seems to have never turned up in Leghorn, but he was in constant communication with the other members of the council.

6. *Camp Darby base and the American officers' quarters in Pisa,* frequented by the commander Laposata, the officers Mary and Katherine and probably also by some influential and rich compatriots. This is the only reference point outside the city perimeter, but the base is still very close, even though in the territory of the Municipality of Pisa.

It will take fourteen years for the dust to settle and for the waters in Leghorn to be calm enough to allow a glimpse of the skeletons buried among the mud in the ditch.

The truth, as the popular saying reminds us, will out, and over time each of the main players in the great deception of 1984 have to face their responsibilities. However, to this day they have only faced moral judgement: never any convictions, although numerous investigations have been conducted since then.

Only three false heads emerged that year from the ditch, but many more were stored in the city and were ready to make their appearance and to seek authentication.

In the *Corriere della Sera* of October 8, the journalist Ettore Vittorini 1998 explains thus: "The word in Leghorn is that it was more than an elaborate joke [in 1984, ed.]; it was an attempt at a swindle organised by some prominent members of the city's cultural world in order to relaunch the name of Leghorn in the field of art. It is said that two heads were ordered from a good forger. Then they were buried in the ditch [...]. Then comes the dredger, which fished up three of them, to the great surprise of the fraud organisers who only expected two. But they remain silent, allowing all of them to be attributed to Modigliani". The article is entitled *Il giallo Modigliani: Le teste sono otto* ["The Modigliani mystery: There are eight heads!" - ed]. In other words, based on what is known, some of those heads are still in the ditch or in a private collection somewhere. The question it is far from being closed.

In short, examining the succession of snapshots taken over time from various newspaper articles, we can get a not-too-cloudy glimpse of many elements that, put together, make it clear how plausible the hypothesis is of a conspiracy aimed at marketing fake works. Hardly just a lampoon!

At the crime scene, there are at least five conceivable premeditated forgeries, not all produced for criminal purposes. The first is the one conceived by Carlo Pepi, which we believe was the seed from which other projects were born. The second we believe may be that of Angelo Froglia. The third was made by the students; the fourth would belong to some municipal employees and the two Durbés, and the last to the Americans.

We have said enough about Pepi's intentions. However, what might have motivated the others? We can think about it by putting events in chronological order. Nevertheless, let's start with two assumptions. That is, first of all, there is some sort of conflict between the Legal Archives of Paris and the Durbé siblings. Secondly (but no less important), economic interests are at play of the kind unleashed every time a popular event is organised, cultural or otherwise. Little has changed.

Checking the timeline once again: The date set for the opening in Leghorn of the Modigliani centenary exhibition is July 1, 1984. In the artist's hometown, the excitement of the organisers is sky high, especially concerning their extraordinary project to verify the "legend of the ditch". Everything is ready: excavation plan A, excavation plan B, the convening of the press, invitations to art critics. However, on May 25 the Superintendence of Fine Arts in Rome, on the advice of its Pisa counterpart, suspends the start of the dredging works. The municipal Administration and Vera Durbé are extremely angry, especially the director of the Museum who has been fighting for three years to get the project approved. Fortunately, after some modifications to the dredger's toothed scraper (which was the main issue, rather than the usefulness of the project, according to Michele Caturegli), the recovery plan is approved and work begins.

On the announced date, the exhibition at Villa Maria opens its doors and it will continue until September 9. There is a lot of coverage in the newspapers. In the meantime, however a second letter from Jeanne is received by the Municipality's Department of Culture and by the managers of the Museum at Villa Maria. The artist's daughter points out the reasons that would have led to her "exclusion from the setting up and the exhibition". Above all, a series of concerns about the authenticity of a painting by Modì included in the exhibition; the portrait of Pablo Picasso, from the Perls Art Gallery in New York, a painting that Picasso himself had already denounced as fake.

Modigliani's heir supports her assertions by underlining that the painting does not appear in any reliable publication certifying its authenticity. In support of Jeanne's genuine perplexities on the subject, an authority intervenes: Professor Maurizio Calvesi, Professor of medieval and modern Art History at the University of Rome, as well as director of the figurative arts section of the Venice Biennale. In an interview with the weekly magazine *L'Espresso*, Calvesi asserts that the head exposed by the Perls Gallery was a fake because "It was not the same as the one photographed in 1911 in the Cardoso atelier". Calvesi himself was one of the few critics to say immediately that the heads that emerged from the ditch were not by Modigliani. Pepi, who saw the collector's works exhibited in 1984 at Villa Maria, defines the American gallery as "a fake factory".

Klaus Perls, let's remember, is part of the scientific committee of the centenary exhibition. With him is Carla Panicali. Parisot, in his typically cryptic manner, writes to us about the latter: "Panicali was the US contact for the whole operation; it was she who brought Perls to Leghorn. And she was also the commercial manager of the scientific committee." It therefore follows that each work exhibited by third parties was evaluated by Panicali, perhaps from a commercial, rather than artistic, point of view. Even before the controversy broke out, London's Tate had withdrawn the head it had promised to loan, saying it had "prior commitments" at other international events. Of course, the Tate's managers could not let their head be placed next to that of Perls, which had already been declared a forgery by authoritative experts.

According to Parisot, Perls' participation in the centenary ultimately enabled him to sell 54 "Modigliani works". This, considering that in the entire Ceroni catalogue there are a total of only 337 artworks. The head brought to Leghorn by the American is similar to the beautiful sculpture exhibited in London, which was certainly authentic. But, Perl's head was not convincing, Parisot says. "Some elements are copied but have no relevance, not everything is round, the base of the sculpture ... the volume..." he muses.

"Vera Durbé was under the control of her brother," Parisot tells us. "I have the letters he wrote me. He had insisted certain members be on the committee: Panicali and the American, as well as Osvaldo Patani, who she did not want." A few years later, we find Osvaldo Patani in Viterbo, surrounded by the Carabinieri. They are impounding the works at the exhibition he has organised, where seventy drawings attributed to the young Modi - but believed to be false - are on display. Our sources in the municipal administration at the time also confirm the role of Superintendent Durbé: "Let's be clear, here Dario Durbé was in charge, the others were under his control. All they were thinking of was the media coverage that would draw thousands of tourists and the lenses of hundreds of cameras from all over the world. That was their only interest, and Dario had free rein."

Analysing the timeline of news and events drawn from the documents and articles of that period a clear picture begins to appear. The actions and declarations of the world's leading art critics, people universally recognised as experts of Modigliani's work, taken together point to a high degree of collusion in the mischievous "recognition" of the fake stone heads, especially made to be found in the ditches. What had seemed like a colossal blunder, in the light of our research takes on the hue of a knowingly organised "crime". An elaborate fraud.

"Come to Leghorn. I will give you further proof [...]. Now I am too afraid. They will kill me." This was written at the foot of the page in the second letter that a concerned Carlo had sent to Jeanne Modigliani.

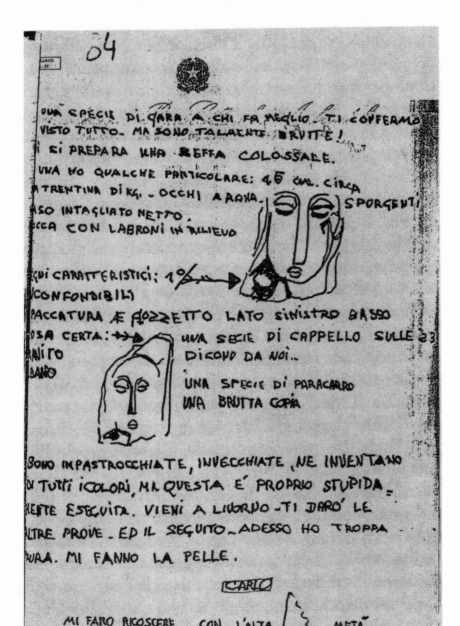

Why was the writer of the letter afraid of dying if it was only a lampoon? Maybe the writer knew that there was much more behind the "discovery" of the heads. According to the material in our possession, and according to witnesses like Carlo Pepi and other sources from the municipal administration of the time, the author or authors of those letters could have been Elisabetta De Paz and/or Massimo Seghetti. Angelo Froglia, who at first remained close-mouthed before the Marshal of the Carabinieri and the Brigadier who had questioned him and showed him the anonymous letters, later stated that Seghetti and De Paz were the only ones who had the heads. In 1993 Carlo Pepi and Giuseppe Saracino (a Leghorn designer) hand over forty-seven items of evidence that a crime has been committed to the courts through the lawyer Nino Filastò. It is the first lawsuit/complaint to contain Angelo Froglia's statements; not in an interview this time, but in a signed statement with legal weight. In the document, Vera Durbé is accused of attempted or actual aggravated fraud and of ongoing violation of the law protecting works of art.

The lawyer is well aware that this act will not be taken into consideration by the judicial authorities. These facts referred to occurred nine years earlier, and the crimes to which they refer have already hit the buffers of the statute of limitations. Even so in 1993 Vera Durbé, undaunted by the evidence and admissions of the key players in the intervening period and now almost verging on absurdity, reaffirmed her belief in the authenticity of the works now proven to be fake. If in 1984, her wild statements may have helped others get rich by fraudulent means, nine years later they could have had few objectives other than an attempt at personal rehabilitation. Too bad that, given the statute of limitations, the complaint was now a discharged weapon. Here, in conclusion, is our hypothesis.

It is a tempting opportunity: the centenary of the birth of the most catalogued and copied artist of the twentieth century. There are plenty of fake art works around the world. They are all certified but they are also kept aside, waiting for the right moment to be presented to the general public in order to maximise their value. Carla Panicali would seem the right person due to her Roman acquaintances. Dario Durbé is looking forward to becoming a star of the art world. As Pepi says, "what can the Macchiaioli be, they cannot be compared to the great Modigliani... In Leghorn everyone is a Macchiaioli expert; Durbé is one of the many. What do you think about being acknowledged as a Modì expert? Come on! A painting by Amedeo is worth millions, not a few cents like Fattori's other apprentices. You only need one percent for those who provide the certification and you're rich".

The stakes are enormous and the operation takes shape. Perls has the shamelessness to bring a painting and a sculpture branded as fakes to Italy; he can afford it thanks to his appointment as the "Scientific" expert of the exhibition. Nobody tries to impound them. The country with the widest artistic heritage in the world remains silent and does not listen to the howls of protest that come from Paris, which are immediately silenced.

Along comes poor Angelo Froglia, addicted to drugs, with his concept of an act that in his mind will be political dynamite against the art establishment. There are several plans that involve him, knowingly or otherwise: the Legal Archives that want to undermine credibility of the Durbés; the municipal employees who play both sides, but more against Frontera and the Durbés; the Americans who have every interest in the event being successful, to give their forgeries the scent of authenticity. If everything goes well, they think, then from that moment on, whenever any of them presents the market with an artwork by Modì, it will be credible. The "fake factory", like Pepi called it, would have produced artistic wonders with all the appropriate certificates. Froglia himself belatedly tells his lawyer Nino Filastò, that he has been contacted by an American who promised him international fame and exhibitions in New York. The key to the mystery perhaps lies entirely in the title of the video that he made during the preparation of the heads: Peitho e Apate ... della persuasione e dell' inganno (Peitho and Apate - of persuasion and deception - ed).

A stars and stripes plot

The shadow of American interests looms over the crime scene, along with a handful of American players. Their presence is not accidental, and could be attributed to a plan to gain authentication for the art works they own. The works do not need to be authentic. Through exhibitions and events, they can acquire more and more prestige, perhaps assuming a value that they do not currently possess at all. This is what the exhibition in Leghorn was for them: a catwalk.

La Notte delle Rose Nere, The night of black roses, a fiction based on a true story and written by the lawyer Nino Filasto', gives a glimpse on this reality. Over the years, the author attended to the legal affairs of first Angelo Froglia and later of Carlo Pepi, becoming to all intents their "confessor".[39] In 1993, together with the journalist Paolo Brosio, the lawyer collected the testimony of someone who was without doubt one of the main actors in the "Leghorn heads case".

In his novel, Filastò changes some names, but he also tells us that all the quotations recited by the main actors through the course of the play are accurate. It is in this play that we meet an American art merchant who pulls the strings of the great deception.

Mr Packard arrives in Leghorn in that spring of 1984, stays there for a few months plotting on how to exploit the programme to celebrate the centenary (including the dredging of the river) with the ultimate time of giving a certain identity, and a value, to the various sculptures attributed to Modigliani that he already owns and which are of dubious origin. In this period he comes into contact with Rofo (Froglia). With the help of a man and a woman from Leghorn (presumably Seghetti and De Paz), he approaches Rofo/Froglia and involves him in his plan. The reason for the parody is not entirely clear to the artist, but he glimpses in it the opportunity to express himself as a sculptor, and to give vent and maximum visibility to his protest against the Italian cultural elite. Packard takes advantage of Rofo's weakness - he too is an addict - and regales him with ideas of artistic fortunes overseas derived from exhibitions and events. A beautiful and rich lady, Carol, also an art dealer, plays a supporting role: she is Packard's lover, also has great interest in the value and accreditation of the sculptures.

We have not yet said who Packard might actually be, but it does not seem difficult to give him a name, and perhaps also to the female character. The great American collector is probably Klaus Perls, who with his brother Frank owned the famous and homonymous Perls Gallery in New York, opened in 1937. The gallery specialises primarily in collections of

---

[39] Nino Filasto, *La notte delle rose nere*, Mondadori, Milan 1997.

twentieth-century French-trained artists, such as Pablo Picasso, Georges Braque, Maurice Utrillo, Raoul Dufy and, of course, Amedeo Modigliani.

The success of the events for the centenary of Modì's birth would certainly increase the value of his art works. Perls is the gallery owner who brought many works from his private collection to the Villa Maria exhibition: paintings, drawings and even sculptures. Jeanne Modigliani, from Paris, railed against the exhibition. She dismisses as false the portrait of Picasso attributed to Amedeo and lent by Perls. She questions the historical traceability of the sculpture attributed to her father and exhibited in Leghorn. But besides Perls, who sits on the scientific committee that gives accreditation to the art works? Who would bring Packard (aka Perls?) to the Tuscan city? As Christian Parisot told us, "who else but Carla Panicali", who also deals in Modigliani works in her gallery in Rome. She sold one in 1962 (authentic) to the National Gallery of Modern Art (Gam) in Rome. A few years later the beautiful and noble Roman lady would be charged over a fake sold in the seventies to the same gallery, then to the Italian state. The shadow that blurs the bright rooms of the National Gallery in the Durbé era is a rectangle of seventy-five centimetres by a hundred and five, hanging in the Halls of the twentieth century. For years, on that piece of wall, the *Donna Seduta* was proudly displayed as a painting by Joan Miró. Augusta Monferini was for years Durbé's deputy despite being in constant conflict with him. When she took over from Dario in the role of superintendent, she decided to remove the Miró, which had always troubled her, from the rooms. David Stein, believed to be one of the greatest forgers alive, would claim a few months later to have painted that *Donna Seduta* owned by the Roman gallery.

"The exhibition, organised by Vera Durbé, uses not only the expertise of Carla Panicali and the supervision of a scientific committee formed by Dario Durbé [...], Jean Leymarie, director of Villa Medici, Paolo Ciardi, a professor at Pisa, Professor Megged, Klaus Perls and Lamberto Vitali [the only true authority on the committee in terms of his knowledge with respect to Modigliani, ed]". Vitali, according to Carlo Pepi who was in his confidence, may have been completely unaware that he was named as part of the committee. The list was compiled in "La Stampa" of January 7, 1984 (which omitted any mention of Osvaldo Patani, later involved in the events in Viterbo).

Returning to Leghorn, those who understand covert affairs know that every US embassy has the specific task of facilitating the business of its fellow citizens, including through intelligence activities. So, finding four Americans on the scene in this story is no coincidence: a businessman and art dealer, personally or through his emissaries, and three soldiers stationed in Pisa.

Angelo Froglia reveals to his "confessor" that he was approached by the rich American, who "took care" of him. He took him around chic nightclubs and fulfilled his every wish. This is why he disappears from his circle of friends, as the framer Filippelli told us, for those two or three weeks that passed between the showing of the video at his father's house and throwing the heads into the water, an act carried out by municipal employees and in which Angelo mysteriously did not take part. Froglia does not tell this secret to anyone else, not even to his great friend and adviser Alessandro Bulgini who, in a long interview with us, claimed he had never even heard of the American.

In this scenario, the United States may come into play - an inevitable presence in every mystery worthy of the name that occurred in Italy's recent history. The US base Camp Darby, located between the Pisa airport and Leghorn, is the largest logistical settlement in the Mediterranean. Copious strategic reserves are held in one hundred and twenty-five underground bunkers. The base is connected through a network of channels and through the Canale dei Navicelli at the port of Leghorn, where it supplies US naval ships. Given its importance it is unthinkable that in the base there is no intelligence service, indeed it is likely that all seventeen stars and stripes agencies have intelligence feeds there.

In those days, the whole of Tuscany was considered a "red" region, especially Leghorn which for decades was ruled by a communist council. Put yourself in the shoes of the base commander, who was most likely also responsible for the intelligence services in the area: he would not waste such a chance. Pepi had by then spread the rumour, which had certainly reached the ear of the American 007. We would be amazed if they were unaware of what was about to happen.

Uncle Sam's interests in that summer of 1984 would have focused on Leghorn and they would have acted with what appears to be a pincer operation: strategic and tactical. First, they needed to approach the creator,

Pepi, then the executor, Froglia. First, the two female soldiers and their commander attached themselves to the more lucid Pepi. The second would be easier to deal with considering his drug addiction: on him, the power of money and vice would do their work.

Let's take a short step back. Pepi comes up with the idea of ridiculing the organisers of cultural events, who had neglected to involve either the committee to honour Modigliani, which he directed, or the Legal Archives headed by Jeanne. He gets three heads produced and tells the Guastalla brothers of his idea. However, Pepi, as we know, renounces the task in the end. But someone else likes the idea and sees the chance of earning some money. It is not difficult for that someone to approach Angelo Froglia, who like all talented and desperate Leghorn artists moves around what the former mayor Filippo Nogarin calls Massimino Filippelli's "smithy". The relationship between Froglia, Filippelli and the Guastalla brothers has developed over the years. The Guastallas have already produced some lithographs from Froglia's drawings in their print shop, and they would later organise the first posthumous exhibition of the former would-be terrorist.

Klaus Perls had lent some of his works - whose authenticity was contested by Jeanne Modigliani - to the Progressive Museum of Contemporary Art under Vera Durbé. Elisabetta De Paz was at the time Durbé's deputy. It would be naive to think that a senior municipal administration official like De Paz, working in the art sector, was not in contact with the merchant Perls or his associates such as Panicali. But it does not end here: De Paz's partner is the very same Seghetti who, together with Bellandi, from a little boat "plants" the two pseudo-works near the dredge on Froglia's behalf.

Some years earlier, Froglia had carried out a bomb attack on the headquarters of a Leghorn trade union and he had been arrested and sentenced for this. In prison, he had continued to nurture his subversive friendships. Some people say he even made the acquaintance of the prominent criminal Renato Vallanzasca.

Keeping the military base safe is the primary task of the intelligence services, so checking all the troublemakers is the smartest first move for a 007. The Americans were definitely keeping Froglia under observation. Moreover, it is certainly not a coincidence that the Commander Laposata approached Pepi, later having him accompanied, not coincidentally, by two young women in official uniform. As any book on espionage will tell you: women can more easily approach the target.

However, the skilled strategists had not calculated that Leghorn is the national champion at "fucking around". An outlandish variable, the four students, mess up their plans. The "secret" project goes up in smoke, leaving the conspirators empty-handed.

1

3

2

4

Modi's Places, today. The last home in which he lived. Rue de la Grande Chaumiere Paris.

5

6

The room of the nude school where Modi studied and worked at the Academy of
la Grande Chaumiere in Paris

The steps of our journey exploring the Amedeo Modigliani Legal Archives, just arrived from New York in Europe, at the free port of Geneve. In particular: the entrance of the vault, the opening of the crates (pic 7-11); details of files with drawings marked in red on transparent cover (12-15); Modi's palette (16); letters, drawings, masks found in his atelier (17-27), in particular the Jewish marriage agreement (ketubah) signed by the respective parents and spouses Amedeo and Jeanne (18), a drawing by the painter Maria Marevna, at the time partner of the painter Diego Rivera who portrays the artists of Montparnasse sitting in a tavern (21), a detail of the certificate of enrolment of the free nude school of Venice (26).

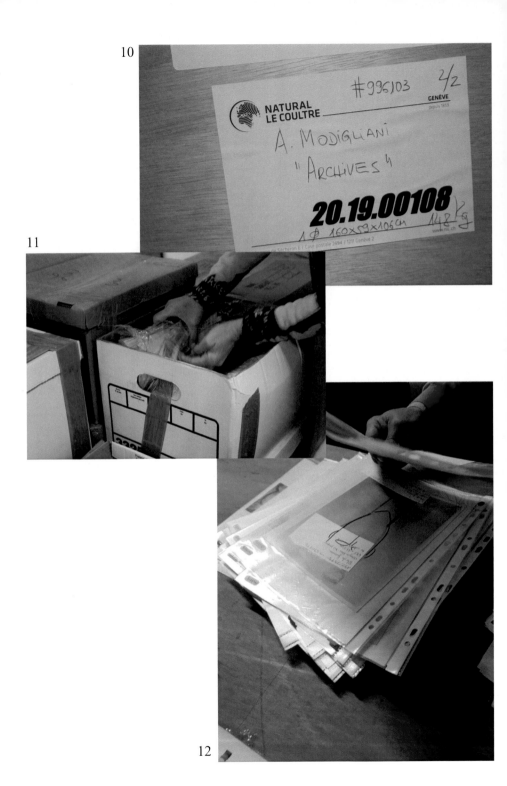

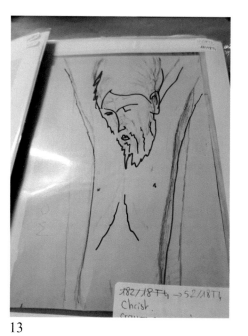

13

14

15

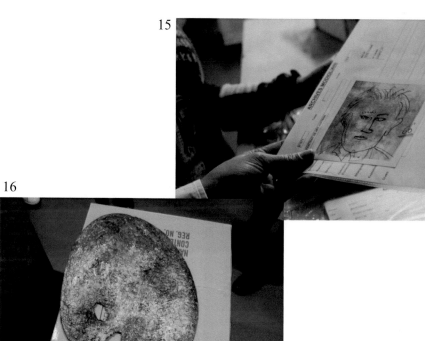

16

17

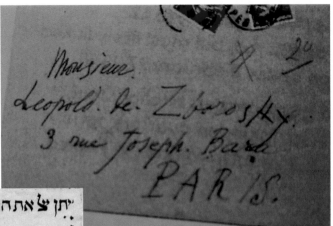

18

19

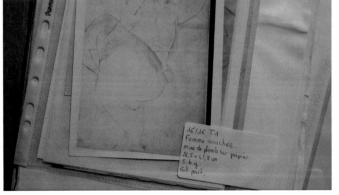

20

21

22

23

24

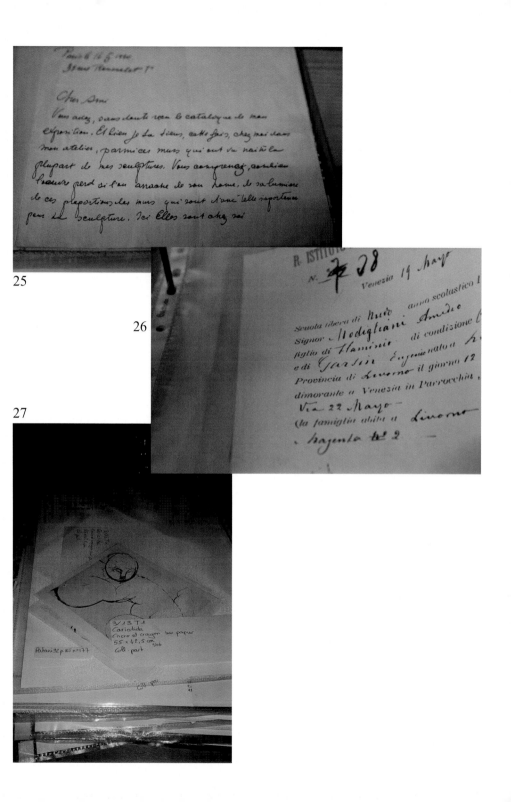

25

26

27

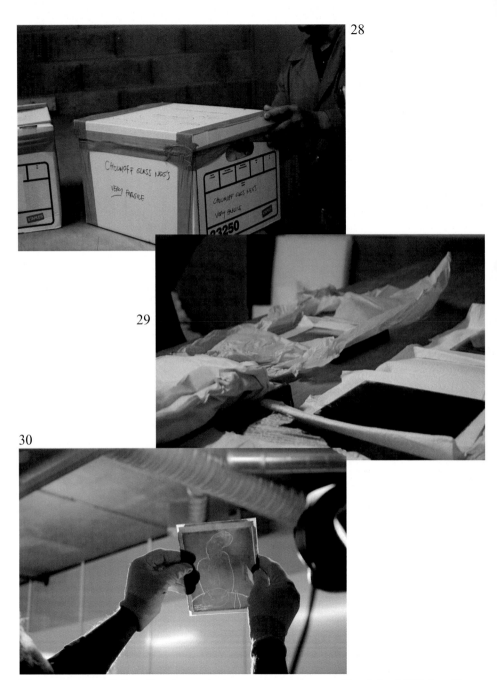

The crate containing fourteen photographic plates, realized in 1919 by Pierre Choumoff, official photographer of the art merchant Leopold Zborowski for the works by Amedeo Modigliani (pics 28-34).

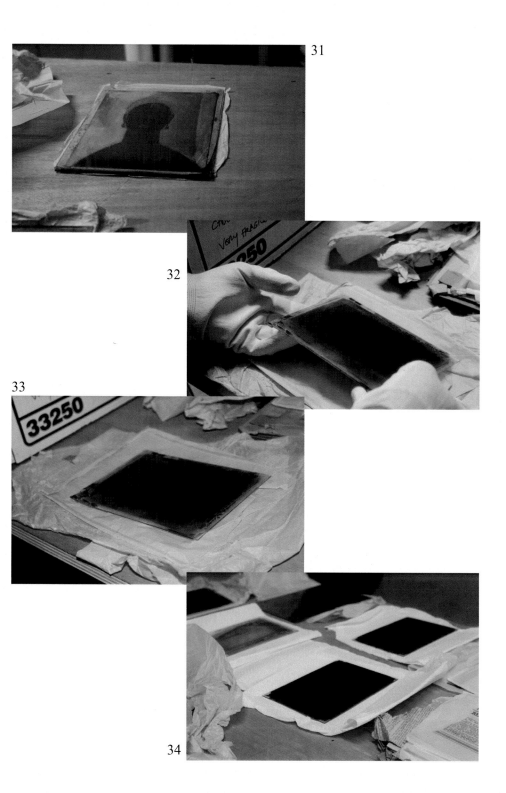

35

36

37

38

39

The two art works attributed to Modi put on display at the exhibition at Palazzo Bonocore in Palermo, seized by the Carabinieri in March 2019 because they were considered fake (pic 35,36); poster held on a pole between Piccadilly Road and Albermarle Street in London for the temporary "exhibition" held on December 22 2018 at Brown's Hotel (37); stone head that the American magazine "Spy" attributes to the art merchant Paul Quatrochi who supposedly bought it in a London flea market and it was used as a doorstop (380; head attributed to Amedeo Modigliani, Perls Private Collection, today on display at the Metropolitan Museum of Art of New York (39).

40

41

42

Livorno, 1984. Steps of the dredging of the "Fosso Reale" (by courtesy of the owner of the pictures, the engineer Michele Caturegli). In particular: the starting of the works with the shifting of the boats (40); the testing of the bucket (41,42); the carriage of the dredger to the "Fosso Reale" (43-46); the starting of the works (47,48); the dredging of the first stone later renamed Modi 1 (49,50); Vera Durbe' emotionally moved by the first head (51); engineer Caturegli and Cesarino with the dredger (52); in the garden of Villa Maria, where the exhibition for the centenary of the birth of the artist is held, presentation of the catalogue Due pietre ritrovate di Amedeo Modigliani with Dario and Vera Durbe' (54).

43

44

45

46

47

48

49

50

51

52

53

54

Fifth Crime Scene: Palazzo Ducale, Genoa
The Rooms of vices and of virtues

CHARACTERS

Marc Restellini – art historian. Director of French museums, founder of the Institut Restellini in Paris, and one of the principal authorities on Modigliani. He has been working for more than twenty years on a new catalogue on the Leghorn artist, due for publication around 2020-21. For his purpose, he uses innovative technologies that have allowed him to classify four hundred works by Modi and to identify two hundred fakes. At the time this book is being edited for publication, Restellini appears to be the curator of the exhibition, *Modigliani, Soutine and the Cursed Artists*, that will be held in Leghorn during the centenary of the artist's death.

Marc Ottavi – He is considered the world's foremost expert on Moïse Kisling. He lives in Paris, where he runs an expert workshop specialising in 19th and 20th century paintings and sculptures.

Isabella Quattrocchi – art history expert. For thirty-five years, she has been an art expert for civil and criminal courts. She works with public prosecutors across half of Italy.

Mariastella Margozzi – member of the scientific committee of contemporary art at the *Roma Tre* University. She is in charge of the early twentieth century painting and sculpture collections section at the National Gallery of Modern Art and she is a former director of the Boncompagni Ludovisi Museum for decorative arts in Rome.

Rudy Chiappini – critic and art historian. For almost twenty years, he was director of the Lugano Museum of Modern Art. Curator of the Genoa exhibition in 2017, he was investigated for forgery, fraud and receiving stolen goods.

Joseph Guttmann – US-naturalised Hungarian collector and art dealer, owner of Global Art Exhibitions in New York. He is member of the board of Leonardo Exhibitions International. He lent works believed to be false to the city of Genoa, which were exhibited in the Doge's Palace. He is under investigation for fraud and receiving stolen goods.

Massimo Vitta Zelman - president of the international giant MondoMostre Skira, an editorial group that manages events related to art throughout Europe. It is based in Milan, Rome, Paris and New York. He is under investigation in Genoa for fraud and receiving stolen goods.

Paolo Blendinger - Swiss painter. From 1975 to 1979, he attended art history courses at the University of Florence. A member of the Society of Painters, Sculptors and Swiss architects, he held solo exhibitions in Switzerland and abroad. Teacher of History of modern art at the Professional University School of Applied Sciences in Italian Switzerland (Supsi), in the applied arts department, from 1999 to 2002.

Yves Bouvier - Swiss businessman and art dealer, tycoon of Geneva's freeport, the largest treasure chest in the world of works of art and luxury goods (it holds over a million works). Under investigation in Geneva for tax evasion totalling some 330 million Swiss francs ($360 million).

Jean Olaniszyn - graduated in History of Art in Paris in the seventies with a dissertation on the life and works of Amedeo Modigliani. Swiss from the Ticino region, researcher and promoter of culture, publisher, founder and curator of the Hermann Hesse Museum of Montagnola, member of the Russian Academy of Sciences.

Vittorio Sgarbi - art historian, a well-known face on Italian television, politician, member of parliament in several administrations. Indicted on charges of authenticating fake De Dominicis works when he was president of the De Dominicis foundation.

Pedro Pedrazzini - Ticino collector investigated in Genoa for fraud and receiving stolen goods.

Paul D. Quatrochi - New York art dealer.

And again: *Jeanne Modigliani, Christian Parisot and Carlo Pepi.*

Genoa, Palazzo Ducale, July 13 2017, 23.00 hours

The Doge's apartments, which overlook the main courtyard, are brightly lit, but it is already night when the Carabinieri arrive on a mandate from the public prosecutor. They get out of their cars, guard the exits, and flood into the halls. It looks like a criminal raid, except there is currently no one to arrest. Even so, the mission is a delicate one. Law enforcement officers work with gloves, their movements slow and efficient. From the walls they remove twenty-one of the forty artworks that have been on display for months in this solemn building so dear to the history of Genoa.

They check the works one by one, to verify that they are precisely those denounced publicly as "cheap daubs" first by Carlo Pepi, then by Marc Restellini and Marc Ottavi, all supported by documents and expert reports. Defining this event as sensational is saying little. The exhibition dedicated to Amedeo Modigliani in the Genoese palace had been anticipated for months, and with it the promise to do justice to the greatness of the Leghorn artist. Instead, it is a disaster.

The public prosecutor's instructions concern paintings and drawings, twenty one as mentioned, of which fifteen are attributed to Modigliani; three are joint works with Kisling and three are attributed the latter. Some are images known to those who work in the world of art, others have never been seen before. Large and small paintings, each of which according to those who own and exhibit them, are worth from a minimum of 10 million euros to over 100 million. A trove that, provided it is believed authentic, is worth around one billion euro.

The Genoa prosecutor's office made a brave and certainly long-pondered choice. Such decisive action is not easy, especially when it risks attracting criticism and countermeasures from powerful adversaries - adversaries who directly with those who holding the sceptre of power in a world, that of the art market, worth hundreds of billions in the international markets. Evidently, the investigators have concrete evidence, and that is why they decide to make their move.

A few more days and the exhibition would have closed. The artworks, masterpieces as they had been presented, or forgeries as they are now believed to be, would have returned to their owners' lounges and vaults, waiting for another exhibition, but with an extra "medal" on their pedigree, that is, a greater value and credibility.

A more prudent tactic would have been to wait for the exhibition to end before arriving with a seizure warrant. It would have caused less of an uproar and attracted less media attention. It would have been too risky though. This time things could not end like they did in Pisa in 2014 or in Turin in 2015. The cities had dedicated important exhibitions to Modigliani, displaying many works of art that visitors would later find at the Doge's Palace.

The accusations of well-known experts had grown stronger, it was necessary to prevent those who might have something to fear from putting the artworks onto the first flight to the United States or to some other destination in the Middle or Far East as soon as the exhibition closed. Because in that case, after a while everything would have been forgotten.

It mustn't happen. History must not be allowed to repeat itself. The seals must be put on urgently. The next day, when the usual line of tourists who throng the exhibition as soon as it is open begins to form in front of ticket office, the clerks will have to say, "the exhibition is closed, the paintings have been impounded". This is the message to the organisers. In short, the party is over. In a few hours, the news travels around the world.

The "circus" of the art world trembles, shaken by an earthquake on a global scale. Four people are put under investigation: Rudy Chiappini, curator of the exhibition; Joseph Guttmann, art merchant and owner of eleven of the paintings exhibited in the Doge's Palace; Massimo Vitta Zelman, president of MondoMostre Skira, the event organiser; and Stefano Zuffi, who had coordinated the organisation of the exhibition. Zuffi is the only one who will escape further investigation.

The investigations by the Carabinieri's cultural heritage unit encompass the crimes of receiving stolen goods, importing fake or counterfeit artworks into the country, material forgery and aggravated fraud. The seizures of the works are backed by four technical reports, signed by Tiziana Mazzoni, Marie Pierre Etcheverry, Mariastella Margozzi and Isabella Quattrocchi, the last expert to be called by the prosecutor. In turn, these reports are supported by the opinions of art critics: the collector Carlo Pepi, Marc Restellini and Marc Ottavi.

The early closure frees the Municipality of Leghorn from a potentially embarrassing situation. It had lent two authentic Modigliani paintings to Genoa. In the wake of Pepi's claims, Leghorn's then mayor Filippo Nogarin wanted to get them back as soon as possible. "The distinction must be very clear. On one hand, there is the heritage of an artist and his city, which is recognised world-wide; on the on the other, there are speculators who want to make money from anything to do with the artist," he said.

Even so, neither the Municipality of Genoa nor the Palazzo Ducale expressed no position even though the controversy had been raging for months amid allegations and denials. And so the Leghorn administration, on July 12, the artist's birthday, responded by asking for the "immediate return" of its property. The Councillor for Culture Francesco Belaise writes to President of Palazzo Ducale: "I trust that our mutual love for Modì and the need to protect his heritage will help you understand our decision." The works of art would be returned only after the seizure of the twenty-one alleged fakes during the late evening of July 13.

Tense hours were to pass before the verdict was signed by Deputy Prosecutor Paolo D'Ovidio alongside his deputy Michele Stagno. But someone may have had advance warning that soon, the sword of justice would fall, and a few days earlier, had tried to tell Rudy Chiappini in a rather careless email which we managed to locate:

> *...everything must be sent back immediately, and I hope you do it very carefully.*

Christian Parisot sent this message to the curator which one of our sources passed on to us. Another confiscation would follow the first; during this time Parisot says to his friend and former colleague at the Amedeo Modigliani Legal Archives:

> *He did not follow good advice ... His image and reputation are badly damaged...*[40]

Modigliani's exhibition is co-produced by Palazzo Ducale and MondoMostre Skira, who entrusted it to the management of Rudy

---

[40] According to the evidence we collected, shortly after the seizures in Genoa, Parisot is alleged to have tried to regain possession of the Archives he had just sold to Marescalchi, perhaps in an effort to "integrate" them. See the Second Crime Scene in this book.

Chiappini. They were all prominent names, and that should have been a guarantee. The Carabinieri look around those great rooms during their search. Who knows if they notice that here and there, above their heads, in addition to the fabulous eighteenth-century stuccos, the frescoes of the four cardinal virtues stand out like a warning. Moreover, one of the most famous works in the palace is the very victory of virtue over vice, by Giambattista Zelotti. A paradox of sorts, that this story about forgeries had its epilogue in a place where art depicts the religious admonitions that underlie the history of our civilisation.

Iustitia, Prudentia, Fortitudo, Temperantia

Justice, Prudence, Fortitude, Temperance: biblical virtues that, if the charges are confirmed, are as complete strangers to the organisers of the Modigliani exhibition - opened on March 16, 2017 and closed by the Carabinieri on July 13. Thousands of eager exhibition-goers, disappointed. Tickets sold to about a hundred thousand visitors would have to be refunded.

The god of Money is difficult to resist, and in the art world, as elsewhere, there are many temptations. Dizzying sums that overwhelm the common sense of many well-regarded experts and perhaps weakens their willpower, rendering them incapable of keeping their lust for money under control. Pepi is one of the first to accuse the organisers of dishonesty: "When I had the Genoa exhibition catalogue in my hands and I saw at least thirteen fake works, I told myself this was beyond the pale."

The exhibition organisers would not get to sleep on the night of the Carabinieri raid. Some of them rushed to welcome the Authorities in the Doge's apartments. The search warrant creates a general furore among the people who gravitate around the exhibition. Between July 13 and 14 cell phones burn with messages trying to understand what do, how to explain. Lawyers are waken in their beds and summoned in haste.

Once they recover from the shock and have had time to sort out their ideas, the organisers and others involved consider how to reply. They take precise aim. They do not attack Restellini directly, but Carlo Pepi, whom they consider weaker because, in their opinion, he has no academic qualifications in this field. Scrolling through the CVs of those who scorn him, attacking his credibility, we note that only one of them appeared to have acquired in-depth knowledge of Modigliani. Pepi may have been self-taught, but he did little else but study Modigliani's work throughout his life, receiving wide recognition. They threatened to sue him: to date we have seen no charges against the fearless 80-year-old Pisan.

All the people involved tell the same story, starting with the former president of the Palazzo Ducale-Foundation for culture, Luca Borzani: "The only painting that Pepi mentions, the *Portrait of Chaïm Soutine,* was exhibited in Paris, Lausanne, Pisa, Turin: all of these details can be found in the catalogue. The curator of the exhibition, Rudy Chiappini is a very prestigious person who signed off on important exhibitions, from Moma in New York to Palazzo Reale in Milan." But his analysis is scant, scribbled down in haste to give the newspapers an improbable image of Carlo Pepi. Borzani fails to address the details of the Pisan collector's claims; in reality, just in the catalogue he had identified not just one but thirteen forgeries, including "the draft of the *Reclining Nude*". The original had been sold for several million euros. Chiappini, for his part, could not be unaware that the *Portrait of Chaïm Soutine* had been branded for decades as a fake.

"The present works had already been in large exhibitions at prestigious institutions," MondoMostre Skira wrote in a press release. "Each one of them has its own dense catalogue, with a bibliography. Moreover, we are willing to present these statements at any appropriate venue." Then Vitta Zelman, the president of MondoMostre, and Rudy Chiappini also go after their other adversary: "Restellini's Pinacothèque de Paris is an empty space, which was closed three years ago," while "Pepi has not published any studies." The reactions continue, right until the plot twists: Chiappini, surprising everyone, begins to distance himself from those who in the past had certified the authenticity of the works he had identified. "It makes no difference to me," he says. "I did not make the attribution for Modigliani's the works, I limited myself to collating information. We will have to track down the source that made the first attribution. In any case, I still think that those paintings are genuine."

However, he well knows who the source is. Parisot himself, the author of many painting certifications, had in fact advised Chiappini that things were turning sour. He had also been member of the board of the Modigliani

Archives after the departure of his Ticino colleague Jean Olaniszyn, and he certainly could not have failed to note the latter's clear views on the *Portrait of Chaïm Soutine*.

Olaniszyn himself said that he had reported it as a fake way back in the seventies.

> *I had been contacted by the antiquarian from Gordola [in Switzerland, in the district of Locarno, ed.], Guido Alborghetti, who had bought it. Years later, I happened to have it in front of me again. Pedro Pedrazzini [currently under investigation in Genoa - ed.] had repurchased it. In the meantime, Christian Parisot, whom Pedrazzini had turned to, took care of the authentication, even though I had already adjudged it a fake. Parisot had the authority, being the archivist of Modigliani, and he could do whatever he wanted. In 1999, he participated in the exhibition put on by Rudy Chiappini at the Malpensata di Lugano, supplying it with material from the Archives. In 2006, he and Pedrazzini were back, presenting the famous Portrait of Chaïm Soutine for a review at the Library of Lugano prepared by Giorgio Alberti and me. We categorically refused to take it.*

Perhaps Vittorio Sgarbi was also among those awakened in the middle of the night by the news that the Carabinieri were in Palazzo Ducale. Indeed, in the early hours of July 14, 2017, he had already posted on his Facebook page: "Genoa, Modigliani's alleged fakes: an investigation is not a judgement. The exhibition must be reopened. The judicial authorities this morning seized twenty-one works from the Modigliani exhibition being held at the Palazzo Ducale in Genoa. I find it outrageous that the organisers, intimidated by the judicial enquiry, brought forward the closure to the exhibition because of alleged, but unproven, forgeries: it is a grave act of submission before the authorities. For the time being, some people are only under investigation. The investigation itself does not mean that the works on display are false."

"Let's say that all this is tied up with Modigliani's curse," he will then comment in an interview, half-ironic and half resigned. However, it is disarming to think that a public figure, who has been a member of parliament and a mayor, should forget that forgery is a crime, and can be an important component in the overall criminal environment.

Yet, Sgarbi is not the only one to refer to the "curse". We were surprised, during the preparatory work for this book to come across people steeped in culture who, in order to keep enquiring minds at bay, like soothsayers, prophesy impending misfortunes ready befall anyone who digs into the Modigliani racket.

A clash of titans

In Genoa in 2017, a no-holds-barred struggle began between some of the titans of the art world which, at the time of writing, is still ongoing. An epic clash in the art market, an attack on the alleged "factory" which produced some of the most notorious forgeries of the last hundred years. The giants of the sector are aligned on either side to defend their own interests: at stake, for all of them, money and credibility. But while on the one side we are talking about income which, though earned in a high-risk field, is derived from knowledge and authority, the other is a vortex of purely economic activity based on a network of fraudulent relationships at the expense of artist and art lovers.

At last the time is ripe. The centenary of Modigliani's death is here, along with a whole circus of celebrations. Everyone has their own good reasons for participating. Marc Restellini is about to complete a project that has taken twenty years. The Modigliani Legal Archives are again for sale on the black market; shady individuals who buy works at exorbitant prices, sending prices soaring and increasing the risk of money laundering, step up their activities in the market; those who present themselves as standard-bearers of the law rush onto the battlefield.

The Herculean scope of the contest was immediately clear when the prestigious Institut Restellini along with Marc Ottavi, the most prominent authority on Moïse Kisling's, sided with Carlo Pepi, a step they had never previously taken. Each one of them had launched their offensive during the preparations for the Genoese exhibition, sounding a warning for those working on the project. After the inauguration, Restellini stepped up his attack. "This exhibition is highly questionable; I had to report the situation to the Italian authorities as soon as I saw the content. The Institute knows these works because they are forgeries, and we have all the documentation to prove it," the press release of May 24 reported. "At least a third of the paintings in the exhibition are known to be fake. Nothing like this has been seen since the arrest and sentencing of Christian Parisot for counterfeiting."

It is a chance that Pepi does not miss. A few days later, on May 30, he himself launches an appeal to Italy's art historians: "Go and see the Modigliani exhibition in Genoa. I would hope that some of you have the ability to identify the piles of junk included in the exhibition, and that for once in your lives you take an unambiguous position and make a concrete contribution to end the indecent, unpunished proliferation of fakes!" Pepi's exhortation goes unheeded. The deafening silence of the academic world calls to the mind the disgraceful position held by many art experts on the discovery of the "fake heads of Modigliani" in Leghorn in 1984 when, over a timeframe of just a few hours, they attributed those poor, purpose-made forgeries to the artist.

The news that there are forgeries is nonetheless sensational, and it soon spreads beyond the Italian borders, from the United States to Russia. In France, the newspaper "Le Monde" publishes an article on Genoa's suspected fakes Modigliani works. The scandal is now an international one.

In order to give a touch of originality, at the exhibition the organisers also included some works signed by both Modigliani and his friend Kisling. Without minimising the affection and friendship that bound the two painters or entering into the artistic merits of the works, when considering just the personality, intellect and individualism typical of Modì, who would even imagine that he might have co-signed works with an artist so different from him? The ambiguity arises from certain stories that ran rife among the painters of Montparnasse, which told that the merchant Léopold Zborowski wanted to entrust some unfinished works by Modigliani to Kisling's finishing touches after Modi's unexpected death. If that were the case, they would surely not have included still life paintings, which Modì would have never even started painting. All this is confirmed by the most renowned expert on the Polish artist, the French critic Marc Ottavi. Ottavi told us what happened in the long interview he gave us.

Among the authentic masterpieces I admired when visiting the exhibition, I also saw thirteen fake works by Modigliani (as Restellini argues), three fake paintings by Kisling and, a rarity, three paintings resulting from a hypothetical four-hand collaboration between Modigliani and Kisling, where the forger had had to test his imagination and invent an intermediate style for the two artists.

Ottavi laughs when he tells us about his surreal experience at the Genoa exhibition, which he defines as "a unique opportunity to check my observation skills" when seeing, next to each other, authentic and fake paintings attributed to the same author. Then, more seriously, he continues:

Now, everything I know about the works co-produced by the two points to them being fakes. As soon as I received the catalogue, I realised that none of the Kislings was authentic. I send a letter to Chiappini. "You have to remove them immediately." However, the curator does not answer me directly, but through the press. He defends himself by saying that he has the documentation where Kisling's son, Jean, categorically attributes the works to his father. Jean was an airline pilot; he did not have the skills to ascertain whether a painting is a Modigliani, or even identify works by his father. At the end of his life, he made many mistakes, authenticating fakes. So much so that I persuaded him to make amends by publicly destroying one of his own books on his father. Then I replied to Chiappini underlining that he seemed to have stumbled upon a fraud. A set up staged by an American forger called Joseph Guttmann. Someone who survives only thanks to his ability to bribe the right people. Guttmann is a thief who steals our heritage and defrauds the community. This information should send him to prison.

Joseph Guttmann indeed: a famous merchant, the owner of an important New York gallery, so private a citizen that he does not even have a website. There is little about him on the web. Among the few news items, there is the sensational case (reported in an article in the *New York Times*) of a Picasso stolen from a wealthy New York woman between 1980 and 1985 and replaced by a copy which was so well made that nobody noticed until the owner died.

In 1991, Guttmann went to Sotheby's to get a valuation for the stolen original. The auction house informed the police and the merchant, when questioned, defended himself explaining that he had received it from a customer, who in turn had acquired it as payment for a debt. We do not know how the investigation turned out. Among the few scraps of news available about him, there is a letter written by another American art dealer, Paul D. Quatrochi, who apologises to Guttmann for reporting him to the authorities for the theft of a Modigliani: the great *Reclining Nude* of Céline Howard, a work that we find today among the Carabinieri's impounded properties in Rome. It was one of the paintings on display at the Doge's Palace.[41]

The painting had already been contested in the past, during an exhibition in Bonn in 2009 and then again in 2012, in Brazil, at the São Paulo Museum of Art. Several newspapers across the globe reported the details and the many controversies about the authenticity of the work. Yet, this was not enough to dissuade the exhibition organisers in Genoa.

And what to say about the famous portrait of the Polish Cubist painter Maria Marevna and the embarrassment in Moscow during the exhibition at the prestigious Pushkin Museum in 2011? They even put it on the cover of the catalogue. A worldwide scandal, since a Russian collector who wanted to buy it, with the support of other connoisseurs, had had it analysed a few years earlier by a laboratory in Switzerland. The examination is said to have established that the pigments used were not yet in use in Modigliani's lifetime. Furthermore, neither Marevna nor her daughter Marika Rivera, who left memoirs covering several areas, ever mentioned a portrait by Modigliani.

In spite of all this the director of the museum, who had opposed the choice, joined the scientific committee of the Legal Archives chaired by Parisot shortly afterwards. The painting later reappeared on the other side

---

[41] The controversy between the two has been going on for decades and in 2003, it reached the Civil Court of California. From our information, it seems that Quatrochi would have been forced to write the famous apology, thus withdrawing his accusations against Guttmann. Parisot also confirms the dispute in Los Angeles. The issue appears much more complex and according to our sources, it would concern a loan that Joseph Guttmann and Guy Vincent Chastenet are alleged to have requested from two banks, Crédit Agricole and Indosuez. Quatrochi in this case is the only plaintiff. Our sources allege that Quatrochi tried to buy the painting in question from Chastenet, to try to document its authenticity. Once he had obtained the loan, probably also thanks to Quatrochi's intervention, Guttmann is alleged to have cut him out of the deal. For this reason Quatrochi might have felt cheated. Subsequently the banks are alleged to have noticed that the painting was not signed by Modigliani, but at least it could be "attributed" to him.

of the world: in Brazil. However, like the nude of Céline Howard in 2012 in São Paulo, it is contested.

We recall what the art critic and Modigliani expert Jean Olaniszyn, artistic director at the Rivellino in Locarno, Switzerland, had previously told us:

> *Yes, it was known. Already years ago, when I took care of the Archives, I reported the presence of several fakes. The works have been shown in other exhibitions and published in the relative catalogues. Often they are certified by Christian Parisot, who has already been sued over forged documents and fake works. It is for this reason that, like Pepi and Restellini, I resigned from the Amedeo Modigliani Archives a few years ago. I could not take part in this farce.*

Meanwhile, Rudy Chiappini tries to explain by providing some data he believes are incontrovertible on the historical validity of the works he selected. With regards to the *Red Caryatid - The Wedding Couple*, for example, he says the attribution has been known since 1930. He adds that in the seventies it was donated by the Perls Gallery of New York to the Metropolitan Museum of Art. Then he quotes three expert appraisals including that of Hanka Zborowska, wife of the one-time merchant of Modigliani's works.

However, the curator overlooks the fact that Klaus Perls had already been at the centre of the Leghorn scandal in 1984, for providing two fakes to the exhibition organised by the Municipality for the centenary of Modigliani's birth: the portrait of Picasso and a caryatid in stone. Modì's daughter Jeanne herself had said that they were not authentic. When he left Leghorn, Perls returned to the US and thanks to the notoriety he had acquired, he managed within a short time to deal in over fifty "works" by Modigliani. We remember that at that time Carlo Pepi himself, without ever being contradicted, had called the Perls Gallery "a fake factory".

We would say all this controversy arises from the confusion and mystery that always accompanied the works of the Leghorn painter, especially in the United States. Only a few are included in Ambrogio Ceroni's catalogue because of the difficulty the compiler himself had in verifying their condition and ownership. It should arouse at least some suspicion that Perls sells such a large quantity of works attributed to the Italian master in the

United States - practically a seventh of those in existence around the world that are considered authentic.

In the early 1990s, Perls had bought, among other things, a stone sculpture from Paul D. Quatrochi (the same person who had accused Joseph Guttmann of theft), which he put up for sale again soon afterwards. It is the same head that we find today at the Metropolitan Museum of Art. A cursory look at the exhibition catalogue prepared by MondoMostre Skira brings us to a stone sculpture, a head attributed to Modigliani and identified as having come from Perls Gallery. The work was not exhibited in the Doge's Palace, yet it was included in the catalogue. A sculpture by Modì in such refined detail had never been seen before. Even the hair is carefully worked, a hairstyle with two locks on the forehead. Everything is so symmetrical, defined and smooth.

With respect to the so-called certifications by Zborowski's wife, it is her closest friend, Lunia Czechowska, who dismantled that theory in an interview in the 1980s, already mentioned earlier, in which she explains that neither she nor Hanka Zborowska had ever signed expert appraisals.[42]

The evidence is built on a mosaic of clues. But then how is it that the event organisers in Genoa never felt at least a pang of doubt? Although in the past, as Chiappini notes, the paintings had been displayed at prestigious exhibitions, this doesn't mean that later investigations could not establish that they were forgeries. If we consider an art exhibition only as an economic business, we must bear in mind all the precautions that a careful manager would adopt before taking on potential liabilities. It is an indispensable risk analysis approach, which includes, among others things, the careful monitoring of news media and of all news published on each topic. None of the suspects, as far as we know, ever assessed this risk.

According to Restellini, who now enters the fray firing on all cylinders, it may have been a risk worth taking. His is a direct indictment of the organisers, willing to do the bidding of the art dealers. The aim would be very simple: to introduce forged works of art into the market, lending them

---

[42] See Santini's interview with Lunia Czechowska, in Aldo Santini, *Modigliani. Leghorn Paris Ultima Bohème*, Rizzoli, Milan 1987.

legitimacy and giving them a value of millions. It is unacceptable for national museums to agree to such deception. Restellini says it loud and clear in his "Institut" press release dated June 15, 2017:

> *Contrary to what has been said, none of the works concerned (have authentications) based on any historical documentation, and none of them appeared before 1970 at best. So what the organisers said when interviewed is absolutely false. None of these art works has the slightest credible, reliable, documentary proof from the period. And if it does exist it is, in all probability, falsified documentation.*

The suspects and the parties involved, such as the Palazzo Ducale Foundation, ready their defence.[43] They prepare the collected counter-arguments in a dossier that appears to be around ninety pages. We don't know specifically what arguments they presented, but we were able to verify that one of the party's expert reports was signed by Professor Paolo Baldacci, an expert on avant-garde art of the twentieth century. Baldacci himself is not completely without stain, he had been sentenced for authenticating fake De Chirico art works, a sentence then suspended on appeal. According to what we understood from the De Chirico Foundation, civil litigation is pending.

For the counterclaims sustaining the authenticity of the art works, the defendants' legal advisers produce earlier certifications signed by Angela Ceroni, Klaus Perls and Christian Parisot. Three recurring names among the plethora of hotly debated expertise. Through their lawyer, they also try to object to the sample of pigments that the prosecutor's consultants are about to take from the canvases. "If the paintings were real, the damage would run to millions," the lawyer asserts on July 24, 2017.

It is common knowledge that such investigations are always carried out with extreme care and attention, and that the tests are conducted by professionals who have been working in that field for decades. They are minute samples that certainly do not affect the overall structure of the painting. If this is the case, what should we say about the American restorers who allegedly worked on some of the canvases as though they

---

[43] The Palazzo Ducale Foundation would say it was a "severely damaged party" in the affair. See "Il Sole 24 Ore", January 9 ,2018.

were painters and decorators, slapping "three layers of clear coat" on the works, as the prosecutor's consultant told us? What was the defence trying to do, if not to prevent the discovery, later made, that titanium white, a synthetic pigment created after Amedeo's death, had been used?

Probably the defensive strategy is to dismantle the credibility of the prosecutor's two expert witnesses, Isabella Quattrocchi and Mariastella Margozzi.

Then Vittorio Sgarbi makes his reappearance. In a newspaper article from March 10, 2018 under his byline in *Il Giornale*, he opens the article with a eulogy to the security contractor Fabrizio Quattrocchi, who died at the hands of Muslims fundamentalist in Iraq with the cry: "I'll show you how an Italian dies" - almost as if he were trying to confuse his readers. There is no connection, apart from the same surname, with the calm and reserved professor Quattrocchi.

The article is inaccurate, perhaps deliberately so, because we read that the public prosecutor's technical consultant is alleged to have been born in 1983, and therefore she would be too "young" to have the necessary experience. He must have misread her curriculum, which incidentally can easily be found on LinkedIn. 1983 it is not the year of her birth, but the year in which she began working with the judicial authorities as an expert witness.

One thing reported in the article is true, however: Isabella Quattrocchi was instrumental in the investigation of the works of art seized from Massimo Carminati in the probe known as "Mafia Capitale". It doesn't seem a shortcoming to us, quite the opposite in fact.

In the same article, Sgarbi also attacks Mariastella Margozzi, the other expert witness. "Known for her modest expertise on whichever artist," he writes, adding: "I don't know if those paintings by Modigliani are fake, but I know the experts who say so are not authentic".

Among other things, during Margozzi's professional career she was, for twenty three years, in charge of the early twentieth century painting and sculpture collections at the National Gallery of Modern Art and director of the Boncompagni Ludovisi Museum in Rome. The famous art critic's article appears to be a clumsy attempt to discredit the investigations. Quattrocchi, who has been a teacher of art-related subjects since the early seventies, replies in kind. "Did he say that I have no expertise on Modigliani? He might be right, I don't know. I don't care what he says. That's also because he is a very peculiar character: he thinks he is top of the class, but he really isn't."

Support for the suspects is minimal, both in Italy and in Europe. Since no national artistic or judicial authority intends to take the side of the accused, someone thinks of playing the American card. Vittorio Sgarbi rushes to the rescue once again. In an article published in *Il Giornale* on February 21, 2018 and evocatively entitled *There! The Modigliani's were originals*, he reports: "The federal judge of Houston, Greg Abbott, after receiving the *notitia criminis* of the "fake Modiglianis of Genoa" from the collector and art dealer Joseph Guttmann, rejected the reports of experts whom he adjudged to not possess the relevant, expertise, such as Mariastella Margozzi and Isabella Quattrocchi [...]. For this reason, the American judge has issued an injunction to remind the Italian judiciary of the principles of rectitude."

In the article, four international art experts are also mentioned, named by the elusive Texan judge, who allegedly certified the authenticity of the paintings. They are Nicolas Andrei (*sic*; the correct name is Nicholas Andrew - *ed*) Serota, former director of the Tate Gallery in London, Glan [*sic*; the correct name is Glenn, *ed*.] D. Lowry, director of the Museum of Modern Art of New York, Michael Govan, director of the Los Angeles County Museum of Art, and an unspecified John Papi. To this day, none of them has spoken out on the case, and the supposed judge is none other than the current governor of Texas, who was a federal judge, but only until 2001. In the internet age, when many things can be verified in a matter of seconds, Sgarbi's article appears imprudent. The prosecutor's office responds dryly: "No injunction arrived from the USA".[44]

A year later, Sgarbi turns up again to lend support to the organisers of the exhibition at Palazzo Ducale. In an interview to Primocanale.it on 30 January, 2019, he comments: "You have had a good experience with fake Modigliani pieces in Genoa. Forgeries always attract a lot of people, too

---

[44] *Falsi Modigliani, Sgarbi ancora all'attacco e la procura chiede una rogatoria agli Usa,* "la Repubblica", February 22 2018.

bad they closed the exhibition early." It is however a matter that pertains not only to ethics, but also to the law: attracting unwary paying visitors to an exhibition of forgeries is the type of deception which in the legal system is called fraud. It was a poor move, which has to date cost Palazzo Ducale at least one million Euro in repayments.

Prosecutors do not limit themselves to reading newspaper articles or social media posts: as prescribed by criminal procedure, they carry out the research needed to identify evidence and proof. The Carabinieri immediately take statements from the accusers, as "people informed in the matter" and they confirm everything they have alleged in the past. Carlo Pepi arrives in Rome from Crespina with his swathes of papers and documents. Restellini and Ottavi come from Paris to explain their position, even paying their own travel expenses. They are under no obligation, but they do it anyway. The volume and coherence of information that the investigators gather from around of the world seems overwhelming.

The woman of the palettes

The colours. The intense pink of the blooming Judas trees, the yellow of daisies, the green of fresh grass, the violets, the hawthorn that breaks the grey of the asphalt, the blue of a clear sky in the first days of spring. A silent road that curves, rises, turns and slopes sinuously down through the middle of the Sabine countryside. Not far away from the abbey of Farfa, where for centuries the amanuensis monks painted and transcribed precious and unique volumes, lies a small farmhouse among the olive groves, whipped by the winds. This is where Isabella Quattrocchi awaits us; she is a woman who for forty years, quietly and without too much media attention, has been devastating the plans of numerous renowned collectors and also of international counterfeiters through her expertise. A Penelope weaving her tapestry in the shadow of Europe's prosecutors; she has been studying artistic techniques and materials all her life, exploring the narrative behind every painting. Her preferred retreat is surrounded by nature. Every window is a landscape, almost a painting by Paolo Uccello. The calm and peace instil a feeling of well-being and a magical stillness.

Despite her seventy-nine years, she is energetic and combative, constantly moving among the thousands of memories that crowd the home. Paintings, drawings, books, records, plates, china, trinkets of every kind. There are two cheerful and lively dogs to keep her company, which immediately make friends. On the walls are dozens of palettes imbued with colours. Almost all of them are square, but each is as different as the stories of the painters to which they belonged. Ancient, modern, old, worn, heavily used, each one of them exudes the ingenuity of the artists whose needs it served. She studied them one by one, seeking to discover their secrets. They are fundamental pieces of the puzzle when seeking to identify forgeries, or indeed to restore a painting. Of each palette, she speaks with pride and affection.

On the telephone, she has a youthful and ringing voice, which sometimes drops as if to leave room for her thoughts. During the interview, she looks at us directly. Two eyes with a sweet and slightly mischievous look, a captivating smile that have preserved the traits of a distant youth. She is like a girl who has aged prematurely, with her jaunty air and her fascinating dialect. Most of all, she exudes passion. Passion for everything: for the men in her life, for her five children, for her grandchildren, for painting, for the work that requires her to take trains and planes from one courthouse to another around Italy.

She comes to meet us, wrapped in a large shiny sweater that serves as a coat.

She talks about herself with gracious self-irony, celebrating her successes without hiding her disappointments.

I came across Modigliani when I was very young, as a result of a number of factors. At nineteen, I married the father of my first four children, a sculptor who was also my teacher. I went with him to see the inaugural exhibition at the National Gallery of Modern Art where some sculptures and a painting by the Leghorn artist were on display. I came across his work many other times in my life as an expert. In 1962, my husband took me to Paris. He introduced me to the beauty of paintings and of the original drawings by Modigliani. Then I saw the exhibition of the works from collection of Paul Alexandre, his friend and patron as well as his doctor.

Isabella Quattrocchi is a woman full of memories and of surprises.

I won a national competition in painting techniques where five thousand people took part. I helped many young people who came after me, who did restoration and learned all about materials. If you start with restoration, you can almost read the biography of the works visually. The prosecutors can barely distinguish a lithograph from a drawing. The best school that I attended consisted of civil courts, where inheritances were involved.

By offering this type of expertise, I was continuing my studies. I went to the experts, so I learned everything. Today my children, above all my daughters, scold me for mother who was so devoted to work. True, I have always loved what I was doing. However, how I could have raised five children with the salary of a history of art teacher? I had to study and get by, day by day. Although today they are all adults, I stay in touch with them as closely as possible, I want to be as present as I can in their lives.

The expert then talks about the exhibition at Palazzo Ducale.

When I found myself in front of the paintings, I wanted to cry. I felt helpless. It was all a big financial game, all of it premeditated, that took place at Palazzo Ducale. A fraud. Of the twenty-one works seized, only one was not a fake, and it was a drawing donated by Paul Alexandre. When I returned to Genoa, I worked for days with lenses, lamps and equipment. Then I reviewed the works impounded in Rome in the vault of the Carabinieri. I was given forty pages of expert opinion on a painting whose observations were doubtful. [signed by Professor Baldacci, ed]. You cannot fill a report with so many "coulds", "woulds", with so many conditionals. The magistrate needs data and certainty to express a judgment, the expert must express himself in a decisive manner.

Modigliani painted by drawing. He had no money for canvases, brushes or colours. He drew on paper. He used blue or sepia lead pencils. He used the pencil because he could not always afford colours. When he used his brush, he used fluid paints; he had to use it very sparingly. The paintings in Genoa, on the other hand, are charged with colour, brush strokes upon brush strokes. Some are the result of a collage of paintings that certainly belonged to the artist: Modigliani was could prepare an outline with a few strokes; he was very skilled at drawing. Wherever he went, he would the free school of nude painting: it cost nothing, he could find materials on which to experiment his technique and he did not have to pay the models.

Quattrocchi met of many people during her lifetime of study and research in the field.

> *My experience, as a woman, mother and scholar, opened many doors for me, it allowed me to meet many people; I crossed paths with men and women that I ran into over and over, for a variety of reasons. Among them were Carlo Pepi and Vittorio Sgarbi. I met the former many years ago during an appraisal conducted on behalf of the Court of Pisa. They summoned me to give my assessment of a work by Mario Schifano that I declared false, while Pepi had thought it was authentic and was therefore disappointed. He is a very particular person. Original. He never got angry. Indeed, there has always been a lot of mutual respect.*

"How come Vittorio Sgarbi is so angry with you? Do you know each other?" we ask?

> *Of course, we know each other. I also worked on the most recent expert reports during the investigation into fake works attributed to Gino De Dominicis, recognised as one of Italy's most important artists in the post Second World War period. Twenty-three people under investigation, all accused under various criminal charges, counterfeiting of works of art and of receiving stolen goods. Two people arrested. Sgarbi was the president of the foundation. His deputy, Marta Massaioli is under house arrest together with Giordano Villa, accused of having materially produced the counterfeits of the works attributed to the painter from the Marches region. She is a prominent player; previously she had been De Dominicis' personal assistant.*

During the investigation, the authorities seized more than two hundred and fifty counterfeit works (worth over 30 million Euro), mostly sold to unsuspecting collectors, as well as the materials necessary for the falsification. The accusations made against the art critic after months of wiretapping and surveillance are no small matter: falsifying and authenticating counterfeit works despite knowing they are fakes, aiding and abetting a crime. The men of the Command for the protection of cultural heritage took pictures of him authenticating recently-produced forgeries arriving from a warehouse in Cerreto d'Esi, in the province of Ancona. Sgarbi, according to the investigators, authenticated the works submitted to his judgment without even viewing them, signing some sheets accompanied by photographs as he sat with Massaioli in a hotel lounge (a public place which could actually be seen from the street through the large windows).

Justice makes up ground

"Twenty out of the twenty-one paintings we seized are fake." The confirmation of the charges made by the Genoa Public Prosecutor and by the Carabinieri arrives on March 13, 2019. It is covered by news agencies, newspapers and television stations. The works are not by Modigliani. Renowned experts say so; analysts from the Scientific Investigations Department of Rome, who also carried out chemical investigations on the colours, determine it. Those colours had never been on Modì's palette. The reconstruction focuses on the appearance of colours starting with the earliest charcoal used through to the most recent finds: quinacridone, a synthetic pigment created in the 1950s. Even the titanium white found on the canvas considered to be a forgery is from a later date, 1921. When it was invented, Modigliani had been dead for over a year.

With high-tech equipment, the Carabinieri also carry out molecular analysis of the fibres of the binders, the glues, the wood, the paints and the paper. They leave no stone unturned. The list of suspects contained six names. Chiappini, Guttmann and Vitta Zelman are joined by Nicolò Sponzilli, a director of Mondo- Exhibitions Skira, Rosa Fasan, an employee of the same company, and Piero Pedrazzini, known as Pedro, a collector and owner of one of the counterfeit works, the *Ritratto di Chaïm Soutine*.

From Genoa to New York, passing through London and Geneva: the investigation into the fake Modiglianis was global. The prosecutor worked on all fronts, seeking international cooperation to acquire more information on the twenty-one works exhibited at Palazzo Ducale. For months, the police forces of the United States, Russia, Great Britain and Switzerland produced documents and certificates and questioned those thought to have information in their respective jurisdictions. They did not neglect the more traditional investigation tools either. Along with multispectral analyses they carried out financial investigations, searches, surveillance and wiretapping. A full-bodied investigation. A probe that will mark the history of art-related crimes, and a point of no return for wrongdoers.

Isabella Quattrocchi has no hesitation when she talks about the exhibition and her belief that whoever organised it knew very well what it was all about.

The exhibition with Modigliani's fake paintings in Genoa? It was planned for this reason, with twenty clumsily faked works. I only had to take a picture of them, back and front, to work it out. Whoever did the job before me had relied on photos they were given. Another important detail, then, is that the exhibition was dark, and this clearly was no accident. There was no general lighting, the light was focused only on the paintings. On each, there were three fingers of heavy, thick paint. It's like when on the road you come across a car with its high beam headlights on: you get blinded and everything seems blurred. If scientific tests claim that that particular pigment didn't even exist in the 1920s, how can you contradict science? This is also why I said some canvases are clumsily forged.

One of the paintings rejected by the expert had been authenticated by the Ministry of Education. "A very serious matter," Quattrocchi comments. In fact, as the consultant explained to us, it was not a formal authentication, but a notification of historical and artistic interest. A document that apparently makes the authenticity of an artwork unquestionable.

We often wondered why certain people avoided our questions, as Rudy Chiappini has done several times. Again on February 27, 2019, a few days before the conclusion of the preliminary investigations, he told us for the umpteenth time that he is not interested in talking to us. At the beginning of our investigation, we heard from Parisot about a sort of conclave held in Lugano to prepare an effective defence. The people summoned were Guttmann, Chiappini and Zuffi, together with the expert Paolo Blendinger. However, what was Parisot doing with some of the suspects, since he seemed extraneous to the whole affair?

Nobody would have expected the FBI to enter the field of play. Federal investigators broke into Joseph Guttmann's home and offices in early 2019, following up on an Italian legal request. Among the many papers they find, they come across a fake document. It was a letter in hastily-written English, which turned out to be the translation of another document that had nothing to do with the matter in hand but which contained the stamps and logo of the Municipality of Genoa. It was meant to be a sort of guarantee that the Genoese administration had given the American-Hungarian merchant, that is to say, an assurance that his painting would not be impounded in the city during the exhibition. Once convinced, Guttmann is alleged to have had it sent via MondoMostre Skira.[45]

It would seem clear that the organisers of the exhibition were under heavy pressure from Guttmann, and fobbed him off by falsifying a document purportedly from the Municipality. In reality, the collector claimed a sort of "immunity", expecting that his property would not be confiscated in any case. Written commitment was also requested from the Ministry of cultural Goods, but they were careful not to grant it. Guttmann's claims, are based on common practice among private individuals. Whoever lends an artwork for an exhibition usually asks for a sort of indemnity whereby those who receive the painting are liable for any damages caused to the sender if, for any reason, the authorities intervene. The practice however must always have a legal basis, i.e. the object lent must have been lawfully obtained.

Like the accusers, the suspects - along with Parisot, who authenticated some of the works in question - arrive in Rome to be interrogated by the Carabinieri. As far as everyone knew, the evidence was based items such as intercepted e-mails between two employees of MondoMostre Skira. One of them, as the Carabinieri report detailed, writes to their colleague "Abandon ship". In an intercepted phone call, Luca Borzani, president of the Palazzo Ducale Foundation, speaks with Vitta Zelman, president of MondoMostre, and says: "I wouldn't swear on (the good faith of) Guttmann and Chiappini".

It will take months and perhaps even years for the trial to reach its conclusion. And it is not guaranteed that in the end there will be convictions for the crimes committed proven: the statute of limitations may yet come into play, as it has many times in the past for crimes of this kind.

We suspect that the failure to bring charges of criminal conspiracy may favour the dismissal of the case. We note that often, when it comes to crimes committed in the field of art, such charges are not brought. Yet, the Italian criminal code is clear when it states, in article 416: "When three or more people join together in order to commit several crimes..." From our

---

[45] Ansa, *Una rete americana dietro le mostre con i falsi Modigliani*, March 28 2019.

understanding, six people are under investigation, the alleged crimes are more than one in number and everyone involved worked to achieve the same criminal plan. It is not our task to replace the judge, but we ask the same questions we believe any reader would ask. Why have charges of criminal conspiracy never been brought: several people, multiple crimes, same goal? We believe that the explanation, beyond a legal one which is beyond our skill set, is the perception - wrong, in our opinion - that similar crimes and related offences pose little danger to society.

"In Genoa there's a gang on the move"

According to Restellini, "there is "a "gang" on the move in Genoa". We decide to go and meet him in Paris. We stop in place Clemenceau to admire the statue of General De Gaulle, immortalised on his pedestal. We cross the Elysée gardens and in a few minutes, we are at 91 rue du Faubourg Saint-Honoré, a few dozen metres from the presidential palace. A building with large windows. This is the headquarters of the Parisian "Institut Restellini".

Marc Restellini welcomes us, sitting in his black leather armchair with a large modern art painting behind him. He has a scarf that covers his neck and his unbuttoned shirt, in bohemian style. With a short, sardonic laugh - he knows what we have come to talk about - he is already enjoying his victory. He has succeeded, at least for the moment, in forcing that "gang" into a corner.

We want to get to the crux of the matter straight away. Whatever the outcome of the trial may be, it is clear that the art world is shocked by the ease with which so many forgeries had, at one fell swoop, been allowed entry to a cultural shrine like Palazzo Ducale. "What happened in Genoa from your point of view? And who might have had an interest in exhibiting forgeries, if they are indeed forgeries?"

Restellini replies calmly but firmly: "I think they are. Now what happened in Genoa is very simple. I had heard talk about the exhibition when it was being prepared. I had seen the exhibitions that had previously been prepared by the curator Rudy Chiappini, especially the one in Seoul, and the presence of paintings that are notorious forgeries - fakes - had already terrified me. If it weren't so difficult to speak out in Korean..."

So, according to the Parisian historian, there are well-known precedents. "Then I heard that the same exhibition would arrive in Genoa; in any case I had immediately refused to take part.

When it opened, I received phone calls from people who told me: "It's a horror show, there are forgeries". I thought: "Oh well, how many? Two or three? If there are two or three forgeries we will do what needs to be done". Then we ordered the catalogue and when it arrived, it wasn't two or three. For me there were twenty-one, totally fake! At that point, the situation took on proportions that could no longer let you believe it was a mistake ... at that level. And that's the problem. A mistake can be understood, admittedly, nobody is infallible. We can all make mistakes even when we are diligent. But twenty one out of forty! There is a problem there, it is no longer a mistake, it is something else. Moreover, we know these paintings; we have known them for twenty years. They are famous forgeries. We know all about these works, we know very well that they have no history, we know well they appeared in the seventies, that they were made with chemical compounds that absolutely do not correspond to the palette used by Modigliani. Therefore, I immediately sent a letter to the Italian Ministry of Cultural Heritage and to the Carabinieri."

"But if it is not a human error, Professor, what should we think?"

"Well, it's a fraud, a manifest fraud. The Carabinieri replied to me in twenty-four hours saying that it was very interesting. Therefore, they asked me to come to Rome to give my version of the facts. Fifteen days later, I believe, the prosecutor ordered the seizure."

"Who has anything to gain by exhibiting fake paintings?"

"Here we are exposing commercial and financial interests. If you have a fake painting worth zero, but you start finding ways to legitimise it, to give it an official place, the painting can be worth something on the market. And its value rises ever higher. These paintings belong to merchants, or at least to an American merchant [Joseph Guttmann, *ed.*], who takes great advantage of the fact that they are displayed in exhibitions. He has a strong incentive for such events to be held, and even in financing them. This allows the organisation of even prestigious exhibitions at an excellent price. Those of Modigliani would usually cost a fortune. One of his paintings today is worth between 50 and 100 million euro. If he has forty paintings in an exhibition, do you realise how much the event can cost in terms of organisation and logistics? But in this case, I found out from the investigators that the cost of preparing the exhibition at Palazzo Ducale was very low."

"Which is? How much?"

"I don't have all the details, but obviously there is a big difference between how much the exhibition actually cost and how much it should have cost. Moreover, when the price paid to set up the event does not reflect what is on display in the exhibition, we are looking at a fraud. I am shocked. The person who organised it has a responsibility. I ran a national museum for twenty years, and then my private museum. There is a deontology: first of all, we must make sure that the content is legitimate. These people know that perfectly well."

"When you speak of a "small gang", who do you mean in particular?"

"I'm talking about the suspects in Genoa, the ones who organised everything."

"What do you think of Christian Parisot's work? In Italy, he has been investigated in several trials and was convicted in France? For years he was president of the Modigliani Archives ...""

"I don't have a particular comment to make about Parisot, I was one of those who helped in his conviction for counterfeiting and fraud. For the law, he is a convicted forger. What annoys me is this idea of hiding or denying the truth, of claiming that it is only a dispute between experts. It is not so: an expert and a forger are not the same thing."

"So he calls himself an expert?"

"He introduces himself as an expert, but he is a convicted forger. The judge has passed sentence."

"Anyway he was president of the Modigliani Archives, what does that mean?"

"I have no idea. It is an entirely Italian concept. For me, these Archives have never been of the slightest scientific interest. Someone from America offered to sell them to me, so I think that today he (Parisot) no longer has them in his charge."

"Someone offered to sell them to you?"

"Yes, they were offered to me but I refused because I have no interest in them."

"So, what exactly are these archives?"

"I have no idea. From what I have seen, they consist of documents that are not original. Or falsified artworks or even fake documents for falsified artworks. They don't add anything to the existing documentation, absolutely nothing."

"Would they serve as an alibi for Parisot?"

"I do not know. What I do know is that in the documentation, there are two or three interesting things, but the rest, in my opinion, is of no account."

"Have you seen them?"

"Yup. Certainly. I saw them in Leghorn."

"Aren't there any stamps to authenticate the works?"

"I don't know, but there are no stamps that can authenticate paintings ... The problem is that we have known of these works [the works exhibited in Genoa, *ed*] for a long time. We know they are forgeries. The biggest mistake that has been made so far was not to ask for them to be destroyed, and it's a mistake I made too. Counterfeiters benefit from a sort of aura, like Arsenio Lupin, the gentleman thief. The forger is not seen as what he really is: that is, a criminal. They are not people who work for the love of art. They act for the destruction of works and artists alike. All for their personal profit, and the potential financial rewards are considerable. Therefore, the general admiration that exists for counterfeiters does not cease to amaze me; I don't like them at all. They are real crooks. If we don't destroy the fake works that are impounded, they will not disappear; one day they will reappear somewhere else."

Concluding the interview, Restellini pauses to outline the profile of the true forger.

"The counterfeiter has an immeasurable ego. He thinks he is a genius, untouchable. Like God, he manages to do what Picasso, Modigliani and the others did without anyone noticing. Do you see the problem with this? A counterfeiter is perfectly capable of lying. Among the many lies [of Parisot, ed], I had the "honour" of being called a pupil of this fellow, when I was already a professor at the time. I was supposedly on the board of directors of the Modigliani Archives, except that I never set foot there. Never, ever."

The Archives? In Geneva to solve a mystery

Under pressure from investigators, Parisot admits during his third cross-examination that the Modigliani Legal Archives are "an empty box without original certifications". Basically, all the authentications he had produced in the last forty years would no longer have any value after this declaration. It therefore remains impossible to establish, solely by virtue of his stamp, if a work can be attributed to the master of Leghorn or if it is a fake. It is unprecedented. Parisot has not owned the archives since 2015: why only now does he decide to admit that they are of no value? Because he has sold them and, despite his persistent attempts, has failed to get them back. He does not even know where they are now. We, however, have been able to touch them with our own hands. As soon as we heard the news of their return, we hurried off to Geneva.

It's a March morning in 2019. For a few hours today, we will be players in this intricate investigation which began a year ago and led us to follow the trail of the Modigliani Legal Archives. From the beginning, we wondered why what are supposed to simply be historical documents should be shrouded in so much mystery. Why hide them in cellars or in locations as secret as the one we are about to visit? Here, between these glass and steel buildings of the most inaccessible museum on earth, we too can attest to their existence and see what they really contain.

A trip organised quickly, in the wake of a phone call. "I managed to bring them back." So Maria Stellina Marescalchi had told us only two weeks earlier. "Are they in Italy?" we asked, eager to know if it would be possible to see them after our lengthy search. "No, they won't be coming back to Italy. I'm at the free port in Geneva. If you want to see them, you can join us." We had looked for them in vain in Rome, at the State Archives in Sant'Ivo alla Sapienza, in Palazzo Taverna, then in Paris and Cerreto d'Asti, in Chiasso and finally in New York, where we had tracked them down but been unable to see them.

Now we know exactly where they are. And so, we prepare to leave. On a grey morning, we are standing in the cold in front of these heavily-armoured glass cubes where over a million priceless art works are kept. We are going into the most secret museum of the world: the free port of Geneva, just a few steps away from Lancy-Pont-Rouge train station. Inside there are immense riches, perhaps far greater than those preserved in the nearby vaults of UBS, one of the country's two huge banks.

Inside are paintings, sculptures, archaeological finds, together worth billions. Among the many, also the *Salvator mundi*, the canvas that, some say rashly, was attributed to Leonardo Da Vinci before being sold for $ 450 million in 2016 to Mohammad bin Salman, the powerful and feared heir to the Al Sa'ud dynasty. In April 2019, someone thought it a cunning plan to suggest the painting had disappeared, perhaps to increase its value and mystery: in March informed sources told us it had always been held in these labyrinthine vaults. Many experts have claimed that, "there is no clear indication that can tie that work to Leonardo's hand, while there are engravings and signs that could suggest it is the work of his first pupil, Bernardino Luini". A marketing operation whose sole objective was money-laundering, according to our sources. Above all, a thick veil of secrecy feeds the suspicion that within this luxury warehouse, the lawful and the illicit are intertwined. Here, too, was found a Modigliani work stolen by the Nazis from a Jewish collector and currently owned by the art dealer David Nahmad via an offshore company created by Mossack Fonseca, the law firm at the centre of the Panama Papers scandal.[46]

This is the realm of Yves Bouvier, Swiss art dealer, billionaire and true lord of the free ports. Not happy with the tax set up in Geneva, he would move his residence to Singapore to evade the Swiss tax authorities. For this, he was charged. Among other things, he bought and sold the *Nu couché (sur le côté gauche* - Nude reclining on her left side*)* by Modigliani, paying about $95 million for it in 2012 and selling it on, in 2014, to the

---

[46] A scandal that broke in 2016, when the leak of a huge volume of information stored electronically (namely the Panama Papers) revealed detailed information on over two hundred thousand offshore companies, exposing tycoons, criminals and politicians who were hiding their wealth and income from the scrutiny of the law.

Russian oligarch and collector Dmitrij Rybolovlev[47], for about $118 million. He organised its subsequent auction in 2016, when the work was valued at $150 million.

What Bouvier has here is a real Fort Knox, inaccessible to anyone who, like us, is not expressly invited inside. When we pass in front of the entrance to the free port, which leads onto a side street lined by barbed wire, we see a black van with tinted windows. It stays there. We notice it immediately, sure that those inside see us, too. We have nothing to hide, we are here on official business, but we do not go unnoticed. Giovanni, the photojournalist, is with us with a huge backpack full of technical equipment. We cross the street and find a bar. Here we begin to arrange the material. While Giovanni pulls out the cameras, a muscular man, with a long unbuttoned jacket and a hat lowered over his forehead, approaches the counter, orders a coffee and, thinking we are not looking, turns his back to us. He pretends to take a selfie, pointing the camera of his smartphone towards us. We notice him immediately. He doesn't stay more than a minute, then goes towards the exit as we watch. He realises he has been seen and gets on the first tram that passes; as he departs, he returns the wave we had given him to show him how careless he had been in his spying efforts.

Carrying the cameras on our shoulders, we cross the street. It is a few minutes before nine, the scheduled time of our meeting. Outside the free port, "Europe's vault", four men and a woman wait for us. Furtive looks, knowing looks, handshakes. Maria Stellina Marescalchi is on time. Her friend Francesco accompanies her with two Spanish "colleagues" who speak neither English nor French, and the manager of the storage warehouses. None of them introduces themselves by name or surname; but everyone knows who we are, and they don't ask our names. After a careful security check, we pass through a steel turnstile, one at a time. Then all

---

[47] Marta Pettinau, *Il miliardario russo Rybolovlev acquista un Modigliani a 118 milioni di dollari. Ma a una festa incontra il venditore e scopre di aver pagato 22 milioni in più: e denuncia l'intermediario Yves Bouvier*, «Artribune», March 15 2015 (*Russian billionaire Rybolovlev buys a Modigliani for $118 million; but at a party, he meets the seller, finds out he had overpaid by $22 million and sues the dealer, Yves Bouvier*)

together, we go towards the vaults. Inside there are areas protected around the clock by CCTV cameras, biometric sensors, super-safe elevators, with five reinforced doors to pass through to get to the vault, which is protected in turn by another five-ton door and kept at a temperature which is never above seventeen degrees centigrade and at the level of humidity required to preserve the art works.

There are also studios of painting and sculpture restorers, equipped with ultra-modern technologies to assess the condition of the canvases. Moreover, there are lounges to display the masterpieces: here, you can organise auctions, galleries and sales. In the courtyard, we notice the inscription "Institut Restellini". Passing it, Ms. Marescalchi comments on Marc Restellini's role in the Modigliani affair. Unflattering words, which we won't repeat here, preferring not to exacerbate the hatred that evidently exists and is based on only one reason: business, and the great financial turnover generated by the art trade, which has caused some friction between the two.

Two large steel doors open in front of us. We enter the safe. No windows. In the concrete cube, there are only two boxes. When we see those miserable, bare crates, unadorned and anonymous, we cannot help but reflect on what remains, after a hundred years, of the life of this singular man, this extraordinary artist, this refined thinker. Many relics from his life have passed from hand to hand for impressive sums of money, but no accompanying emotion for what they really mean that wasn't feigned or venal. No respect for what they represent. Is this what Jeanne Modigliani envisaged when she collected what was left of her father's life? When she appointed Parisot as the guardian of Amedeo's memory, did she imagine seeing his heritage wandering between customs houses, from Paris to Chiasso, to New York, to Sao Paulo, to Shanghai, to Geneva? No, she dreamed of a museum, a place where the world could finally appreciate her father's genius. Perhaps, like Pepi, she wanted them right in Livorno.

Here, however, there is nothing to remind us of him. On the boxes, there are just some tags with the sender, Ifl-Art Service 97 Horton Avenue, Lynbrook, New York, and the recipient, Natural Le Coultre S.A., 6 Avenue De Sécheron, Genève, Switzerland. On another label, the handwritten inscription: "A. Modigliani Archives".

There is no trace of Maria Stellina Marescalchi's name. The material had been delivered on December 5 to Ifl (International Freight Logistics), a transport company which oversaw the transfer from Glenn Horowitz's "bookshop" to the courier, where it stayed in storage for over a month. Then its departure to the Swiss free port. While everyone is talking, the two warehouse workers are preparing to remove the screws that seal the first crate. Giovanni sets up the video cameras and his photographic equipment.

These are moments of great anticipation as we wait to ascertain the integrity of the precious contents. Ms Marescalchi points out that she has given instructions for each package to be properly sealed and countersigned. Carefully, as if they were surgeons, the two workers remove the packaging and protections. The side of the crate is finally opened. It is immediately clear that in one of the boxes the tape has been cut, it is not sealed, it can be opened. Moreover, underneath, at least two others bear clear signs of tampering. Giovanni films everything; including the reaction of Marescalchi, who does not seem too surprised at the discovery.

At that moment we feel like unwitting witnesses to some trickery. Maybe she needed someone outside her entourage and she chose the eye of our camera. She approaches the crates, and lifts the lid of the upper box to check the contents. "Here are Parisot's files." In the lower one on the left, however, only books. Our doubts increase as the boxes are opened; the merchant appears know their contents in advance.

Whoever surreptitiously cut that tape was obviously looking for Parisot's files, and knew more or less in which box and in which crate they were contained. All the others, in fact, are perfectly sealed. There are four groups of folders wrapped in a light film. It is clear that the first two were opened and then hastily closed. The other two are intact. Whoever handled them knew what to look for. A new *coup de théâtre*. The Modigliani Archives never cease to amaze us and every day adds a fresh mystery to this story that resembles a Russian matryoshka doll of crime and skulduggery.

We pick up Parisot's "renowned" files. We've been wondering what is in them for months. We scroll through the transparent folders that contain black and white copies of the catalogued drawings. They seem to be just a bunch of photocopies. There are 271 of them, but they are certainly not all that the archivist had collected in his time: the progressive numbering reveals several gaps.

"When I saw them at the free port of Chiasso, in 2006, there were a thousand files," Jean Olaniszyn told us, explaining that, as far as he knew, Parisot had sold a part of the Archives to a collector in Sao Paulo in Brazil and another part ended up in China. In truth, on closer inspection there seems to be some sort of code. All the files have an identifying mark, but there is no key to decrypt the numbers and letters with which they are catalogued. The most readable thing is the name of the owner whose work is depicted on the file. For example 3/13T1 *Cariatide-Encre et crayon sur papier* - Patani 92p165 n ° 177 (Caryatid - ink and pencil on paper).

Given the name on the tag, we forward the photo to Carlo Pepi, who in 1991 reported Osvaldo Patani for exhibiting fake drawings in Viterbo. He replies immediately "No, I have never seen this utter rubbish."

It is precisely this type of material that would seem to be of most interest to those who need to reconstruct the history of a work in order to pass themselves off as "experts" on it. From here the archivist Parisot could reconstruct his own "extracts", providing a story behind a hand, an eye, a nose, a sculpted head. Among the many transparent folders, there are many that catch our attention. On the plastic folders someone has traced a few carefully chosen lines of each drawing with a red marker, those that somehow "characterise" it. That well-defined red outline could also have been used to make other copies, such as a matrix. Just like we did as children when we wanted a nice drawing to take to school, and produced it by tracing the lines of someone else's better drawing.

The two warehouse workers take a box that has remained sealed in their gloved hands on. They open it before our eyes. They take out, one by one, some yellowed newspaper sheets that have been used to wrap some small photographic glass plates of a type common in the early twentieth century. It is a real thrill to see them against the light. They themselves are a work of art: many were produced by Pierre Choumoff, a famous Belarusian portrait photographer. In those early years of the 1900s, he wandered through the alleys of Montparnasse, immortalising paintings by Modigliani, Utrillo, Picasso and others, often still on their easels. He also went down in history for his portraits of Auguste Rodin, Igor Stravinskij, Claude Monet, Marc Chagall and Albert Einstein in those times of avant-garde and experimentation. Choumoff forever preserved the works of Modì in these negatives, which bring to light all the magic of his painting. They enrich the Archives, offering the proof that everything on these plates belonged to the painter from Leghorn.

Another box is opened. Lots of bags. In one, the rag doll that Amedeo had given to his daughter. Then a wooden statuette and huge masks that his brother Umberto had brought him on returning from his travels. The long noses and bulging eyes that had converted him to primitivism and that had inspired so much of his sculpture, his heads so different from the canonical Western images of the time. It seems to us that now they are almost part of our life too; familiar objects that we have read and written about, that we have seen in many photos, and that we can now touch. There are also many postcards and photographs not previously seen.

Here we have some new sealed packages in the second box that has just been unscrewed. In one, we find a large bundle wrapped carelessly in paper. Once opened, an elliptical wooden object emerges covered in several layers of colour. There is a hole in the lower part. It's Modigliani's palette. This find alone would be enough make worthwhile the effort that kept his daughter Jeanne busy for years. You could exhibit it anywhere in the world together with Choumoff's negatives and it would attract queues of tourists and art lovers.

Forget the virtual exhibitions that inspire little emotion apart from that of the organisers, whose pockets they fill. Perhaps they are not exactly fakes, because they are only photographs (although not always high quality ones), but we can say they are illusions, because in those images there is nothing of the artist; his brushstrokes are not there, the colour has no texture, nor the sculpted strength of his lines, nor poetry, passion or his wayward folly.

There is also a less romantic aspect to this palette, assuming it is original. That dense colour contains not only Modì's chromatic magnetism, but also the chemicals pigments of the composition of the colour itself. It could be a decisive factor in establishing the authenticity of the works of the Leghorn painter. This is particularly important in light of the latest report from the specialist Carabinieri unit Rome on the paintings and drawings seized in Genoa and deemed to be fake, partly on the basis of a chemical analysis of some of the colours.

Ownership of the original source would be especially tempting for those who want to speculate on the authenticity of the works. For a palette it is very large and heavy, and the colour is not as clearly distributed as you would expect from a painter of that calibre. It indicates a real waste of colour, all smeared on one side. Modigliani had no money to spend, and none to waste. He used all the colour, Isabella Quattrocchi tells us, and he used it well and sparingly. But even so, that simple piece of wood stirs up our emotions.

Our time is up. One minute before the automatic closing of the vault, we cross the threshold and head for the exit. We are almost hypnotised by what we have just seen. We are aware that we have been inside Amedeo Modigliani's history. Outside, we briefly say goodbye, we leave with the impression that everything that is now there will soon take wings to an unknown destination.

For months, Maria Stellina Marescalchi has insisted that her goal is to give value to the Archives, to create an institution that can deal with its care and management, as well as the "authentication" question. We believe in her good faith and we hope she is willing to allow access to highly-regarded experts and critics, scholars and admirers who are free from purely financial interests in Modigliani's work. We will see. Meanwhile, on March 15, 2019, Jean Olaniszyn, tells us: "They are on sale for about two million Euro [we recall that just recently they had been valued at over 4 million euro, ed]. I don't have that much money, but with the help of a friend and a grant from a Swiss public institution, I think I can do it. I couldn't buy them in 2006, when Christian Parisot himself offered them to me. Then, too, the asking price was 2 million."

It is a plan that would deny Italy of a heritage to which it can claim a right, and which would make available to a select few something that should be open to everyone. Because, just as Modì wrote, "life is a gift, from the few to the many: from those who know or who have to those who do not know or who do not have".

Sixth Crime Scene: London
A Shadow over Piccadilly

CHARACTERS

Elmyr de Hory – A Hungarian Jewish aristocrat, a great forger to whom several art works in circulation are attributed. He was active from at least 1940 until the seventies.

Arthur Pfannstiel – A German Nazi infiltrator in Paris, art critic and author of catalogues on Modigliani.

Albert C. Barnes – doctor and famous researcher, the first great Modigliani collector in the United States.

Frank Perls – the owner, with his brother Klaus, of an important art gallery in Manhattan; a German Jew who fled Germany before the war.

Fabrizio Quiriti – an Italian art dealer involved in various scandals concerning forged art works. Director of the Skema-Arte Art Gallery in Cuneo and of JZ Art owned by the former footballer Jonathan Zebina, in Milan.

Alberto D'Atanasio – an art historian under investigation in Palermo for exhibiting two fake paintings, co-conspirator with Luciano Renzi.

Silvia Benini – forensic graphologist.

And again: *Jeanne Modigliani, Christian Parisot, Carlo Pepi, Isabella Quattrocchi, Luciano Renzi* and *Paul D. Quatrochi*.

Tate Modern, January 2018

Between the water tanks and smokestacks of Bankside, on the south bank of the Thames, where until 1981 ships docked with cargoes of coal destined for the thermoelectric power plant, post-industrial architecture has carved out a beautiful area. There, in the international art gallery, the Tate Modern, between November 23, 2017 and April 2, 2018, paintings and sculptures by

Amedeo Modigliani are on exhibition. The works have arrived from all over the world, but mostly from Paris and New York. It is an authoritative exhibition, never challenged by any experts.

An exhibition such as this took courage, particularly after what had just happened in Genoa. The curators, Simonetta Fraquelli and Nancy Ireson, are very keen on disclosing all the research and in-depth studies that preceded the exhibition.

The chosen place is fascinating, the scene of a careful reclamation that projects the past into the future. It recalls to mind another place when, in 1919, paintings by Modigliani were seen in the English capital for the first time. Then, they were exhibited in the Mansard Gallery, an attic at 196 Tottenham Court Road. Then, as now, his nudes drew the attention of art critics and of the general public alike. The two brothers who had organised the exhibition, the baronets Osbert and Sacheverell Sitwell, sparked this early enthusiasm of Londoners for Modi. The success and the magic that still surround his story began here.

The twelve nudes that a century ago caused scandal and created a sensation are back on the banks of the Thames. We have come to see them. Who knows if they will be the same works? We buy the catalogue, curious to see if the works just released from the Palazzo Ducale that have not been impounded are also on display. In these cases, one can never be too careful, and certainly, the events will have convinced the supervisors of the Tate to be extremely cautious. Isabella Quattrocchi, whom we invited to accompany us during the visit, told us "she had arrived late in Genoa, when the seals of the Carabinieri had already been affixed following the evaluation of others," which she had simply confirmed. According to the expert, however, there were not just twenty fakes at the Genoese exhibition, but "many more". We do the maths as we wonder if any of those canvases arrived in London.

The portraits of Jean and Paul Alexandre, Modì's two great friends and the first collectors of his works, welcome visitors at the entrance of the exhibition. The first one is in the centre of the great hall we pass through after the entrance; as we proceed, Paul's smaller portrait hangs on the wall. We enter a long room where we can admire all the nudes in sequence.

It is a labyrinth of corridors that leads us to those paintings leaning against the walls just a foot from our faces. In front of the *Nude*, 1917, which also appears on the cover of the catalogue, our expert shakes her head, somewhat discouraged. "The choice of this nude is very questionable. The colour does not convince me, nor the woman's face. Many other details cause me to think he didn't paint it." She makes a comparison with a painting exhibited a little further on: *Seated Nude*, also from 1917. "Here we have Modigliani's complexion," Quattrocchi tells us. We are surprised to find this artwork here. Its full name in Italian is *Nudo seduto su un divano (la bella romana)* and it has a long history, which some attribute to the Nazi raids in Paris. It disappeared in 1937; it reappeared fifty years later, in 1987, and was sold by Sotheby's in 2010, for 69 million dollars.

The exhibition seeks to amaze visitors with its special effects. At one point, as we put on our virtual reality headsets, we are transported into the old atelier on the top floor of rue de la Grande Chaumiere. Technology takes the visitor back in time. However, contrary to what really happened, here everything is still in its place: the brushes, the paintings, the bed, the coal stove, the large windows. Today, those who actually visit the tiny Parisian apartment once inhabited by Modigliani see something entirely different. The interiors have undergone a dubious restoration, nothing retains any of its old charm; there is no sense of history anymore, not even in the floorboards. A very long, narrow wooden staircase with smooth, worn steps, climbing from a dark and deserted entrance hall and up through the galleries, is all that remains to remind us of a sick man and a pregnant woman climbing up to the fourth floor. Modernity in Paris did not leave much space for history. On the facade of the modest building at number 8, a marble plaque reads "Atelier Gauguin & Modigliani", as if it were a business concern.

The Tate exhibition is very engaging. Catalogues in hand, we move through the rooms. As Isabella Quattrocchi looks around, some of the nudes make her start. "This is not right. The hand in some cases is still recognisable, but what have they done with the colour? Do we want to say Modì painted it? But, where is his brushstroke, where is the delicacy of the complexion? Here, the colour is too thick in my opinion, too many reds on these bodies. I wouldn't define some of them Modigliani. At best, they can be drawings finished by others. When you study his drawings extensively, you can discern the characteristic notes of the artist, the stroke, the hand, the taste of perfect proportions. Nobody, with so few strokes, can convey the sensuality of the nude like Modì. The paintings I see here do not convince me at all. If I could carry out a closer analysis I could give a conclusive assessment."

Room after room, the court and prosecutor's counsel does hold back her judgement. Only before some paintings does she lingers with a smile, convinced and fascinated: for these she would no doubt confirm the attribution to Modigliani. "Who knows if the certifications, the so-called supporting documents, are from the same experts who documented the paintings confiscated in the Palazzo Ducale" the professor muses.

We came here already disenchanted by our previous experiences and by the evidence gathered during this investigation. Yet, we did not expect to find what we are witnessing. The expert's comments echo in our heads. Is it possible? Glasses on her nose, wandering through the halls, she runs into an insider who she knows by sight. "He is a professor of ancient art," she explains at the end of the short conversation. "He was sure there would only be authentic pieces. But in my opinion too many paintings come from the same collections" Quattrocchi says.

With our catalogue of the latest Tate exhibition and with many questions still in our heads, we decide that on our return to Italy, our next meeting will be with Carlo Pepi. We go back to Crespina, on a grey and rainy day. In the farmhouse-museum it is usually very chilly, but Pepi always manages to warm the environment as he regales us. Before we can explain why we are here again, he beckons us to follow him. He takes us to the best-lit room. Then he walks away and, moving among the hundreds of paintings he keeps everywhere, he takes a big green binder.

"There, I'll show you how Modigliani drew. After this, you will understand better how it is not very difficult to identify fakes. And how different so much of the rubbish floating around is." The volume that he is holding is a large format boxed edition, made of canvas (60x47x70). Einaudi published it in 1959, in a limited edition, just seven hundred and fifty copies, edited by Lamberto Vitali, a great expert, a patron and enthusiast of Modigliani. It contains sixteen pages and forty-five loose boards of drawings reproduced in their original size, in phototype. "A feast for the eyes. These are the only reproductions from real drawings in circulation, because they come from the Vitali collection. Lithographs made on the same paper used by the Leghorn painter for his drawings. The stamp is dry." Our host is not wrong; it is a unique and special work that does justice to the great artist.

Thus, still a little enthralled by such beauty, we take out our Tate catalogue to get his views on it. He had called the canvases of the exhibitions in Genoa and Palermo seized by the Carabinieri "Horrendous fakes". He flips through it, curious but suspicious. "What do you want to know, if I think there are some forgeries? Yes there are. Some of them are better made because the underling brushstroke could have been produced by Modì. I recognise it from the hands. Modigliani had a unique way of outlining hands. However, the colour is thick, it's not his. Some of the others are really ugly."

Another head, this time in London

But that's not the only surprise that London has in store for us. The news comes from our usual source: Luciano Renzi, with the art historian Alberto D'Atanasio, was alleged to have authenticated forged Modiglianis. The two supposedly went to England, at least that's what they would have us believe, to carry out an expert report directly and then confirm, or otherwise, the authenticity of a wooden head. It was allegedly a small sculpture, partially damaged by woodworm. It seems that it is just one of many similar pieces. Amedeo Modigliani sculpted only stone, but the research that led to the drafting of Jeanne Modigliani's book indicate that he may also have worked with wood using the sleepers found in the Parisian underground station of Barbès, then under construction.

Today the station is called Barbès-Rochechouart, a name that somewhat ironically juxtaposes two very different French citizens: Armand Barbès was a nineteenth-century revolutionary, while Marguerite de Rochechouart was a Benedictine abbess who lived between the seventeenth and eighteenth centuries. Here, in 1903, five months after the inauguration of Line 2, the short circuit on a stationary train triggered a terrible fire that is reported to have caused almost a hundred deaths at the Couronnes station, the worst disaster ever in the Parisian subway. Here, too, in 1941, the first shot was fired at a German soldier, which heralded the beginning of the French resistance against the Nazis. Amedeo Modigliani's connection with the town would just bring it added glory.

Historiographic investigations tell us that this may actually be possible, at least if it took place during the artist's first sojourn in Paris, around 1909. The year before, work on Line 4 had been completed in the station, where Line 2 already stopped. It is therefore plausible that some tarred sleepers could have been abandoned along the subway route, which also runs above ground in that area. And that, just as he had wandered the docks of the port of Livorno in search of stone slabs to work with his hands, the Leghorn artist may have used material available to any passer-by to sculpt the wooden head. This story, told by both Jeanne and Parisot, may have given ideas to the counterfeiters, who over time had tried to pass off as authentic works made of wood, bronze and sometimes even plated in gold.

The story, or legend, is that all trace of that head dated 1909 was lost after it was exported to Australia. But it is on this "phantom" work that Parisot had the famous, gigantic, *Tête de caryatide*, modelled, a work donated to Rome and now on display in Cosenza.

"Renzi sold that head, he sold it to the Municipality of Cosenza after it had been removed from the Forlanini gardens": this is Parisot's grouse against his former partner who supposedly now travelled the world to certify forgeries. Yet there is no sure documentary evidence that Modì sculpted anything other than stone. We search for confirmation, for anything that might confirm that Renzi performed an appraisal in London, certifying what appears to be a forgery as authentic. We finally get our hands on three documents: two on headed paper from the Amedeo Modigliani Institute of Spoleto, signed by Luciano Renzi. The third, however, is on headed paper from Pegasus Cataloguing of cultural heritage, signed by Professor Alberto D'Atanasio on June 25, 2018. Let's start with the latter.

Professor D'Atanasio may not have had time to do any in-depth research on Modigliani. Otherwise, he wouldn't have indulged useless academic quotes or sought unlikely connections between the trees of Senegal and the primitivistic African inspiration which characterised a brief period of Amedeo's life and works. "The type of mark left by the gouges and scrapes on the neck and face were considered perfectly compatible with those found in the sculptures already known as works of the Master and included in the official catalogues," writes the expert. Who knows if one day he will find the time to identify the sculptures and catalogues where he detected such compatibility.

After quoting the evidence of a certain Bruno Albertino - an expert of African culture - and the laboratory results performed by Di.Ar (Diagnostic for images for cultural heritage) of Modena, D'Atanasio states: "Considering the comparison of these finds with others that have already been codified and deemed to belong to the Master's body of work, I certify that the work is attributable to Amedeo Modigliani and was produced between 1910 and 1915 ".

D'Atanasio attaches the Di.Ar report to support his declarations. We contacted the owner of the diagnostic centre, Andrea Rossi, who immediately took his distance from any presumed authentication of Modigliani's works. He writes to us that at the beginning of 2018 D'Atanasio, after contacting him, sent him some samples of materials in test tubes by courier. The analyst did not know from which work they came, and carried out tests on three samples of colours and a wooden sample. He then sent the results, again by courier, to the client. Rossi is keen to clarify that his analysis concerns the dating of the findings based on radiocarbon diagnostic investigations.

Let's see to the two other documents. The first document from the Amedeo Modigliani Institute of Spoleto, dated June 25 ,2018, refers to "Certificate of attribution no. GRZRBT0718". It contains a series of photos. The first portrays a kind of shrine inside which is a small wooden head in typical Modigliani style. Sizes are not reported. The author of the text, Luciano Renzi, in addition to listing his own academic qualifications, declares he is a member of the *concept board* of the Amedeo Modigliani Institute and responsible for laboratory analyses for the attribution of works of art. From now on, according to this certification from the Amedeo Modigliani Institute, and thanks to the *motu proprio* provision signed by the president - Luciano Renzi himself - the "anthropomorphic sculpture" made of worm-eaten wood owned by the Graziosi family, as stated in the report, which has kept it for years as a family heirloom, is finally acknowledged as a "work by Amedeo Modigliani's hand".

Seeing all these academic skills and supporting documents, who would ever question such a certification? However, it is useful to carry out a verification, to line up facts and dates.

After the official registration date of the documents, Renzi feels the irrepressible urge to express "all his scientific skills" through the third document we discovered, dated August 1 2018, registered like the previous one at the Institute of Spoleto: "From the physical examination I found all the stylistic and formal characteristics of the sculptural work of the master Amedeo Modigliani, in particular in the exceptional nature of the formal qualities. Of unmistakable primitivist derivation, the work attains the maximum synthesis of forms ..." And where does he say he saw this caryatid? In a small flat, apartment 7 at number 31, Jenner Road in the north London suburbs, on an unspecified date: "Towards the end of 2016".

Therefore, we decide to go and visit the neighbourhood. We cross the city of London by tube, from the city centre to Liverpool Street. We arrive at Rectory Road. We immediately notice the striking contrast between our search for such a valuable object and the run-down neighbourhood in which we have arrived. From the tube station, we take Jenner Road, on the sides of the road the typical three-floor buildings. We approach number 31, gazing upwards trying to identify which apartment it is. While we check the intercoms, a man with Arab features and a long beard trimmed in the Koranic fashion gets out of a parked green Volkswagen minivan covered with snow. He immediately asks us who we are looking for, if by chance we are looking for him. We get by with a little improvisation, telling him that an Italian friend of ours gave us an appointment there but he didn't show up. He looks suspicious. No Italian has lived there for many years, he says, and he has met all the tenants who have recently lived in the small apartments. Indeed, after thinking about it for a while, he can say with certainty that no Italian has ever lived there. He repeats it at the end with a laugh. Clearly, out request seemed strange.

So, where is the owner of the caryatid and his precious artwork? According to the certificate, the lucky potential millionaire is thirty-five year old Giuseppe Graziosi, a Roman artist specialised in restoration, conservation and woodcarvings. He has lived in the Italian capital for years, in the working-class district of San Lorenzo, having spent some time in London. We call him to see how he reacts. We talk about this and that and he gladly tells us of his life as an artist and his new job at an Art gallery. At this point, we fire our first shot, asking him point-blank if he ever had anything to do with Amedeo Modigliani. He replies: "I may have". We decide to be more direct, stating that we know he is the owner of a carved head attributed to Modigliani. Our young interviewee is clearly embarrassed and his voice stiffens. He gets defensive, saying it isn't a subject to discuss over the phone. And so, we propose a meeting, though it will never happen. We play our trump card as we try to get him to open up. "We know that you had an appraisal done, we have a copy". The man insists that such subjects should be dealt with in person, but does not deny it. We ask him if he believes Modigliani had produced any wood sculptures. He replies, "Yes, he did, look it up."

Whatever the reason for his reticence, there is no doubt that if that work were authentic, or if it could pass as authentic, his life would change. He would become a millionaire overnight. Graziosi continues to insist: "We can't talk about it on the phone." At this point, we throw in a remark he is not expecting. "We know about the head, we saw it at an exhibition in London." "Impossible, it has never been put on exhibition, certainly not in London. Where did you see it? As far as I know that's not true," he answers. However, he sounds worried, and insists on us telling him where we came across it. We explain the place precisely; he is interested. Probably he entrusted it to some middleman who did not tell him about the exhibition.

During our return from Jenner Road, as we arrive in Piccadilly from Green Park station, a poster, we have never seen anywhere else in London catches our attention. It was held precariously in place by a green lace on a pole, at the corner of Albermarle Street. A very colourful poster. You could see Marilyn Monroe's iconic portrait by Andy Warhol, and on it the name Modigliani and then many other of the great names in twentieth century art. The poster intrigued us mainly because it contained a mixture of French and English terms. The site of the exhibition was not a museum, but the historic Brown's Hotel, located fifty meters from Piccadilly Road. It is one of the oldest and most exclusive hotels in London, where the town aristocracy takes afternoon tea. The *exposition* advertised in the poster would take place over a few hours, on the same day, from 10 am to 7.30 pm. It would only last one day.

Obviously, we went there, and here is how we recall what happened. We immediately realise that it is an unusual exhibition. Our attention focuses on the single piece presented as a work by Modigliani: a small wooden head illuminated by a spotlight. Some members of staff approach us immediately, closely observing our movements and preventing us from taking pictures. There are no catalogues or organisers' business cards, no posters, not even a guide. What is the purpose of putting on such an event without any advertising, or any real promotion? If it were authentic, that head would be worth a fortune and would have deserved a much longer exhibition and much more advertising, if only to recover the expense (certainly high) of renting such a prestigious location.

Someone who seems to be in charge comes towards us. He speaks very basic English, with a strong French accent. He asks us what we want. Mischievously, we reply that we are there to review the exhibition for our boss, to see if there is anything interesting there. We will be back in the afternoon to talk about it we reply. Our interviewer is not very enthusiastic about it; rather, he sends us off with a cold shrug.

The exhibition was likely an attempted "sting", hastily organised with a single poorly-produced advertisement and no credible organisers. It makes us think it was a purely commercial operation, an effort to convince some already-targeted patron to part with their money for a fake piece. That piece we saw could have been Graziosi's sculpture. What is certain is that it was very similar to the one described.

Since, in our opinion, it was likely to be a fake, we could not restrict ourselves to simply mentioning it in the pages of this book. Given that we were dealing with an alleged crime, we saw it as our duty to contact the authorities. So, we presented a complaint to the Carabinieri unit in charge of the protecting Italy's cultural heritage, and we sent a report to Interpol.

We understand things better now. When we talk about fake Modiglianis, we don't just mean paintings that are identical copies of originals by Modigliani. You often come across new works modelled on authentic pieces by the artist but produced in a different size. You might find subjects similar to those in the original paintings, rendered in the style of Modigliani. You may even find drawings prepared by the artist but painted later by other artists, talented and otherwise.

Or you might come across high definition photocopies that have been coloured over to make them look and feel more realistic. You might even find drawings expertly copied by skilled hands on paper aged with coffee. This is precisely what has happened in the case of Modigliani's paintings. A fake body of work that, according to Marc Restellini, totals about a thousand specimens scattered among private collections and museums from all over the world.

"The number of forged Modiglianis is increasing every day, in Paris there must be a production line: in the last sales note published in the Société de gestion des droits d'auteur (a copyright management company), I'm told there was an *Étude à Tunis*. Now ... poor Dedo never went to Tunis!" Thus, Margherita Modigliani wrote in 1932 in a letter to to Giovanni Scheiwiller, the painter's first biographer. Back then, it was she who had the right to provide authentication for the works of her brother.

Little Jeanne was in fact still a minor. Not much more than a decade had passed since Amedeo's death and these grubby fakes were already rife. However according to Restellini, the production of fake Modiglianis reached its apex between the fifties and eighties. Overall, in a hundred years, dozens of hands have imitated Modigliani while a number of cunning art merchants with no incentive to study the works carefully saw how huge profits could be generated by mixing originals with fakes. It was a slow but steady distortion of the artist's heritage that to this day distorts the art market and confounds experts, to the extent that few of them are any longer able to identify the authentic strokes of the author.

Among the most famous forgers of all time, you can certainly find the Italian Alberto d'Atri, "who used his role as a critic and essayist as a cover for his much more profitable business as a merchant and authenticator of Modigliani's paintings".

Then we had the Hungarian Elmyr de Hory, an aristocrat gifted with the ingenious ability to imitate the greatest artists of the twentieth century. An eccentric, enigmatic forger who heavily influenced the world of art collecting and the international market of the last century. His life was like a novel. He was raised in Hungarian high society in the early twentieth century (his mother belonged to a wealthy family of Jewish bankers, his father was ambassador to Turkey), and he was trained as a painter first in Munich and then in Paris.

There, in 1926, he attended the Académie de la Grande Chaumière, the same school of nude painting in which Amedeo Modigliani had studied and taught. He often went to the Rotonde: he lived with the great artists of Montparnasse, spending his days between art schools, cafes and bistros[48].

Hitler wanted a Modigliani, too

At the beginning of the twentieth century, it was not only the great and lesser painters, sculptors, photographers, models and merchants who flocked the alleys of Montparnasse. For about twenty years, a Nazi spy wandered amongst them. He was one of the most loyal followers of a man who would later become the Führer. He loves art; he is himself a painter.

Arthur Pfannstiel is one of the young men who in 1923 was part of the Nazi paramilitary group Stosstrupp-Hitler, disbanded after the attempted Munich coup, later known as the "Beer Hall Putsch" of November 8-9 that year. Shortly after, probably on the orders of Hitler himself, he arrived in the French capital ago spy on intellectuals and Jewish artists. Modigliani had been dead for a few years, but he was already a legend. The German spy would play a role in Amedeo's story whose effects would be felt until the 1990s.

Like all those who have to hide their real identity and their mission, Arthur moves with skill and fits in well among Modì's friends and the models who pose for his works. He knows Zborowski, and maybe does some business with him. As a matter of fact, he published his first work on Modigliani in 1929. It is a narrative list of his exhibitions and a catalogue with six colour paintings, one hundred and thirty eight reproductions in black and white, four photographs and four sculptures. Even today, his publication and his expertise are considered more than reliable. It is unlikely anyone even considered digging into his past, a past which casts a dark shadow on his memory.

---

[48] The profile of both characters is outlined in Meryle Secrest, *Modigliani, l' uomo e il mito (Modigliani, Man and Myth)*, Mondadori, Milan 2012.

We thought we would. From the information we gathered, it is not difficult to guess that he was sent to France as a secret agent, his task to make an inventory of the cultural and artistic heritage to be plundered once the country had been occupied.

Fates sometimes travel in parallel, but often they end up crossing like the tracks in railway stations. The Nazi spy and the Jewish Hungarian forger De Hory both depart from Munich. Both young, students and art lovers, they attend the same schools; they are peers, neither with many scruples. In 1926, we find them again at the Rotonde among the shining lights of twentieth century Parisian avant-garde. Fifty metres from the bistro, at number 4, rue de la Grande Chaumière, De Hory studies at the Académie and takes part in the Salon d'Automne. Their acquaintance begins in Paris, or perhaps already in Munich, and is renewed in various parts of the world, from South America to the United States, once again in Europe. There are enough coincidences for to us suspect that the De Hory was also the spy's best source, later becoming the greatest forger of the twentieth century.

Already in those years, widespread anti-Semitic persecution had understandably convinced Europe's Jews to keep a low profile. Gaining access to the closed circle of Jewish artists was definitely not easy for an "Aryan". We can assume that the key used by Pfannstiel to open the doors of that world may have been the Hungarian Jew himself. His biographies speak of border crossings even during the Nazi occupation, a hazardous enterprise even against payment. It is however true that De Hory was interned in a Gestapo concentration camp; but, with almost unbelievable good fortune, or perhaps a fat bribe or the help of an influential friend, he managed to escape by the main door.

Time passes for Pfannstiel, too. Soon his former band of paramilitary rabble rousers will become an army of eight hundred thousand men that invades almost all of Europe. Together with Adolf Hitler, he wrote and translated the propaganda book *Principes d'action*, published in 1936. The path of Arthur Pfannstiel, the SS man who will be revealed to all as a fervent Nazi only after the French occupation, also crosses that of Jeanne Modigliani. She had returned to Paris to join the resistance, but when the capital fell, Jeanne was forced to flee to the South of France. While she fought alongside her companion Victor Leduc, organising the escape of many Jews with passports she herself forged, Arthur became an officer of the Einsatzstab Reichsleiter Rosenberg, the department in charge of looting anything deemed to be of cultural or political interest, including works of art, in the occupied territories of France.

Arthur Pfannstiel was the right hand man and probably the closest associate of Kurt von Behr: an unscrupulous baron placed at the head of the fine arts special unit, the infamous department of Nazi raiders. Few works from the Montparnasse artists escaped their clutches, the stolen works include pieces by Picasso, Utrillo and obviously also by Modigliani.

Hitler himself wanted a Modigliani, but perhaps he didn't enjoy it. We looked for the only painting mentioned in the US Army Report of August 1945, which reports the US investigation on the looting of works of art in Paris. The document contains the list of many of those stolen by the Germans during the occupation.

After the world war, the Nazi Pfannstiel is has to flee for his life. He is caught and tried for war crimes in Paris in 1950, but is acquitted and is allowed to leave for America. His role was not getting his hands dirty with blood ... but with colours. His "friend" Elmyr left before him: in 1948, he arrived in Brazil, and then moved to the US shortly afterwards. He has a three-month tourist visa, but he remains there eleven years. Arthur probably manages to steal many Modigliani works which he brings with him to the United States, some perhaps from the private collections of Paris Jews from whom, as we know, everything was taken away. Many of them were rewarded with a trip to the concentration camps. The diabolical intelligence of people like Pfannstiel was hidden behind the dreadful brutality of the Nazi soldiers.

In 1958, he adds, in one of his publications, over one hundred works to those already present in the catalogue by Ambrogio Ceroni, then considered the bible of Modigliani attributions. Paintings that only he himself may have seen, knowing where they had been taken after they were pillaged in Paris. Even today, many people still have art works stained with blood in their own private galleries or exhibitions. But there is more. Many of these paintings could also be excellent forgeries made by De Hory, of whom Pfannstiel had been a client and partner.

Among the stolen art treasures that have reappeared, several were recently recovered from the vaults of the law firm Mossack Fonseca, the key player in the Panama Papers scandal. Among these, there were various works by Modigliani such as *L' uomo seduto con bastone*. Some say the work had belonged to Oscar Spettiger, a Jewish art dealer who fled to the US with the painting and little else; others say it was one of the many canvases stolen by the Nazis and hidden in America. Who, if not Pfannstiel, could know where it had come from?

Ambrogio Ceroni was right to omit many "American" works by Modì from his catalogue. It wasn't a mistake. Evaluating the details we now have, of which the great art historian and Modigliani expert was probably also aware, we think it possible that he purposely excluded dozens of works by the Leghorn painter marketed in the United States.

The paths of the Nazi spy and of the Jewish forger later cross that of Klaus Perls, president of the American Art Traders Association, a character we have already seen in the "hoax of the fake heads". His gallery, we repeat, was defined by Pepi as "a factory of fakes".

Perls was Elmyr de Hory's first American client, as the writer Clifford Irving writes in his biography *Fake!*[49] The brothers Klaus and Frank Perls, both of German origin, owned art galleries in New York.

Frank Richard Perls, born in Berlin from a Jewish family, son of the gallery owner Hugo, graduated in History of Art in Freiburg. In 1937, the family left Germany and moved to the United States. Together with his younger brother Klaus, Frank founded the Perls Gallery in Manhattan. During the Second World War, he landed in Normandy with the allied troops when and became an interpreter for the army. In 1945, with the US Military Intelligence officer Martin Dannenberg, who was also a Jew, he recovered the Nuremberg law documents signed by Hitler in 1935. Frank, who died in 1975, used to say that it was two Jews who had found that document, one which presaged the mass extermination of Jews, his own people. As he told the story, he could not hold back the tears.

---

[49] Clifford Irving, *Fake! La vera storia di Elmyr de Hory, il più grande falsario di tutti i tempi*, Lupetti Editori di Comunicazione, Milan 2011.

The interests of the Perls brothers, Jews and gallery owners, and of Arthur Pfannstiel, Nazi and art critic, converge on one focal point: Elmyr de Hory, the forger. The Hungarian sells counterfeit works to everyone.

First Picasso, then Modigliani. But he wasn't going to underestimate the gallery owners and the art experts. "No technique was too difficult for Elmyr to imitate, who was able to switch with ease from a Picasso to a Renoir, from a Modigliani to a Matisse; his canvases were then resold to the most prestigious art galleries and museums in the world."[50] He travelled everywhere and sold dozens of his paintings. He was well known; a great director like Orson Welles made a movie inspired by him (in 1973) with the title *F for Fake*.

The Sao Paulo Art Museum in Brazil was one of his clients. Who knows if he placed some of his own "Modiglianis" right there, given that the institution boasts four Modiglianis and that among the works that De Hory attributed to himself there is also a famous self-portrait. According to professor Quattrocchi, Modigliani's 1919 *Autoritratto* self-portrait, which has been exhibited around the world, is in fact a fake. "I don't recognise the way the hands are done as the style of Modigliani," she told us.

The art-forging genius surpasses himself when he returns to Paris in 1961. As revealed by his business partner Réal Lessard, indeed three of his most important Modigliani fakes were sold with a certification from Jeanne. "They met several times and Elmyr brought some drawings by Modigliani to the representative of Mademoiselle Modigliani, daughter of the painter; he obtained a declaration of authenticity, then sold them to an important art dealer in avenue Matignon."[51] He had managed, with his confident air and his magnetic charm, to convince her that these were works produced by her father.

This forger, who deceived and polluted the entire art world with hundreds of works attributed to great masters of the twentieth century, was to die in Ibiza in dubious circumstances in 1976, possibly by suicide. He left behind him a trail of crime for which he never took responsibility, justifying his

---

[50] *Ibid*

[51] *Ibid*

actions by saying necessity had forced him to become a forger rather than a proper painter.

The records tell us that Arthur Pfannstiel died some time between 1986 and 1988. But even in death his name served a criminal cause. In the eighties, just before the centenary of the birth of Amedeo Modigliani, things are moving in the United States as well as in Livorno. Onto the star-spangled stage arrives "a true genius of the scam"[52]: Paul D. Quatrochi, whom we have already met when discussing the Guttmann affair.

The fog seems to fade before our eyes. Many of the paintings seized by the Carabinieri in Genoa have come from the American collections of Perls and Guttmann, and some are even certified by Klaus Perls. The investigation documented by the Carabinieri and the evaluation of the experts Margozzi and Quattrocchi identified them as fakes made in the 1950s and 1960s. A clear thread therefore seems to lead us to the Hungarian Elmer de Hory. If this is the case, they would at least be "authentic forgeries" ... But who is the author of the two Modì pieces believed to be fake and seized by the Unit for the protection of cultural heritage in Palermo in March 2019? We await of the outcome of the investigation, because it could be they are "simply" inexperienced and opportunistic counterfeiters of today.

Human reptiles

"The dealers in paintings and statues get rich by exploiting the genius of poor artists and paying them a pittance." An emotive view. One which he shares, underlining it to better remember it. *Human reptiles*, the volume from which it is taken,[53] was among Amedeo Modigliani's favourite books. One of his *livre de chevet*, which he read and reread.

---

[52] John Connolly, Nick Rosen, *Scumbag Descending a Staircase*, «Spy», October 1992, pp. 56-63.
[53] Alberto Costa, *Rettili umani. Libro in difesa della morale*, Libreria Editrice Massimo D'Azeglio, Milan 1891.

Exploited and plundered: this is the fate that the merchants dealt him for never abasing himself, never complying with their requests. For his inflexibility and stubbornness in pursuing only his own artistic projects. Amedeo does not bend to the spirit of the times, which prefer to reward artists like Pablo Picasso who are prepared to be more "flexible" in their work. Alberto Costa's quote seems appropriate, almost prophetic when remembering Modigliani's path and the lifestyle he shared with the other penniless artists of Montparnasse.

The reasons for such cynicism become clear in good time. While his body burns with fever and he is transported to the Hôpital de la Charité, his studio in the rue de la Grande Chaumière is emptied of canvases, sculptures, drawings. On the same day of his funeral, his paintings are sold by the merchants of Paris at ten times the price offered for them twenty-four hours before his death. They looted those same works that, only a few days earlier, hardly anyone had wanted to buy and in which few discerned the mark of the great artist.

In the immediate neighbourhood of the path followed by the hearse that takes his body to the Père-Lachaise cemetery, on the *rive droite*, the first Parisian exhibition dedicated solely to his works opens its doors. The Galerie Devambez, managed by the father-in-law of the merchant Guillaume Chéron and considered one of the most important in the city, exhibits about twenty paintings by Modì. Perhaps they were the ones kept in the Chéron's house from the days when Modigliani worked for him for a few francs per day. He was however the first merchant to see the potential of the painter from Leghorn, even if the relationship between the two was short. After all, he was also a bookmaker, as such, accustomed to taking risk, to betting on the "thoroughbred".

Francis Carco, writer, poet, friend and supporter of Amedeo, told of the frenetic bargaining between the merchants that accompanied the coffin. "They talked about it completely openly as they followed the coffin: "8000, 10,000, damn you're a tough one," they complained as the cart wheels screeched along the avenues of the Père-Lachaise. "All right, I'll go to 11,000, here you are."[54]

Thus behind the coffin, two very different processions followed, even though they were walking together. A sad huddle of friends and women who had helped and loved him, and a group formed by those who were there only to bargain over his works. His "employer" and great collector Léopold Zborowski is partly in one group and partly in the other.

The evocative illustration on the cover of Francis Carco's book.

---

[54] Francis Carco, *De Montmartre au Quartier latin*, Litterature, Paris 1925.

He had done his utmost for Amedeo, taking great pains because he firmly believed in the enormous potential of the Italian artist. From 1916 to 1918, he had spent difficult weeks knocking on all the galleries of Paris trying to sell paintings that no one wanted, even for a few francs. He sold off some personal property to guarantee the Leghorn painter 15 francs a day and pay for colours, brushes, models and some of Amedeo's family expenses. In 1918, with the birth of little Jeanne in Nice, Modì finds new inspiration and begins to sell some artwork in the South of France. Zborowski supports him by also contributing to the maintenance of the child.

However, we cannot take it for granted that his commitment to the extraordinary artist was only driven by esteem or affection. Who knows if between the two there had ever been true friendship; a pure and profound bond such as Amedeo had with Paul Alexandre, the doctor and patron with whom, between 1907 and 1914, he shared both dreams and everyday needs, hardships and ambitions.

Paul and his brother Jean help Modì through the difficult years after his arrival in Paris. Amedeo draws and paints, then throws away or burns everything each time he changes lodgings to avoid paying too much when moving from one place to another, which in any case he cannot afford. The two brothers fall in love with his technique, his intelligence, his philosophy, and they support him. They collect everything he produces for years, buying him canvases, pencils, colours. Sometimes they recover the drawings that he throws away. When no one wants a Modì, not even for 5 francs, they buy whole notebooks full of his unmistakable charcoal strokes.

Four hundred drawings from the Alexandre collection are not publicly seen until 1962. There were at least seventeen oil portraits dedicated to his friend and members of his family. There were also dozens of watercolour drawings using varied techniques. It was the Great War that separated them. When, amid a thousand difficulties, Paul Alexandre returned to his city following the general demobilisation of 1919, Amedeo was coming to the end of his life. They never saw each other again.

His friend Paul was his reference point and guide in an unknown and hostile Paris of those years; and Paul's closely kept private collection is perhaps today the only "archive" not polluted by crime, the only reliable observation point of the beauty of the most authentic Modiglianis: a heritage currently worth between 600 million and one billion euros.

Léopold Zborowski, unlike Alexandre, could instinctively spot a business opportunity. Although aware that its fruit would be slow to ripen, he also knew that the harvest would be very profitable. Between Amedeo and Zbó (as Modì and Lunia called him fondly) there was honest solidarity, but probably never true empathy: it was always a very formal relationship, a distance between them that kept the relationship within strict parameters, where money was the demarcation line. Modì was grateful to him, but at the same time, he felt the weight of his dependence on the money Zborowski gave him that every month enabled him to survive, as a man and as an artist.

Léopold certainly understood the contempt that the Italian had for the "dealers", for feeling like a "slave" to that perverse mechanism that bound him and at the same time made him free; he knew he could not make it alone and that his thirst for independence was limited by his need to survive. Modigliani was not the only one in who Zbó invested, in his "stable", we also find the names of Chaïm Soutine and Moïse Kisling. The merchant's sound instincts are confirmed when in London, in the summer of 1919, he finds himself in possession of 60 pounds of gold in exchange for the painting *Il Contadinello* by Modigliani. Among the forty artists of Montparnasse who crossed the Channel with Zborowski, Modì, with fifty-nine works, has the lion's share. The British critics shower him with their flattering reviews and, for the first time, there is talk of "masterpieces".

Along with Maurice Utrillo, Modì was the artist most highly esteemed by visitors and international merchants. His paintings, which arrived at a London exhibition at the Mansard Gallery - without frames or stands because they were too expensive - are sold for between 30 and 100 pounds. Kenneth Clark, who later became famed art critic but at the time was just sixteen years old, is the first to fall in love with a painting, to the point of investing sixty coins of gold. A king's ransom at the time for one of for Modigliani's works, who nevertheless was not there to bask in the success because, being ill, he had remained in Paris.

In those days, it had started to become clear that there would be a difference between the value of one of his works while alive or after his death. During the exhibition, in fact, news of a worsening of his condition reached the Polish merchant. Paul Guillaume, who owned many paintings by Modì, cynically to Zborowski asking him to stop the sales. If Amedeo had died in the next few hours, the price of his works would have doubled. As Osbert Sitwell, one of the two organisers wrote with typical British sarcasm with respect to the London exhibition, "Unfortunately, Modigliani did not comply with the program that had been prepared for him." He probably meant that, given Amedeo's worrying state of health, those who organised the event were perhaps hoping that the artist would pass away.

Léopold returns to Paris in haste. Modigliani miraculously recovers. For him, there are some good reviews in the newspapers, a few francs and a nice pair of English shoes. Zborowski must have had much more left in his pockets. A single coin with King George V's face on it weighed about eight grams. It was then the gold price that determined the value of coins in circulation. At the end of World War I, when the "Franc Poincaré" was introduced (before that the silver coin was in circulation), estimates attribute it a value of about 0.06 grams of gold, meaning that 60 pounds were worth about 8400 francs. To earn that figure, Modì would have had to work 560 days.

The merchant's investment begins to pay off. The last two years of the Leghorn's life painter witness the best of his artistic production. From July 1919 to January of the following year, Zbó also sells more, and at a better price in France. He no longer needs to make sacrifices for Modì. Indeed, his production certainly provides good income for the Pole. Modigliani, however, does not change his lifestyle; evidently, there are no great gains for him. Not to mention the collection of paintings that grows in number and expressive quality. Amedeo continues to keep his illness a secret from everyone until the end.

How far does the speculative cynicism of the merchant go? Does it stops before Amedeo's conditions worsen irreparably or, considering that in any case he is fated by the consumption that lays him low, does he leave it to fate? Was it just a dramatic coincidence that kept him away from Modì when the artist needed him most?

Can a man who also sent his wife to work, just to support his dream of beauty linked to Modigliani's work, refuse to pay for his funeral? The family of the artist, from Italy, fails to intervene immediately. Zbó has many paintings in his house, some even taken from the studio now abandoned by everyone after Amedeo's hospitalisation. In those hours the value of his paintings continues to rise, the requests multiply. Maybe it would be enough to sell one to give a dignified burial to his painter friend. But on the day of the funeral, Zborowski refuses to sell and instructs Kisling to take a collection among their friends to raise the 1350 francs necessary to pay for the burial costs.

His behaviour was as abject as it was cynical. He resisted because he knew that Modì's paintings would soon rise in value, and by a lot. With great surprise Emanuele Modigliani, who would be able to reach Paris to cry over his brother's grave only a month later, would find himself looking for traces of the paintings that not only disappeared from the atelier in rue de la Grande Chaumière, but have already largely been sold. He will have to turn to Paul Alexandre to see some of them.

Within a few years, the works of the Leghorn artist have landed in America. Like Zborowski, collectors and merchants from overseas make a fortune.

An American success

In January 1923, Albert C. Barnes, a physician and researcher who loved the artists of Montparnasse, decides to invest a part of his wealth in works of art by emerging French painters. He wants stand out from the other American billionaires and focus on contemporary artists. Paul Guillaume takes him in hand. With Modigliani dead, just Soutine was left to paint for him. After seeing some unusual works by the Russian painter, Barnes decides to bet everything on him and goes to meet Léopold, who at home has dozens of paintings, piled up and unsold. The American buys them all for 35 dollars each. A real fortune for Soutine and Zborowski: until then the canvases had been brought the artist from 20 to 50 francs. The meeting is a turning point in the life of the pair.

The merchant begins to offer Barnes works by other artists. The American does not go crazy for Modì, but he grasps his value and also buys all the Italian paintings still in Zborowski's hands. Then he buys up the sculptures by Jacques Lipchitz. We are talking about an unimaginable investment for those times: 3 million francs for the works of unknown artists, who from that moment will begin to gain a reputation.

When, thirty-eight years later, Barnes first made his collection public, he amazed the educated and snobbish America but also the America of businessmen for the wealth of the collection, which in the new continent was unprecedented, as was the value of his investment. Standing out among the many paintings, there were over seventy Picassos and many of the most beautiful works by Modigliani and Soutine. The Barnes collection remains a milestone to this day.

However, in the grey area of American art collection, where it was more difficult to make a census of all the authentic works (be it paintings, drawings or sculptures), for half a century a flotilla of gallery owners and dealers sail in the uncertain seas of counterfeit certifications, unchecked attributions, clumsy restorations and counterfeits. For them it is not difficult to invent an overseas "curriculum" for these works, since it is not always easy to find evidence.

In 1989, we find Paul D. Quatrochi who would try to sell works by Amedeo Modigliani together with a self-styled New York lawyer, Tom Andrews. As a mainstay for his plan, Quatrochi conceived the publication of a catalogue on the Leghorn artist[55]. A project that we might ironically define as "scientific". It begins with the creation of a study centre: the Bibliothèque Modigliani, of the Namega Corporation of Jacksonville, Florida, which in 1986 published *Modigliani: A Study of His Sculpture.*[56] A publication in which he presents artworks whose historicity finds no other evidence, but which will nonetheless be mentioned in the literature in which Sotheby's presents its works of art for sale.

The book names its authors as the practically unknown Bernard Schuster as well as Arthur Pfannstiel. We know the second one. The first one

---

[55] The following reconstruction is partially taken from the American magazine "Spy", which is considered satirical. To convey the idea, we can compare it to Dagospia. Satire it is safeguarded in the United States by the First Amendment. We found moreover specific evidence that make the story very plausible; we consider that the magazine reports through quoted sentences declarations that would have been freely granted by the protagonists and were never denied by them.

[56] Bernard Schuster, Arthur Pfannstiel, *Modigliani: A Study of His Sculpture*, NamegaCorporation, Jacksonville 1986.

appears to be the author of Pfannstiel's autobiography as a Polish child who escaped the death camps, *I Will Die Tomorrow, But Not Today*, which also contains an interview with Steven Spielberg.[57] He is also quoted by the USC Shoah Foundation Visual History Archives.

The whole complex infrastructure of the alleged Quatrochi orchestration rests on these pillars. Giving an identity to paintings and sculptures in order to sell them later. Among the customers, we find once again Perls, Ms Panicali and Guttmann, names also known in the Italian chronicles. Hence begins the incredible story told by the American journalist-investigator John Connolly, about a stone caryatid that from worthless a souvenir bought in a London flea market becomes an unlikely Modigliani sculpture worth millions of dollars. Among the art works that Quatrochi tries to sell, ultimately with success, there is, according to the periodical, a head sculpture that they had inserted into a catalogue, described thus: "Amedeo Modigliani, *Tête*, 67 cm, light grey limestone, around 1913".

He would initially try to sell it in New York, at the Gertrude Stein Gallery in Madison Avenue, which is said to have considered it "not authentic", and refused it. Quatrochi would then have asked for help from Carla Panicali, who has galleries in the Big Apple and in Rome, as well great connections. Panicali supposedly sold the caryatid to Klaus Perls for 1,200,000 dollars. When he found out that it was probably fake, Perls let it be known through one of his employees, Barrett Owness: "Mr. Perls does not intend to sell the Modigliani, which is now part of his private gallery. For him it is authentic". The hope, perhaps, was a recurring one: to resell the artwork when everyone has forgotten the affair.

Carla Panicali and Klaus Perls are the same couple who appeared in Livorno with the forgeries of 1984. In the interview given to "Spy" magazine, Quatrochi would claim he had found that head during a trip to London. It was a doorstop in a shop in the suburbs, and he had bought it for a few pounds. After cleaning it, he wanted to put it back on the market. However, this wasn't his only masterstroke. At that time, he said he had taken a young researcher from Moma to dinner and convinced her to

---

[57] Bernard Schuster, *I Will Die Tomorrow, But Not Today*, CreateSpace Independent Publishing Platform, 2013.

include the Tête documentation in the museum's archives, passing it off as authentic. If anyone had any doubts about it, they would find proof of its historicity in the library of the famous museum.

The head does not, however, appear in the collection of the twenty-six works listed in and photographed for Ambrogio Ceroni's catalogue. We believe we recognised a photograph of it in the catalogue of the Genoa exhibition, on page 28. Usually only art works present at the specific event should be included in such repertoires. In this case, nonetheless, they dedicate an entire chapter to sculptures by Modì which have not even been on display, and here, among the various authentic ones, appears that curly-haired piece supposedly bought at a London flea market by the American. Quatrochi himself proudly confirms that it is now displayed in the Metropolitan Museum of Art. In order to check if we had got it right, that is, if the head appeared in that farcical catalogue is the one currently displayed in the famous US museum, we ask for the opinion of the consultants who, with strict but authoritative judgment, identified the twenty fakes of Genoa: Carlo Pepi and Isabella Quattrocchi. Neither has any doubts. "They are very similar to the fake from the flea market, they have the same features, only one is coarser ... They could have worked on it," Pepi says. The expert Quattrocchi says she is certain, too: "It's an outrageous fake. Modigliani never did such well-defined hair, at the back or on the sides. Usually there's just a hint, here they've gone for real hairstyle. For his sculptures, he prepared studies, as witnessed by dozens of drawings, especially in the collection of Paul Alexandre which is now a bible for those who want to know how he sculpted. There is no trace of these horrible details."

It may be that Klaus Perls's history and long experience did not help him much in this case. It is likely, however, that he realised he had bought a worthless trinket. The important thing was to exhibit it in his gallery or in his private collection. It was enough that it looked like a Modigliani, maybe it wasn't essential that it really was. The very fact that he owned it gave that object the magnificence of a work of art. There may have even been a reason behind the remarkable sum he is thought to have paid for it. It could be taken as proof that he had not bought it from a second-hand dealer; only in extreme circumstances would he have perhaps admitted that it was fake. In fact it seems that, even after Quatrochi's comments, reported in "Spy" magazine, Perls is said to have insisted that "to his eyes, it was an authentic art work".

This is how many dealers see a work of art: a simple tool to make a profit and, in recent times, an excellent way to launder money. According to Connolly, it would not be the first time that Paul Quatrochi tried to sell a fake Modigliani. In 1987, he is said to have sold the world famous president of the Health and Tennis Corporation of America, Roy Zurkowski, a fake drawing by Jeanne Hébuterne, for 685,000 USD. After a few months, the entrepreneur is said to have noticed, because he had heard gossip about it, and attempted to get his money back, even using unorthodox methods like sending a former police officer to recover his money. In response, the merchant is said to have told him: "Go fuck yourself". He may himself have enjoyed some protection, and so could afford such arrogance.[58]

Italian Merchants

Italy's art market is not free from frauds or scams. There are many legal proceedings pending against gallery owners, merchants and self-styled experts. There are many associations, foundations and companies that buy and sell Modì's paintings and drawings. The investigations conducted by the Guardia di Finanza and the Carabinieri tell us that from Palermo to

---

[58] We find it hard to believe that it is only playful banter, irreverent as it is, because there are many indications that it is not. We found out in fact that between 1998 and 2003, Quatrochi himself initiated a civil lawsuit in Los Angeles against Guttmann, Guy Vincent Chastenet and the banks. From our sources, we ascertained that Carla Panicali acted as an intermediary between Perls and Quatrochi himself for the head that later ended up in the Metropolitan Museum. There is one publication by the elusive Jacksonville library quoting as authors the two Germans. We learned that Quatrochi knew the two and that he had collaborated with Klaus Perls in some research. We believe it is unlikely that the magazine could have invented a story with so many correct names and a photograph of a sculpture very similar, if not the same, to the one currently exhibited in the Metropolitan Museum. We would never have dared to make such a comparison if we had found official denials by the main actors. Quatrochi also confirmed to us that he had never sued the periodical that allegedly portrayed him as a forger.

Venice, passing through Cuneo and Arezzo, not all that glitters is gold in our galleries.

Ever since word of our investigation got out, they are now many people who want to put us on the trail of alleged scammers who until now have not had to worry about being discovered and ensnared in the web of justice. One of our informants gave us "an authentication for a drawing and watercolour on cardboard with dimensions 100.5x70.5". The document in question, which the authoritative source tells us is fake, bears the signature of Fabrizio Quiriti and the stamp of the Skema Srl Gallery - Modern and Contemporary Art. The matter would concern two drawings and a third watercolour which has been retouched, accompanied by two handwritten letters by Jeanne Modigliani, probably forgeries, dated June 25, 1978 and June 15, 1979. We ask for Carlo Pepi's opinion, and he replies straight away: "All fake, I already conducted an appraisal for the Carabinieri in Rome. They are badly copied from the Paul Alexandre collection or from the catalogue of Vitali's lithographs." Junk, in short, that once again we find being marketed by the usual "expert".

We wonder who Quiriti is for him to claim the right of authenticating. From what we learn in newspaper archives, he appears to be a friend of the wealthy Italian businessman Flavio Briatore, but he allegedly didn't hesitate to cheat him too, or at least that is what the news reports say. Prosecuted for embezzlement and fraudulent bankruptcy.[59]

A strange bankruptcy, that of Quiriti and his five companies that touted art works. For years, he had continued to obtain huge bank credit lines. One of the alleged guarantors of his credit was Briatore, who promised through a letter presented to the bank, to back him with one and a half billion of old Italian lire to his friend from Cuneo. Apparently only a fifth of the

---

[59] Sentenced in first and second degree, Quiriti escaped a definitive sentence thanks to the statute of limitations. In fact, the crime dates back to September 2009. Shortly after the failed appeal (2017), the deadlines for reaching a definitive sentence expired. Gianni Santucci, *Milan, Briatore compra e il direttore incassa. Il Gallerista Zebina non sarà pagato*" Corriere della Sera", April 4, 2018. The events do not concern works by Modigliani. Barbara Morra, *"A Fabrizio Quiriti tanti soldi dalle banche senza avere garanzie"*, "La Stampa", November 12, 2013. See also *Bancarotta finita in prescrizione. Assolto il gallerista cuneese Quiriti*, "La Stampa", November 9, 2017,

guarantee was handed over (300 million). Meanwhile, however, the loan went through.

Quiriti, with his "impeccable" curriculum, was then artistic director of the JZ Art Trading gallery in Milan, owned by the former soccer player, the French international Jonathan Zebina. Just in that role, Quiriti allegedly sold at least one fake work, apparently produced by Michelangelo Lanza, and was accused of unduly taking possession of the proceeds from other sales to the detriment of the shop owner. Lanza owns a shop of paintings and carpets in Viguzzolo, in the province of Alessandria; he is friends with various footballers and on his LinkedIn profile, he claims to be an "expert in national and foreign carpets and tapestries. Expert in contemporary art". In 2005, he was convicted, along with Maura Lari, the wife of the great footballer Franco Baresi, for marketing a fake De Chirico.[60] In 2011, we find him again involved in a new episode of art galleries and fake paintings. The investigations were triggered by a report from the Arman Archive, which protects the memory of the well-known French artist Armand Pierre Fernandez, known as Arman, for the transaction of a fake sculpture passed from the hands of Lanza to those of the gallery-owner and footballer Zebina. Among those cheated, again, was Flavio Briatore.[61]

An exhibition dedicated to Modigliani is scheduled to open on November 21, 2015 in Arezzo, curated by the art gallery of Rimini Rosini-Gutman, with the participation of the municipal administration. However, the exhibition, entitled *Quando conoscerò la tua anima dipingerò i tuoi occhi*, was postponed for a fortnight because, according to an announcement by the mayor and other organisers, the art works, arriving from Paris, got stuck in France because of the terrorist attacks. Could they all be in Paris? It appears to us that some of the art works had already been exhibited in Naples some months earlier.[62] Romano Boriosi, artistic director of the local art gallery La Chimera was called to curate the exhibition. In reality, he has

---

[60] In a 2005 plea bargain, Lanza was sentenced to two years in prison and a fine of 2,800 Euro. See Sarah Martinenghi, laRepubblica.it, October 19, 2011.

[61] Alberto Gaino, Grazia Longo, *Stock di quadri falsi, Briatore in procura: «Mi hanno bidonato»*, "La Stampa", October 19 2011.

[62] Paolo De Luca, *Modigliani in mostra all'Agorà Morelli*, "la Repubblica", May 22, 2015.

no particular expertise, certainly not on Modigliani, and he claims to have graduated in journalism at the University of Urbino, as well as being a painter and sculptor. As soon as the exhibition is inaugurated, Carlo Pepi publicly denounces it: "It's all fake"[63].

"I had the misfortune of going to see the exhibition in Arezzo; as I feared, I did not even see one authentic work," Pepi writes on his Facebook page in those days. "I've seen reproductions based on from sketches that themselves were not authentic, fakes based on fakes, including the various bronze sculptures which the artist never have even considered creating." According to the argumentative Pisan, who would be called to testify in Arezzo against Gianfranco Rosini, owner of the gallery, the Carabinieri seized everything. We did not find any confirmation in the newspapers, but Parisot too confirmed the existence of the proceedings. First of all, we tried to understand the origin of the alleged works on display. It appears the Amedeo Modigliani Institute in Spoleto was again involved.

In Rome, meanwhile, the frauds have taken on a film-like quality. The Institute of the Modigliani Legal Archives Paris-Rome, run by the partners Parisot and Renzi, weaves its plans with moderate success, organising exhibitions and sales. In June 2009, for just one week, they prepare a small exhibition at the Attorney General of the State building, in the Vanvitelli room. The curator, Massimo Riposati entitles it *Un amore segreto*. The catalogue is written by Claudio Strinati, Michael Mezzatesta, Francesca Ramacciotti-Sommati, Christian Parisot, Vladimir Goriainov and Massimo Riposati himself. They present only one painting, exhibited for the first time in Italy: *Jeune femme à la guimpe blanche*. The only portrait of Simone Thiroux that, according to the catalogue, Modigliani painted in 1916.

From that moment, it begins to travel from one art gallery to another. Modì, as far as we know, never authored such a painting. It is only after six years that the Carabinieri unit for Cultural Heritage realised, blocking an attempted sale in 2015. The auction was in progress and it involved a wealthy American and an unspecified art dealer. The American buyer had

---

[63] See also Dario Serpan, *Maledetto Modigliani, ad Arezzo una mostra sospesa tra arte, tecnologia e polemiche*, «Blastingnews», January 20, 2016.

probably also sponsored the exhibition at the Attorney General's building, through which he would have acquired the right of pre-emption on the purchase from the presumed family owner of the portrait. According to news reports, it was a clever fraud, well planned, to steal 9 million euros from the art lover's account. This year the court finally ruled the destruction of the artwork, despite the great critics who had praised its beauty and specially created the catalogue and the exhibition. If the parties do not appeal, the picture will soon be sent to be pulped.

An attempted coup in Piazza Affari

Friends-enemies. Partners-adversaries. Christian Parisot and Luciano Renzi have been arguing over the inheritance for over ten years and also on the ownership of the Modigliani brand. It is worth about 100 million euros, but it would not belong to either of them. The courts are battlegrounds, but so are market and business; and so too the world of forgeries and certifications. Their common goal in 2006 had been to conquer Rome. Their Trojan horse, as we know, was the Modigliani Institut Archives légales Paris-Rome.

The big deal that the two partners envisage is not just about paintings or exhibitions, but also on the name. With the centenary of his death, 2020, in sight, they begin to work on the registration of a Modigliani brand. The offensive starts in 2009 with an agreement with Fiat to launch a new model of the Cinquecento car. At the presentation, in front of a blown-up image of a work by the Leghorn painter, Christian Parisot smiles next to the Romeo Ferraris racing team and Anneliese Abarth, wife of the fondly remembered Carlo and the current director of the Carlo Abarth Foundation. In 2010, the Institute signed agreements with the best-known exporting companies: first with the Tuscan cigar manufacturers, the Customs Agency and state monopolies, which created a cigar named Modigliani to follow those dedicated to Garibaldi and to Soldati. And again, with Richard Ginori, producer of precious ceramic works, founded in 1735. The collaboration will lead to the creation of exclusive Ginori products inspired by Modigliani's unmistakable style and with Jeanne Hébuterne's likeness. "Activities that the Institute [Amedeo Modigliani, *ed.*] will accompany abroad: Renzi & Partners, the worldwide licensee for the use of the brand, has obtained funding from Simest [one and a half million euros, *ed.*], a public financing company for the promotion of Italian companies abroad, to verify the real potential of the American market."[64]

In December 2012, the Carabinieri stormed their headquarters in Palazzo Taverna following the arrest of Parisot, president of the Institute; and so, Renzi transfers its operations centre from the capital to Spoleto, to the same building where Spoleto Arte is based and where the TV art critic Sgarbi exhibits and often curates exhibitions. He transforms the name into Institute Amedeo Modigliani Spoleto, but he keeps the same company registration name. Here, alone, he tries to put from his mind the inconvenient partner accused of forgery and receiving stolen goods, renaming his association but taking with him the digital copies of the Archives, which he would later use for his "Modigliani Experience" exhibitions around Italy. In March 2019, in the middle of his peregrinations, justice catches up with him, too. The Carabinieri once again block his way in Palermo. On March 31, they break in and close the exhibition *Les Femmes Modigliani Experience* at Palazzo Bonocore. Only twenty-four hours earlier, the Ministry of Cultural Heritage had announced that it had never granted patronage to the exhibition. It was a "virtual event", supported by the presence of only two paintings that experts who appraised it considered fake.

Meanwhile, following his "split" from Parisot, Renzi continues to use the brand and tries to make one last big deal. In 2016, he strikes an agreement with WM Capital, a company specialising in business format franchising and listed on the Milan stock exchange. The arrangement should take the Modigliani "franchise" a long way. It covers the trademarks of Modigliani, Modigliani Brand and M, in all their iterations. The agreement concerns the concession of exclusive licenses worldwide relating to the Legal Archives and the licensing of trademarks to third parties, including allowing the licensee to register other trademarks. The contract is valid until 31 December 2023 with respect to access to the Archives, to 2033 for the licensing of trademarks to third parties, and provides for the royalty

---

[64] Daniele Autieri, *Il marchio Modigliani per sigari e ceramiche*, "la Repubblica", July 13 2010.

payments to the Modigliani Institute with a guaranteed annual minimum of around 15,000 euros.

"The agreement has been suspended," the founder and chief administrator of WM Capital, Fabio Pasquali, explains shortly. "We soon realised the characters' lack of seriousness, and a company like ours cannot afford to compromise its own image." However, the underlying asset may certainly be appealing. In 2010, the Amedeo Modigliani Institute commissioned Interbrand to research on the potential value of the Modigliani brand. The brand value specialist identified huge possibilities for market penetration, particularly in the United States, Brazil and Japan. It put the value of the Modigliani brand at around 18 million dollars in the United States, 16 million in Japan and 7 million in Brazil, a total of 41 million US dollars with solid growth potential. These entrepreneurial projects were ambitious and seemingly legal, were it not for the fact that the entire business was born from a probable fraud against Modigliani's legitimate heirs, as well as against the new partners. Renzi has no archive, apart from the one created with the contested artistic curator Alberto D'Atanasio, which allegedly included false certifications. Neither has anything to do with Modigliani's works, least of all with the "moral rights" to exploit them. Their focus returns to the paintings as they try to stimulate Italy's interest in the painter, particularly in light of the events organised for 2020.

And so in June 2017, at the same time as the exhibition in Palazzo Ducale in Genoa, Modigliani House is inaugurated in Spoleto, one of the events of the Festival of the Two Worlds. "Our goals ... to celebrate, to remember, to spread Amedeo Modigliani's story and work in Italy and abroad." This is the mission statement on the website of the Amedeo Modigliani Institute in Spoleto. First event, the exhibition *Modigliani and Art Nègre*. An exclusive presentation: a Modì drawing depicting Jeanne Hébuterne in 1917, never seen before. The inevitable Carlo Pepi, who had already been fighting for months against the fakes in Genoa, was quoted in the most widely read Italian newspapers that it would be another fake. "I don't believe this drawing was produced by the hand of Modigliani. The lines, the atmosphere, the composition all correspond to the false works of Modì that have been circulating since the 1980s."

Back in his home town of Cerreto d'Asti, Parisot too is agitated and brands the drawing as "a remarkable fake". Scrolling the images of the video presentation of the exhibition, we notice other suspicious paintings, including that *"L' Uomo col Cappello"* which has already been identified as a "lousy fake". We consult our sources and discover that once again Renzi, supported by the Spoleto professor D'Atanasio, man have certified more "obscene filth", as both Pepi and Parisot define it.

"He ruined my life, Renzi; he's an impressive character, and his bare-faced front has no limits. He showed up in Paris and had a secretary introduce him as president of (the respected news agency) Adnkronos." Christian Parisot seems to feel the blow when, during a long sequence of messages, he tells us about his old partner, now a bitter enemy. It is only two years since the inauguration of Casa Modigliani, but a lot of water has passed under the bridge. Exhibition-focused activities have proliferated around Italy. Casa Modigliani has a prestigious location in the Festival city, and two exceptional ambassadors in the popular videos of the celebrations: Vittorio Sgarbi and Philippe Daverio.

The art historian D'Atanasio and Renzi himself certify Modigliani's paintings and sculptures in the name of the Institute, thus stealing space from Parisot and diluting the value of his skill. But here, at least the archivist gets a small revenge. We tell Parisot the news that the Carabinieri Unit for the protection of cultural heritage, sent by the Palermo Prosecutor's Office, have raided Palazzo Bonocore to shutter the exhibition *Les Femmes Modigliani Experience* on its last day of opening to the public and impounded its only two paintings. These are paintings that, like Carlo Pepi, he himself had lambasted several times as "horrendous fakes". The news of the raid in Palermo had just come out. Renzi was under investigation, along with D'Atanasio. The searches had turned out well. We ensured that charges would be pressed by filing complaints the Ministry of Cultural Heritage and to the Carabinieri.

The news is music to Parisot's ears, and he decides to open up to us. So, we begin a conversation via WhatsApp. "He (Renzi) called himself a business lawyer and a communications specialist. He had come to Paris by car, accompanied by a driver and a secretary." Everything fits, just like in a movie plot. What better coverage than Adnkronos? Of course the agency knew nothing about it.

"From 2006 to today, Renzi has perpetrated a series of Modigliani-related scams that are only now coming to light," Parisot continues. "The most important episodes are characterised by events where fraudsters passed themselves off as respectable people who were part of the "system", thus avoiding suspicion. These were extensive scams, all based on the unauthorised use of the Modigliani Archives [which are neither his property nor in his possession, *ed*]. The "Modigliani Institut" logo has been pirated by Luciano Renzi, who in addition to performing many 'expert appraisals' of notorious forgeries, was now trying to sell the name "Modigliani" as if he were the legitimate owner."

It was a hoax founded on the improper passing of the "moral rights" to the work that Laure Modigliani Nechtschein herself had in her time passed to Parisot, who in turn had gifted it to the company he established with Renzi. This concession was deemed invalid by the Court of Rome. According to Parisot, and to basic logic, Renzi took possession of a non-transferable right, the moral right that is the right of Laure Modigliani and her descendants, and which encompasses the defence of the Master's image, honour and the integrity of his works.

Parisot contradicts himself in his correspondence, however, because on the one hand he admits that the moral right cannot be sold, but on the other, it was the archivist himself who took advantage of it first, at least until 2009 (we have proof) by exploiting the brand in partnership with Renzi. He took Laure to court and she was then ordered to pay compensation, as we have already written. When Parisot in his turn left the scene in handcuffs, Renzi took advantage of the situation and cheated him in his turn.

On the eve of the centenary of Modigliani's death, a plethora of associations and foundations compete for authority over the work of the Leghorn master, often receiving funding. They include the Amedeo Modigliani Scientist Research Foundation in Vietri sul Mare, in the province of Salerno. Given Carlo Pepi's "reputation", they decide that he must be their ambassador. They visit him in Crespina and submit some drawn images to him from catalogues, then ask him to select works that they will transform into two- and three-dimensional animations to be projected during an exhibition. An exhibition without paintings.

We were curious, so we checked the videos that they produce and publish on the foundation's Facebook page. Some of the photographs depicted questionable works attributed to Modì. We then consulted the Pisan collector, who seems to be a guarantor of this enterprise, of its transparency and quality. But Pepi, responds, "They are filth, inspired or derived from authentic works: recent drafts and therefore false. They photographed and reproduced fake drafts. I do not want to be associated with this stuff here, I have already sent them a notice to cease and desist." The president of the Foundation is Fabrizio Checchi, a member of the scientific committee and one of a long list of names unknown in the world of art, but with excellent academic credentials. The president of the scientific committee is Greta García Hernández, introduced by a local newspaper as the main expert on Modigliani's work, who has allegedly patented yet another technologically advanced method for authenticating the paintings and detecting any counterfeits. It is likely that this umpteenth foundation, born in March 2018 in the name of Modigliani, is looking to be accredited to perform authentications. As the art historian Claudio Metzger explains, "technology is not enough, there are many skills (including, importantly, experience and artistic sensitivity) that are indispensable in attributing a certification of authenticity to a work."

One thing is certain: around all these affairs - Modigliani, his archives, his paintings - some order is needed. France, which like Italy is not willing to allow the Leghorn painter's image be damaged by swindlers, has set up a serious academic and scientific committee managed from the University of Lille. To begin, twenty-five paintings and three sculptures will be studied by French scientists, X-rayed and subjected to an analysis of the materials. They all come from state museums and the results will not be disclosed before next year. If this were enough to decree a work false, Italy could use the expertise of its scientific police and the specialist Carabinieri unit, the envy of the world. However, a painting is also emotion, colour, brushstroke, perspective and the soul of the artist. It is above all a philosophical work, while science is limited to the materiality of its observations.

The long deception

Donation deeds, expert appraisals, letters. In months and months of work and research, we have examined dozens of documents. We have spoken at length about some, others have remained in our drawers. All raised many doubts. Concerns and questions that in some case undermined the credibility of people and institutions. Our curiosity and intellectual honesty led us not to judge in advance, but to trust in good faith, and to believe in it unless we saw proof to the contrary.

The material signed by Jeanne Modigliani and Christian Parisot that we have gathered has increased our questions from time to time on the attribution of certain finds. Parisot is now seen as a suspected forger, while Jeanne Modigliani conjures the image of a fragile and easily-manipulated woman. Certainly, their psychological profiles are not enough to mark them as actors, victims or executors of probable crimes. What made us suspicious were the shape, the style, the timing, those signatures and those muddled annotations, those scribbles, those altered dates. So we looked for other manuscripts and documents signed by Jeanne.

We found them at Carlo Pepi's house. The origin of these objects is in this case certain. From the book by Enzo Maiolino, *Modigliani, dal vero*[65] and from certain catalogues we have collected other letters that were undoubtedly written by Jeanne. Three brief documents produced by Parisot in support of his claims stand out among the court documents.[66] We therefore had dozens of signatures examined by an expert.

Silvia Benini calls us on the morning of March 25, 2019. She is the professional that we have engaged to examine the documents attributed to Jeanne Modigliani with the tools of graphological analysis. A consultant who was chosen with care for her absolute credibility and also because she is an expert trusted by the judicial authorities.

Through those contracts, Christian Parisot had obtained the "seal" of the Roman judges. He had taken definitive possession of the Modigliani Legal Archives claiming that they had been donated to him by Amedeo's daughter. This apparently incontestable tool had allowed him to open the doors of ministries, museums, State Archives and other shrines of Italian and international culture.

---

[65] Enzo Maiolino, *Modigliani, dal vero. Testimonianze inedite e rare raccolte e annotateda Enzo Maiolino*, De Ferrari, Genova 2017.

[66] Letters dated September 23 1974, October 9 1974, October 3 1982, October 12 1982.

The graphologist contacts us having completed her work. "It's all lies; Jeanne did not write a single word of those donation deeds. Everything was written in Parisot's hand," she tells us over the phone.

We catch a flight to Turin and arrive at Dr. Benini's studio. Her investigation was meticulous and highly technological. She highlighted every letter, every number, and found the discrepancies. "The writings of texts and signatures with the apparent name Jeanne Modigliani affixed on documents corresponding to the dates of 23 September, 1974; 9 October, 1974; 12 October, 1982; 3 October 1982; and July 26, 1984, classified from X1 to X5, were fabricated. The five scripts are stylistically similar to each other. They were produced by the hand of the same forger and not by that of Jeanne. *The fakes are compatible with the samples of Christian Parisot's handwriting that were provided.*" Thus writes the scholar in her twenty-two page report. It is a shot to the heart. Our assumptions are confirmed by the handwriting expert's report.

"Stylistic differences and different graphic form" between the Jeanne's authentic writings and those papers which we were led to believe had been written and signed in her own hand. The turning point for Dr. Benini is when she analyses and compares those papers with Parisot's handwriting. Whoever wrote the dates had a "hard, stiff writing style, with angles; angles Jeanne didn't have in her soft curves, while there is a correspondence between the style and the shape of Parisot's hand". At the bottom of the 1974 deed, he gives himself unequivocally by using his trademark "a", which he writes as an italicised capital letter, even in lower case words. Yes, it is that document dated 1974 on which we have long reflected in these pages, the one that aroused our curiosity in the first place. That document which our investigations had already to be an historical fake. It had been enough to verify that the agreement with Graphis-Arte, mentioned therein, was only struck about ten years later.

"I conclude with an overall parallel from which the lexical compatibility of the recurrent use of the words "I beg you" in the letter of 3 October, 1982 and in many of Parisot's communications can also be seen," writes the graphologist Silvia Benini, who documents her detailed and pondered analysis with photos.

"And so I beg you to contact me for any loans ... I beg you to take over all the roles of archivist ...," reports the donation deed of 1982, which according to this report is fake, and was not signed by Jeanne Modigliani. A kind, obliging, respectful manner which hides a betrayal, that of the trust Jeanne had placed in Parisot for years by putting him in charge of the Archives, her most precious asset.

"I beg you to add, as agreed ... I beg you to excuse me for my absence ... I beg you to take up your role ..."; Parisot wrote to Pepi in more than one letter ... and he was betraying him too, by making him believe that Jeanne's last letter was for her friend Carlo. The letter delivered to Crespina a few weeks after the death of Modì's daughter, the one Carlo has kept at home for decades as a reminder of her. According to the graphologist, that letter too was written and signed by the archivist on the day of Jeanne's death.

This latest discovery brings us back to the crime scene of July 25, 1984 in Paris, in boulevard Vincent Auriol.

Digging in the mine that is Carlo Pepi's personal archive in Crespina, documents emerge from time to time, which would point to Parisot's guilt. There are many letters destined for the Ministry of Cultural Heritage, the Municipality of Livorno and the Guastalla brothers in which Jeanne Modigliani's signature has been forged by Parisot. Among the forged documents, again according to the graphologist, the expert appraisal supposedly signed by Modì's daughter was actually signed in her name by the archivist. Parisot's hand also emerges on at least one of the evaluations attributed to Victor Leduc.

The investigators wrote that the archivist was a forger, confirming it indelibly on the papers with which they brought him before justice. Like Sisyphus, they loaded the boulder on their shoulders and tried to climb the steep and slippery slope of criminal proceedings. But they did not succeed. Just like in the myth, the stone rolls back down every time, and everything starts again on its endless cycle. What we have discovered brings sadness mixed with anger when we think of the theft from the heirs and the damage done to the memory of one of the most important figures in Italy's artistic aristocracy. Laure Modigliani had said it and had it put on the record: "This is not my mother's handwriting. Those acronyms are not mine. I can't say if my mother's signatures are real or fake." It was January 2016 when Modì's granddaughter came to Rome to speak out for the last time in what was supposed to be an important witness statement following the arrest of

Parisot, accused of forgery and of receiving stolen goods after the seizures of paintings and drawings at Palazzo Taverna and in Palestrina.

While it is understood that all these indications emerged in our own investigation and with the help of a forensic graphologist, we wonder why no one ever thought of raising questions about the papers that a person convicted of specific crimes, a forger, has used as his defence before judges and lawyers. Counsel for the defence should tell us whether they consider that they have taken all the necessary precautions, in a deontological and ethical sense, to ensure that justice was served. Why ever did they not contest those papers, how come they did not appeal? "It seems like making a mockery of misery", to paraphrase the Italian author Piero Calamandrei, in his doubt that the law is equal for everyone. Evidently, he was not wrong.

Who will pay for this injustice? Who can, who must protect the image and work of the great Amedeo Modigliani?

Seventh crime scene: 205 boulevard Vincent Auriol, Paris
Chronicle of a death foretold

CHARACTERS

Daniel Cornibert – former owner of the cafe restaurant Renoir, in Paris, today La Place, 194 avenue de Choisy. Friend of Jeanne Modigliani.

Mister Mainovsky – Concierge of the building where Jeanne died.

Maurizio Silvestri – journalist from *Il Tirreno*.

Valdemar Nechtschein, aka *Victor Leduc* – intellectual, philosopher and partisan of Russian origin. Among the founders of the French Communist Party and the International socialist, Jeanne Modigliani's former husband.

And again: *Jeanne Modigliani, Christian Parisot, Carlo Pepi, Giorgio and Guido Guastalla.*

July 26, 1984, 205 boulevard Vincent Auriol

It is almost 8pm and there is still daylight in Paris when an ambulance with blaring sirens arrives outside the seventeen-floor building overlooking place d'Italie. The stretcher bearers take the elevator and stop at the eleventh floor. They enter one of the small apartments. The woman is lying on the ground in a pool of blood. The doctor, making his way through a group of people, bends down and notices that she is still breathing. However, several hours must have passed since the accident that caused the very serious injury. The face is a mask of blood: the bleeding has not stopped, but the blood on the floor is congealed in some places. Still and dying lies Jeanne Modigliani.

It will forever remain a mystery who or what her eyes they saw for the last time; why and how she slipped in those few square metres that were her home (practically a one room apartment, a *studio*, with the accent on the last vowel in the French way). So many questions: who did she talk to before the accident? Was it actually an "unsuspicious death", as they later called it at the police station? According to some reconstructions, her ex-husband, Valdemar Nechtschein may have found her in that condition. With him are the concierge, Mr. Mainovsky, and a doctor who lived in the same building. In the building, few others would have noticed what was happening since most of the tenants were on holiday.

Right away, the condition of the woman seems desperate. The nurses set about their work, the ambulance whizzes through the streets of Paris with sirens blaring as they attempt to save her life. At 20.50, she arrives at the Hôpital de la Pitié. "Intracerebral haemorrhage" is the diagnosis, and Jeanne Modigliani is immediately taken into intensive care. However, these efforts have no effect: at 16.45 on July 27, the woman stops breathing. In the report that records her death, doctors also report that there was an "alcoholic imbalance".

The small apartment on boulevard Vincent Auriol, the presumed or at least possible crime scene, should have been cordoned off. It should have been secured. They should have prevented anyone from entering and polluting the scene before they could carry out an accurate analysis. Jeanne may have fallen as a result of a fight, as the result of a blow or a push, or she could have got dizzy and lost her balance. She could have been struck by a strong and sudden cerebral haemorrhage due to natural causes, and consequently lost consciousness and hit her head, aggravating a pre-existing head injury. Who can rule out any of these possibilities? The blood loss is compatible with all these circumstances.[67] The first-aiders find

---

[67] In this regard, we asked for guidance to Dr. Riccarda Giraudi, coroner and consultant of the Court of Turin. When you have a head injury following a bruise due to a fall on a large surface, for example a table or the floor, but also when you are hit with a blunt wide object, like a wooden club or an iron bar, you can often observe the formation of an extradural hematoma (ie between the skull bone and the dura mater). The blood shedding progressively compresses the underlying brain, until the victim loses consciousness. However, this can also happen at a distance of hours or even days from the trauma, after the injured person has walked or is dragged even for many meters before falling and losing consciousness. Moreover, in case of diseases affecting the liver (alcoholic liver disease, liver cirrhosis, hepatitis), bleeding is particularly easy and even a small and insignificant head injury can lead to the formation of subdural hematomas which cause progressive compression.

themselves looking at a "pool of blood", but they could barely understand precisely where it had come from and above all why.

What is certain is that Jeanne, just before hitting her head, had drunk too much. According to the reconstruction we will perform, based on the information we have collected, the fact could date back to before 11 am on July 25.

Her daughters and ex-husband are at her bedside. The archivist, Christian Parisot, is not there. On the morning of July 28, however, he will call Carlo Pepi in Crespina asking him to pass the news of her death to the news agencies. The funeral held is a strictly private affair and a few hours later, the body is cremated. In short, three or four days after the accident, on July 29 only memories, a hospital report and perhaps a police report are all that remain of Jeanne Modigliani.

While the world goes crazy for the "rediscovered" heads of Modigliani in the "Fosso Reale" in Livorno, the newspapers dedicate limited space to her. The news articles published are few and confusing; the address of the accident is even wrong, since some say they had sought her at 55, boulevard Saint-Michel, or even that she had been found there, dying.

At the time other reporters, attempting to get her comments on the heads found in Livorno, had tried to call on her at that address. For "three days", a male voice answers. It is probably Valdemar Nechtschein, that is to say, Victor Leduc, her ex-husband, who lives at the address. The laconic voice repeats: "Madame is not in Paris, she is not available."

The man on the other end of the phone has answered a call from an Italian reporter who works for "La Stampa". If it is her ex-husband, does he not know yet that his former wife has died? It does not escape the journalists - at least the more experienced ones - that behind so much reserve coupled with such scant interest in the investigation, behind the lack of an autopsy, they might not find an "unsuspicious "death" at home or the fall of a frail and slightly drunk sixty-six year old. They might be looking at a murder.

Modì, un "giallo" anche la morte della figlia. Alcuni sospettano che Jeanne Modigliani sia stata assassinata. ("Modi: the death of his daughter is also a mystery. Some suspect that Jeanne Modigliani may have been murdered" - ed). This is the headline in the *Corriere della Sera* of September 16, 1984. Years later, on October 14 1992, the Milanese newspaper will return to this story: *Modigliani, un giallo senza fine. "La figlia dell' artista? Uccisa" ("Modigliani, an unending mystery: was the artist's daughter murdered?" - ed).* The questions are not answered: no one follows up, no one undertakes an investigation.

After the separation from her husband, Jeanne had taken refuge in the studio of boulevard Vincent Auriol, which had at first been rented by Leduc for their daughter Anne. Her relationships with their other daughter, Laure, had never been easy; but after Laure's daughter, Sarah, was born in 1979, the tension in the family had become unbearable. Jeanne had to find a new place to live, so Anne had to give up any idea of moving: the room was too small for two people.

There is nothing beautiful about the building to which Modì's daughter moves, alone; it is as modern as it is anonymous, all concrete and windows. The door overlooks a blind corridor, where there is only artificial light. The other flats are all the same, but as Jeanne's is close to the elevator, it is perhaps the nicest. It is difficult to meet someone there, or to invite anyone in.

It is a sultry summer in Paris. The woman has been walking with a stick for about a year after a fall left her with a limp. She has been alone for some time, and she is drinking more; she is less and less lucid. In her rather untidy apartment, she tries every now and then to concentrate and paint, but she can't. In general, she doesn't like talking to anyone, and she doesn't find it easy to get close to others.

All the more when the heads are found in Livorno. Many newspapers seek her comments and the news agencies continue to report her few statements about the events in the Tuscan city. Everyone thinks she is reflecting on what to do. She certainly never believed that her father would have wanted to get rid of his sculptures, however ugly or half-finished they were. But who knows if she really ever understood what was happening in Livorno in those days? Reconstructions suggest that on 19 July she received the anonymous letter that may have upset her, telling her of the discovery of four (false) sculptures by Modì. But as we have noted, the heads had not yet been found.

What is certain is that Jeanne Modigliani' had not been in control of her life for several years. In that period someone had managed to turn her into some sort of icon, a remote figure who only appeared at certain ceremonial events tied to exhibitions of her father's works. She was always accompanied by Parisot. As if to make people think that she was the one who made the decisions, dictated the press releases, selected the paintings to exhibit in Barcelona, in Madrid, and Naples...

The death certificate tells us this may not be so. The effects of substance abuse are evident in body of the victim. We use this word advisedly because, even if it is not possible to provide all the details of a possible crime, Jeanne is a victim. The victim of a world, the art world, which often devours the weak, feeds on their talent and then throws them away.

It is certain that on arrival at the hospital she was subjected to careful analysis, and it is also likely that all her values were found to be out of balance, warning signs, perhaps coming too late, of a tired, fragile liver, now incapable of expelling the toxins. The enemy is called ammonia, a compound produced from intestinal bacteria and body cells when you digest proteins. If the liver metabolises it only partially and badly, it can give rise to confusion, the inability to perform manual functions, psychomotor agitation and aggression. This disease is called hepatic encephalopathy and no one affected by it can keep their self-control, that is, they cannot maintain the abilities and skills needed to effectively control their affairs. Those obvious effects on Jeanne's brain were all there, and her former neighbours told us so.

Heads, letters and anonymous calls

The last official document to record her thoughts is held at the Ansa news agency. The Guastalla brothers, on July 27, receive and publish the press release arriving from Paris:

> *The discovery of the submerged sculptures in Livorno is too important [...]. I believe I now have the right and duty to ensure that the verification of authenticity and the dating of the sculptures recovered from the Fossi has to be entrusted to a committee of experts, which should also include the Archives, regardless of the passions it arouses in us [...].*

However, when her words reach the world, from Livorno, Jeanne is already dead, after being in a coma for one or two days. Who is it that spoke in her place? This is not the only questionable document. Had everything been decided beforehand? The reconstruction of her last days and the timeline which may corroborate the hypothesis of an accidental death pass through three written documents: the anonymous letter received from Livorno on July 19, the ticket dated July 20 that Jeanne allegedly gave to Christian Parisot, and finally the letter delivered to Carlo Pepi and dated July 26, that is to say the day before her death, the same day she was found and taken to hospital.

Thirty-five years have passed. Contradictions and doubts have not been clarified over time. Quite the opposite, the story seems to have crystallised. Even the places remained the same.

It is raining and windy in Paris when we exit the subway in place d'Italie. We are in front of 205 boulevard Vincent Auriol, a building built in the seventies. Well cared for, no names, only numbers on the two rows of intercoms - except for the names of a medical practice and a physiotherapist. If you do not know the code to open the glass doors, it is impossible to enter. Rather, you have to wait, as we did, for someone to come out in order to get in. In the large hall, in the centre, there are two stone partitions that host the letterboxes and list the many tenants. Then there is the office of the concierge. First of all we take a look at the entrances and stairs. Two side corridors lead to the four elevators: two for even-numbered floors and two for the odd ones.

We have come this far with our many questions. While we explore our surroundings, we think once again about the many riddles, yet unanswered, that surrounded that tragic death. From all we have read, from our interviews, our research, we have almost made up our minds. Parisot lied. We just have to understand why. Why so many contradictions every time he recalled those events, supposedly from memory? We entered the building to look for answers and details.

We meet a man in his eighties, fit for his age. We stop him. He is reserved, but straightforward. Then comes a woman of the same age, who also listens to our questions. They are unaware that the apartment in which Jeanne died is in this building. A tall man, slightly younger, seems better informed, but he tells us he had not been in Paris in those days.

Once in the elevator, we on ring all the doors of the eleventh floor without getting any useful information apart from learning that all those apartments are now occupied by young couples who know nothing about Jeanne and who have often never heard of her illustrious parent. We decide to return to the place two days later. We have forty-eight hours to reflect before resuming our detective work.

In Montparnasse, sitting at the Rotonde with a beer, we look closely at the world that once belonged to Amedeo Modigliani. We lose ourselves for a few hours in the poetry and beauty of the Académie de la Grande Chaumière, where time seems to have stopped in 1909. The room of nudes, in which Modì learnt the art of depicting the body, the same stools stained with colour, the same stove, the chandeliers, the large windows, the benches. That canopy above a platform on which a blonde girl, covered only with a bathrobe, is about to undress. It's a few steps from there: above what was the other famous academy, the Colarossi, there is the attic where Modì lived with Jeanne Hébuterne. The steep staircase, the vertigo of that sloping ramp that climbs up to the attic.

At the end of our walk, we think again about the main players in our story. From our backpack, we take out dozens of newspaper articles and interviews with Jeanne Modigliani: we arrange them on the table and we try to recompose the mosaic. The waiter notices Amedeo's photo, smiles and invites us into the bar. Impressive. The red velvet, the tables, all just like a hundred years ago. On the walls the nudes, all the nudes by Modì. Basically, every corner of the two floors of the famous cafe is almost exclusively a reminder of him. Of the other artists, from Picasso to Soutine, to Brancusi and many other great artists of Montparnasse who frequented the area assiduously, there is little trace. But Amedeo Clemente so elegant and aristocratic, really left his mark on this place.

Back at the table, where our documents are spread out next to our beers, we realise that the only common element among all the articles that we brought with us is Parisot's face. He is the only one who tells stories, gives accounts, offers justifications. We reread all the articles. Is it possible that none of Jeanne's daughters, her ex-husband, close friends, relatives, her cousin Luc Prunet, said anything about the tragedy or even just offered an anecdote about her life? Nobody talks, only him. Just one voice, for years.

His statements are all conflicting. He claims Victor Leduc gave permission to immediately cremate Jeanne's body. However, he could not have legally done so, as the two had divorced some time earlier. Parisot hides safely behind words attributed to a man who can no longer contradict him: Leduc has been dead for twenty-five years. The archivist repeats over and over, as though seeking to remove any suspicion, that "as her husband had warned journalists from 'Le Monde' who wanted to publish that Jeanne had perhaps met a different end: Jeanne died by accident, that's all, there is no mystery".

It may be so, but we do not find any trace of Leduc's public stance in the French press. On that death there is only a small and unobtrusive article.

In the meantime, we go back to the building at 205 boulevard Vincent Auriol. We resume our search for other witnesses. This time the fate helps us. A tenant tells us that he did not know Jeanne, but he tells us that a former policeman lives on the first floor. We ring and find out that it's the same man who helped us two days earlier. He's a former chief commissioner from the Paris judicial police, now retired. He and his wife welcome us into their living room with kindness and cordiality. They have lived there for ages, ever since the palace was built. The woman remembers her former neighbour and tells us: "Jeanne was on the eleventh floor, she was a very shy and suspicious person, and she did not let anyone into the house. She was very aggressive. In the last period before her death, when I met her in the hallway, the signs of the problems alcohol was causing her were evident. She had a yellowish complexion; her liver was probably malfunctioning." She pauses as if to think, then she adds: "She was so surly and jealous of her privacy that we all thought she was hiding her father's paintings in her house and was afraid of being robbed".

Few people enjoyed the trust of poor Amedeo' s daughter. Probably a relative trust. Her eldest daughter Anne, the one with a severe handicap, was the closest to her. She had the keys to the apartment, but could not live with her mother, because the house was too small. It was a single room, which included a kitchenette and some furniture that serve also as a living room. With the exception of the bathroom, everything fits inside an environment of less than thirty square meters. We met the person who took care of the cleaning: "Small but always in disorder, often very dirty," Maria tells us. She is elderly now, but has a very vivid memory. "There were young boys who frequented the house, some were coloured. In the building it was rumoured that one of them might have killed her," she confided to us, with some embarrassment and concern she might tarnish the memory of the deceased.

Perhaps Jeanne had a kind of bipolarity: suspicious when sober, uninhibited when in the thrall of alcohol. We dug up this apparent contradiction in her behaviour with the invaluable help of the journalist Luisa Nannipieri. According to what she learned from her sources, the police followed various lines of investigation, but without success, and they ultimately closed the case. It must have been a hurried investigation, however, because Maria tells us that she was never questioned.

The perfect plot of a cold case

Trying to learn more, we go to consult the criminal archives and check with the local police station. "The documents have been destroyed: the trivial incidents on file date back no more than twenty years. If there were any, they would remain confidential and would only be available to family members, not to journalists." This is how the police respond.

In France, therefore, it would be impossible to reopen the case. The writers of TV series will have to find other subjects, other places, this cold case cannot be re-examined. Yet the plot would fit perfectly.

No one can rule out accidental death, but it would be negligent, as it has been so for many years, not to look at the bigger picture. If it wasn't for the crazy variant of the four students, the "Froglia project" in Livorno, the broader plans of the forgers would probably have remained a secret. A group of misshapen caryatids would have inflated the economic assets of art merchants and traffickers. After the party, the celebrations of the centenary, that committee of "experts" would have definitively held a pre-eminent role on any academic matters regarding Modigliani. The Legal Archives would be excluded - that is to say Jeanne Modigliani and her "faithful" colleagues, already subjected to a media lynching.

There would be no trace of Christian Parisot, of the Guastalla brothers or of Carlo Pepi, the later guardians of the Amedeo Modigliani birthplace.

Farewell to the requirement of credibility when certifying artworks, a mouth-watering business coveted by many.

They had to find a remedy. Jeanne was certainly not prepared to give up over those chisel-sculpted rocks produced by a docker. Nevertheless, she would have to be gentler with those now in charge of the game. A more subdued tone would perhaps be useful to get closer to the "winners". A letter attributed to Jeanne recommends "Caution... and let us hope that we can soon set up a committee of experts." You could earn admission into the procession of those great "luminaries" who, when the first stone emerged from the murky waters of the canals, glimpsed the "mystical" signs and "the unmistakable" touch of the Leghorn master. There was only one obstacle to overcome - they had to convince Jeanne not to launch a counterattack.

We begin to imagine what happened that day before the closed door of the *studio*. Standing at the eleventh floor elevator door, we reconstruct the possible dynamics, starting with the newspaper articles from those days. On July 29, when reporting the news of Jeanne's death in Paris, Lorenzo Bocchi of the *Corriere della Sera* wrote: "At first the condition in which she arrived the hospital led them to think it might have been a crime". Words repeated and accentuated with passion, anger, resignation and a pinch of horror by Carlo Pepi: "I immediately thought that they had killed her, she was an inconvenient witness. She was a danger to the counterfeiters. I got two phone calls from Paris, in the first one from Parisot who told me she had fallen down the stairs, and a second telling me she had fallen off a step ladder and hit her head on the refrigerator handle. "Parisot, be careful on what you say!" I reply. "Don't worry, they've cremated her," he replied".

The spider's web

Alibi. It is the Latin term for "elsewhere". I was elsewhere. It was just such a shaky alibi to stir our initial doubts: there was a body; there were many possible motives; and there could have just as many suspicions, and suspects.

We step back thirty-five years. We contact Parisot and ask him to tell us what he remembers of those days. He starts explaining that it was July 25 when he went up to the eleventh floor, but he does not explain how he got inside the building. He said he had come directly from Turkey, and arrived that same day after a night stopover in Rome.

He tells us he was still in Paris on July 19 when he picked up the anonymous letter from Livorno. He claims to have shown it to Jeanne and left immediately afterwards for Livorno in order to deliver it to the then councillor Claudio Frontera, though stopping first in Turin to see his parents. Then he left for Stromboli, from there to Rome, where he embarked for Istanbul. From the Turkish capital he moved to a beach about four hundred kilometres south, also in Turkey, where he was stopped by the police because his girlfriend was wearing a bikini. Therefore, he decided to leave for Rome. In the capital, the Guastalla brothers telephoned to tell him about the heads that had been found. It's July 24th. The Guastallas have never said they contacted Parisot in Rome. How would they know which hotel he was staying in? At that time there were no cell phones. Meanwhile he learns of the letter in which Jeanne, on July 20, had asked him to return immediately. How? He claims that someone had given it to his ex-wife and she had tracked him down. But where? How did he get a phone call while he was in Turkey, traveling between Istanbul and the beach?

Let's try again on our own. If the anonymous letter arrived on July 19, Parisot was supposedly in Paris, at or near Jeanne's house. The mailbox of the Institute Modigliani Archives was in fact a few steps from 205 boulevard Vincent Auriol. We can imagine that he left at on the 20th at the latest. Between the 20th and the 21st he would have met the Councillor Frontera in Livorno, to hand him the letter. Then he supposedly left for Stromboli. Unless he teleported, he would have arrived on the island on the 22nd. He took his time to water the garden; then he went go to Rome, his destination Istanbul, where he clearly suggests he arrived on the 23rd. Then he resumed his journey towards the south of Turkey. He arrived at the beach, put on his swimsuit. The police of General Kenan Evren, a president democratically elected only two years earlier after a coup d'état and two years of dictatorship, pointed their Kalashnikovs at the two half naked Italian tourists. Parisot and his partner decide to return to Italy. They hurry back to Istanbul and from there they set out again for Rome.

This reconstruction is less than plausible. Let's start with times: unless you own a private jet, it wouldn't have been possible for Parisot to tour half of Europe in less than five days, especially thirty-five years ago. Three of the six destinations he claimed to have reached are far from airports and two of these, at least in those years, were not particularly close at hand. Claudio Frontera categorically denies meeting him alone for that letter. The Guastalla brothers don't remember calling him.

Let's go back to the documents and to the press releases from Paris. Anyone who has heard one of the rare television interviews with Jeanne, like the one broadcast a few years earlier by Italian state Television, will have noticed her vocabulary. She expressed herself in Italian prose, as if reciting passages from a novel. Perhaps she really lived in a bubble of fiction, detached as she was from reality. The press releases, sent to the agencies from Livorno on July 25 and 27 by the secretaries of Casa Natale Modigliani in Jeanne's name, are instead flat, uninformative, even ambiguous. It is unlikely, indeed impossible in our opinion, that Jeanne could have dictated them. She certainly wouldn't have used phrases that could suggest that she, while recommending caution, wanted to appoint a committee of experts: as was widely known, she was convinced that any sculpture eventually found in the canals would be a fake, because in her opinion her father would never have thrown them away.

In fact, those statements they are not hers. Giorgio Guastalla, with his characteristic concision and caution, tells us today: "Many years have passed and I don't remember it well. It is however possible that it was Parisot speaking in Jeanne's name. Every time they called us they were together, and after greeting us, he would put her on the phone". Parisot himself confirms this: "We were always together to take calls. We had a headset linked to the receiver". We reiterate that by his own admission, Parisot has admitted that on the 25th, Jeanne was dying and on the 27th, she was in a coma in hospital until her death in the afternoon. On the 24th, according to the same archivist, he was not yet in Paris, at least so he says. It would therefore seem to exclude that the poor woman had spoken with Giorgio Guastalla so shortly before her death.

Other fundamental documents to clarify the dynamics of those days are: the ticket dated July 20, which would be made public only a number of weeks later; and the famous letter dated July 26 and intended for Carlo

Pepi. The same hand, the hand of a forger, is likely to have written them: probably that of Christian Parisot, according to the report of the graphologist that we commissioned. For a few days, we were allowed to borrow the letter from Carlo Pepi, who has held it as a keepsake.

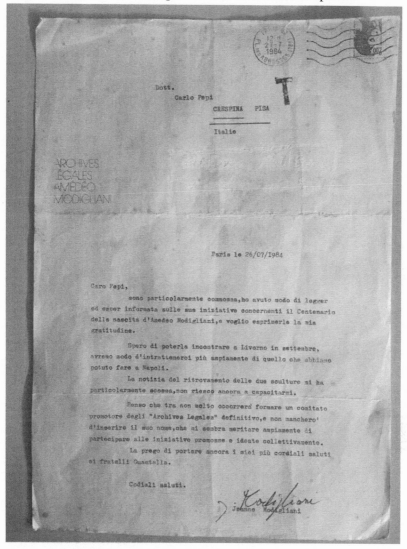

It is accompanied by the envelope in which it arrived in Crespina some time later. It was sent on the 27th when Jeanne was in intensive care in the hospital. Someone posted it in place des Abbesses, in the 18th arrondissement, certainly before 12 noon on July 27. The place is located a few junctions from Pigalle, towards the Sacré-Coeur and Montmartre. About seven kilometres from boulevard Vincent Auriol. It takes at least forty minutes to get there from Jeanne's house, by subway or by car.

The only one who has always said that the letter is false is Parisot. Too bad he didn't also say that the signature may also be fake, and it could be his.[68]

"Jeanne only signed with a black pen, the Pilot ... its name is ... here it is ... it's called Ped ... Pad Clear ... that's it," he tells us. His pauses between "here it is" and "it's called" cause us to assume that he is reading the name of the pen, which he is probably holding while he's on the phone with us. The letter is in fact signed with a black fine-tipped pen.

We had wondered how that envelope got there, so we did some research. "Neither now nor then has there been a sorting centre in that zone. It is impossible that a letter posted in the thirteenth district was sorted in the eighteenth district," we are told by the Paris post office. But it was posted by someone who on July 26 knew Jeanne was forever out of the game and could not deny it.

Let's assume that the archivist had a meeting with Jeanne precisely at 11 am on the 25th. She would have been the one to open the door and let him in. Parisot was bringing startling news: the previous day two heads had been recovered from the ditch in Livorno. Now it was necessary to

---

[68] Parisot wrote us an email dated April 1, 2019 at 10.51: "in order to understand Carlo Pepi's position in all this, it will be enough for you to verify his "origins   " in Crespina, and his utopian position in 1983 in Livorno. Then check the date of the famous "letter" (now known to be a forgery) signed by Jeanne Modigliani (never) sent to him by Jeanne Modigliani. Why does Pepi boast about his affiliation and written appointment by Jeanne Modigliani, when in reality, at that date, the lady was already in a comatose state, hospitalised in Paris, as evidenced by the date of her admission to hospital ...".

understand which position would be not only the fairest and most correct for the Legal Archives to take, but also the most favourable for everyone.

It was necessary to keep Jeanne away from Livorno to avoid ruining the "business". Furthermore, the letter that reaches Pepi is an effort to enlist his inadvertent support in some sort of proxy war. Whoever wrote it - certainly not Jeanne - wanted to use him in the role which so many newspapers had attributed to him: Don Quixote. And unfortunately, he was destined to run into the rotors of many windmills over the years to come.

Unlike Jeanne, Parisot had been to the Tuscan town several times during that period; he understood the power of the Durbés. Perhaps he also knew how dense and intricate the plot was. Maybe he had other ideas about what to do. "Jeanne wanted bring forward her departure for Livorno, which had been scheduled for September," Giorgio Guastalla told us. Thus, we might imagine (although it remains a hypothetical reconstruction) that, in the face of the woman's stubborn insistence, voices were raised. This could have resulted in a heated discussion and even a quarrel. Hence, perhaps an accidental fall, which was fatal.

But the overall picture also opens up a different scenario. In giving the news of the death to Carlo Pepi, on the morning of 28, Parisot provides three different versions, as Pepi himself tells us: "She fell off a ladder and hit her head." At home, there is no built-in bookcase, let alone a ladder to access the upper shelves. "She hit her head on the refrigerator handle." And the more imaginative story: "She fell down the stairs to the cellar ... and died." To us on the other hand the archivist, calling those days to mind, says he remembers going there at around 11 in the morning, knocking on the door but getting no answer. "So I went down and told the concierge," he declares. "I asked her: 'Have you seen Madame?' She said no. That's it, I left. Then in the evening Leduc called me to see if I had any news." This is a change from the first version he gave us in June 2018. "The concierge herself told Victor Leduc, her ex-husband, the next day. I left, and later received the message that she had died in hospital. They had found her dying. She hadn't answered the bell and so they knocked down the door."

The press agency Ansa breaks the news exactly at 14.17 on July 28. A second news release follows at 2.20pm. It is assumed that the second release was made after someone confirmed the news, perhaps Parisot, when reached by telephone. An article from October 10, 1998 by Maurizio

Silvestri of *Il Tirreno* highlights the contradictions which appear regarding what has been said about Jeanne Modigliani's death by Christian Parisot in the immediate aftermath. In the interview reported by the same newspaper on September 17, 1984, again by Silvestri, the archivist had in fact said: "The day Jeanne died, we had a meeting. In the morning around 8.30, I called her, but no one answered. I tried twice a little later, but the line was busy. On the fourth and fifth attempt, the line was free again, but there was still no answer. At that point I got worried and went to Jeanne's house; the woman was bleeding to death, and perhaps she had been lying on the ground for a few hours." In 1998, however, he denies this: "How can you claim that I found Jeanne dying? I was in Turkey and arrived in Paris the next day. I never saw Jeanne in that condition. I was not there ... I don't know they got confused, added something, misunderstood".

In the interview, reproduced in a book by Giovanni Morandi,[69] the journalist Silvestri recorded a longer conversation with Parisot. "I arrived in Paris after Jeanne's death, I met her ex-husband thirty-two hours after the accident and he explained that unfortunately the lady was already in a coma; the news made me fold up in pain." "I was in Turkey during the dredging of the Ditches, I came back thirty-two hours after what happened."

The journalist argues that in the statement at the time he had reported other details and that the interview was never contradicted: "Unfortunately the lady was the victim of a very serious accident due to certain matters. She was hospitalised and unfortunately, three days later, she died". "I arrived a day later ... I didn't even see her in the hospital." "I had an appointment with her, not on the day of the accident but the following day: I had scheduled it before I even left, around June. Then she sent me some letters which I found and she said: 'Come quickly,' and I went immediately. But it changed nothing in any case, because the accident had already happened ... Jeanne did not fall down the stairs, she just fell." The journalist reminds him of "that famous letter announcing the discovery of the heads". He replies, "The police did not find it. It was sent to the

---

[69] Giovanni Morandi, *La beffa di Modigliani*, (the Modigliani Mockery), Polistampa, Florence 2008.

Archives, to Jeanne Modigliani. She handed it to me and I gave it to the Carabinieri in Rome".

"The letter is dated July 19, didn't Jeanne give it to you?" "No, I had already left, I found it later, and she left it to me among the letters that we exchanged in our common secretariat."

"It might have been true, but he would have answered anything else in the same way, because he had a way of speaking that served to conceal rather than to reveal." Thus wrote Gabriel García Márquez describes a character in *Chronicle of a Death Foretold*. Someone like Parisot. In effect, all those we had met before speaking to him had warned us: "Be careful, you will see, in the end he will convince you. He will try, and he will succeed with his way of speaking and with his manner, that he is right, that he is telling the truth". At the end of our phone call we wondered not once but several times: what if he is right? What if things really went just like Parisot says? He has however given too many different versions for us not to keep looking for the truth.

The right to truth

A long time passed and the friends, the people Jeanne knew and spent time with in the neighbourhood were mostly her peers. If we want to find them, therefore, we will have to seek them mainly among the elderly, many of who would be around a hundred. It is hard to find anyone still alive or able to provide us with the sequence of events of that July 1984. But in the end we got lucky when we managed to contact Daniel Cornibert.

Daniel was the owner of the café-restaurant that was at the time called Renoir; today it is known as La Place, at 194 avenue de Choisy, overlooking place d'Italie. He has been retired since 2007. He is himself a painter and art enthusiast; he had named his restaurant after Pierre-Auguste Renoir.

Today he lives between Paris and Avignon. His passion for art brought him together with Jeanne: the two became friends. We reach him over the phone and he seems to want to let it all out, finally, after so many years. To free himself from those thoughts on the death of his friend which still trouble him today: "She was a good person. Like me, many think she was killed. Her ex-husband, whom I only saw once, never wanted to put in a report. A doctor friend of ours, who lived in the building, told me they found her in the house with her head smashed. It seems she had hit it on a low table, where she put the colours for her paintings. But, she was five feet tall, how could she have fallen so hard that she injured herself? Many people used to visit that house. Many Italians, they seemed to me like mafia members; all well dressed, all looking to have her authenticate paintings by her father. They also offered her forgeries. She drank a lot and obviously, she wasn't often sober. She also dated young boys from the area; she was seeing a black man who worked at the town hall".

"But did you ever tell the police these things?" we ask him. "No, they didn't ask me, I don't think there has ever been an investigation." The house was cramped, and first Maria, the housekeeper of that floor, then Berta, the wife of one of the concierges at the time, and finally Daniel have all confirmed that there was no stepladder in the apartment.

Let's assume that the room, the only one in the house, had a surface of 25 square meters, so say, 5 meters by 5 wide. Let's try to draw it in our mind. A kitchen, with at least the essentials: a hob, usually 60x50, a countertop of some ten centimetres, a sink, another 40 centimetres, and the refrigerator, another 60, so at least 200 cm x 60 cm . A French bed, 140 cm x 190 cm. A small table for two people, one square meter. A tiny sideboard, and finally, measuring at least 200 cm x 60 cm, this portentous low table.

There is little space to move around; it is easy to stumble, but you certainly cannot run or move at a fast pace, lose balance completely, and then fall heavily, hitting the edge of that damned small table. Jeanne, we recall, had been using a walking cane for months, which would imply moving slowly, reducing any chances of stumbling and falling heavily. These details, if they had been analysed at the time of the events, would perhaps have been enough to justify further investigation. However, no one noticed them; no one seemed to have any interest in spotting them. It was too much effort to coordinate an investigation between Livorno and Paris. Then the crematorium furnace, hurriedly lit, obliterated what remained of Amedeo's unfortunate daughter.

The tragic event took place a long time ago. As well as Jeanne, other key figures have passed away during these long years: Victor Leduc, her daughter Anne, the concierge and the doctor who took care of Jeanne. The other concierge is now retired and has returned to his country of origin, Portugal. We tracked him down, but he said he didn't remember anything about those days, and that he had probably been on vacation. The police did not keep the records of what they had done in that case. In the hospital, the only clue we could find lies in the poor annotation on the death. No one can say if it was a murder, there aren't many clues left, but we know that in those days someone must have lied. He would have done so knowing he could not be proven wrong, at least until this moment.

We do not know what role Parisot played in the affair of Jeanne's death; we can't say if he was in that apartment, if they had a fight or if they simply witnessed her fall. However, we can argue that while she was dying, he had no scruples about impersonating the poor victim for the umpteenth time in a letter to Pepi. What made him act like this? Is it a random concatenation of events or is it the result of a project planned out over a long period of time?

Since at least June 1984, Modigliani's daughter had initiated a correspondence which indicated a stiff conflict with the city administration and the ministry, but today we know from the graphologist's report that these documents may not have been signed by Jeanne, but by Parisot. The same thing applies to the communiqués on the discovery of the fake stone works. We believe that the clues we found, although not strictly connected to the death through a specific causal link, are consistent, precise and grave.

There are many of them, and they converge on the same point: the falsification of deeds and letters. We are convinced that our reconstruction can withstand any possible objection, at least according to the facts we know. Handwriting expertise is a scientific fact. The chronological phases are well documented. The deeds and documents we have analysed are in our possession. Every word we exchanged with our counterparts were recorded, for our own protection and theirs. We made use of highly-respected experts who gave their valuable contributions. We therefore tried to demonstrate, papers in hand, how the business that revolves around the world of art, in this case the works of the Leghorn master, have often been tainted by impropriety and crime.

We tried in every way to speak in person to Laure or Sarah. When we found their addresses, we were very careful not to overstep the limits of respect for privacy and the unwillingness to reopen old wounds. We asked them to give us a hearing, but it was in vain.

We would have liked to tell them what we discovered, what we know today about what really happened in their family past. With a letter delivered by a courier, we tried to explain the importance of a meeting that could have changed their lives for the better.

Over the phone Laure, in a gentle but firm voice, told us she does not want to return to the subject, she doesn't want to talk any further about that painful story; she will knows it is unjust, but that she wants to forget it. Even so, we went to her home in the hope of convincing her of our good intentions. We took a letter from a lawyer who was willing to assist her in France and Italy.

We even went up to the fourth floor of an old Parisian building in the 11th arrondissement and stopped in front of her closed door. We remained on the landing, observing and contemplating the modest means of a pensioner who was now alone and elderly. The paintings of her grandfather are sold in record breaking auctions; merchandising evaluations of the Modigliani name alone are worth millions of dollars around the world; the exhibitions of the great Leghorn painter enrich those who engage, even unduly, in evaluating his work. On top of that flight of stairs, between one door and another, so much normality. A corridor of the building leads to a row of flats where the bathrooms are external and shared.

Laure's daughter, Sarah, having graduated in Sociology, now sells homemade perfumes that she makes with some friends. She didn't want to meet us either, and she even blocked us on Facebook. Today, given the conditions in which Modì's granddaughters live, they cannot perhaps afford to fight to reassert their rights. We believe, and not just because of Christian Parisot's statements, that he is the one who, since the early 1980s, has provided financial support for Jeanne's daughters and granddaughter. After the arrest of the archivist in 2012, the situation between the parties changed. Since that time, there has been a lengthy legal dispute between Parisot and Jeanne's heirs, who were ultimately forced to succumb. For now, the only winner in this complicated affair is Christian Gregory Parisot.

Post Scriptum. The possible reasons for a non-trivial death

A death is never trivial. The error is already in the adjective with which it was classified that led to possibly criminal motives and clues being ignored, the same ones that made us suspicious. What were the motives, impulses and reasons, if any, for which someone could have been induced to commit the crime? The motives have their roots in the personality of the person who acts. They are psychological factors that pertain to the affective sphere: instincts, feelings. Like jealousy and revenge, so too can the instinct for self-preservation be a motive.

"Self-preservation" should not be understood exclusively as the instinct to protect one's own life. The benefit to be preserved can also be power, honour, money, relationships. When we think of Jeanne, of the crime scene that we surmise may have been "set up" in boulevard Vincent Auriol between July 25 and 26, 1984, we are reminded of that block in the centre of St. Petersburg where the two sisters, principal characters and victims in the novel by Fyodor Dostoevskij, *Crime and Punishment,* died. When Raskolnikov enters the house of the old usurer, he can't foresee that in the other room there is the younger sister, a stranger to the shady business of her loan shark sibling.

Jeanne's hypothetical murderer may also have planned his crime but was faced with unpredictable factors. In Dostoevsky's book, the unexpected is represented by Raskolnikov's encounter with the workers who were renovating an apartment on the floor below.

If anyone left poor Jeanne on the ground, dying, he may have done so for two reasons. In the first case, the crime was not premeditated and was, rather, the consequence of an instinctive gesture during a quarrel; the injury appeared so serious that death must have seemed immediate to the murderer, so he would have fled leaving behind that supposedly lifeless body. Like the Russian student in the novel, the aggressor, leaving the scene hastily and with his heart in turmoil, will certainly have left traces somewhere, even if he tried not to. When he walked away from the site of the accident or crime, the hypothetical killer must have sought to provide himself with an alibi and to ensure the range of possible motives was as wide as possible.

If, on the other hand - and it is the second conceivable reason - the murder was premeditated, who might have had an interest in killing Jeanne? The discovery of the heads in Livorno, as we said, would point to a plot that reads like a detective novel.

Eighth Crime Scene
Worldwide Interbank Financial

A *turnover worth 15 trillion*

Even in crime, the virtual overlaps with reality. Today we live in a sensational paradox: everything is based on money, real money but it has been dematerialised and lives inside the digital meanders of the internet. It hops like a virtual grasshopper from one corner of the globe to the other, shifting from account to account at the speed of light.

We decided to set this last crime scene in a metaphysical space, the immaterial scenario of money transfers. To do this we borrowed the name of the company that invented the Swift code (Society for Worldwide Interbank Financial Telecommunication). Of course, we would like to stress that this does not imply any accusations of connivance on the part of the respectable company born in Brussels in 1973: it has no part in the events we are discussing, and it is totally unrelated to the Modigliani affair. However, it is precisely thanks to the interbank system, guaranteed by the important Belgian institution, that small or large sums can be transferred virtually from one point of the planet to another. The title only serves to explain how this can happen with a simple click, in complete safety and lightning fast.

Now the certifications, the expert appraisal that give value to artistic works, enter the scene. We believe that in international money laundering cases that are perpetrated through works of art, the authentications, simple pieces of paper, have taken the place of those IOUs and of those post-dated checks once examined by Giovanni Falcone, the investigating magistrate murdered by the mafia in 1992. By studying these scraps, he began to understand how the mafia could launder rivers of money bathed in blood.

Today authentications of works of art have effectively become titles of credit that are difficult to trace. Those who own them hold a store of value that is hidden from prying eyes. Alternatively, they can simply pass it on to others, sending them by post and then receiving the equivalent in cash on any current account, at any bank, in any country. In these cases, the transaction is always screened through an offshore company or nominee, so it often remains hidden from government authorities. But with that piece of paper, even weapons, drugs or trafficked human beings can be bought using just a postal package and a mouse click.

The turnover produced by traditional crime, concerning precisely the cases we mentioned above, is estimated at up to $2.5 trillion per year. The amount creamed off by professional money launderers, who among their other tools of the trade can use real or forged artworks for this purpose, is 10 percent, that is, $250 billion per year. An immoral profit of outrageous proportions: "just" $260 billion would be enough to settle the debt that African countries "owe" to the rest of the world.[70] There are few risks for those who perform these trades, which are as easy as they are sophisticated. If anything, the problem is ours, given broader society's almost complete lack of alarm when faced with criminality of such proportions.

This type of business is unknown to most. There are no obvious casualties; bullets do not fly, and there are no moped snatchers, drug dealers or prostitutes on street corners. Yet, the value of such crime is very high. The noise it produces is subdued and muffled, that of clinking cocktail glasses, of business lunches, of chatter in sophisticated lounges. These people don't bother anyone, they do not scare anyone with a balaclava pulled over their heads, yet they rob billions every year that should be paid into the state coffers for the common good.

The most serious aspect is that these gentlemen (so to speak), with their soft-shoe embezzlement, are an indispensable tool in helping to make mafia crimes profitable. In fact for any crime committed by criminal organisations (but also by isolated criminals), the financial revenue has no value, because it cannot be used until the loot is "washed". While for crimes of a small or medium size, for example petty theft, the proceeds can be used immediately by the material author of the crime (he can resell the stolen goods independently or through a fence), in the case of large illegal

---

[70] See *Il debito dei paesi africani*, «Atlante», Treccani, February 2 2018.

income, such as that deriving from typical mafia activities, the use of the money can only take place after the proceeds have been reintroduced into the legal economic circuit.

International money laundering found that this modern technique has an extraordinary value: the trade in fake works of art, the falsification of documents, as well as the fraud that sometimes accompanies it are crimes that when discovered, are rarely punished with jail terms and, as such, they are often dismissed relatively quickly. Thus the whole circus is feasible, and involves minimal risk. It is quite another thing when using traditional money laundering channels such as, for example, those that require the direct transfer of capital through the material movement of money.

By way of example - a hypothesis that we have also put forward in the academic field - the simulation of money laundering to disguise tax evasion. Let's take a company that at the end of its budget year has 10 million euros. The general manager, who in this case could also be the beneficial owner, proposes to the board of directors that the company invests the profits from the year just ended in works of art in order to increase its assets while reducing its declared profit for the year and hence its tax bill.

Let's say he then makes contact with one of the many fraudulent structures around. For a few thousand euro, this structure obtains both a counterfeit artwork and the related certification of authenticity; the fake artwork, endowed with a tailor-made record of its history, is then secured in a Swiss safe. Upon the proposal of the general manager, the board of directors authorises the purchase of the painting in question for 10 million euros. Further along the line, the manager will have built up his own beautiful money laundering network with offshore companies and trusts that, through a cunningly structured transaction, will appear to be the owner of the work, while hiding whoever is really behind the purchase.

The investment is therefore recorded in the financial statements as an asset of the company. After a few months, before the close of the following financial year, the general manager stages his comedy. He appoints an art critic, preferably a famous one, to go and visit the precious artistic heritage, which in the meantime has remained in the Swiss safe. As soon as the expert checks the work stored there, he notices it is a fake. The result of the consultation upsets the directors, who suddenly discover they have been scammed.

All the managing director/scammer has to do now is file a complaint against the seller, the one who was behind those companies which sold the artwork and authenticated it, and who may in fact turn out to be a Burmese farmer. The result of this is that the company has been swindled, the Burmese farmer can never be identified and in the meantime 10 million euros have been shipped to the offshore account of the director of the company in question. At the same time, the operation is recorded in the balance sheet as a loss and as a result, no-one will ever pay taxes on the money.

According to "The Independent", 20 percent of art in most large British museums is fake. At present, these percentages are only inferred, but they might turn out to be even higher if you consider that there are at least three channels, the ones we have described. The first concerns the attribution to famous painters of works made by students in their workshops. These are always beautiful works which, as the art historian and expert Claudio Metzger explained to us clearly, were often meticulously monitored as the work progressed and sometimes even refined by the hand of the master. They are not considered forgeries, provided that the true author is named. The second channel includes works completely made by other artists based on sketches, drafts or even freestyle reinterpretations of original works. This is the case with Modigliani, who died prematurely. Finally, we find the work of very skilled forgers, who, as we have seen, possess and have demonstrated an exceptional ability to imitate the style of others.

A false work, introduced into the exhibition circuit - as happened in the events that we have described in this book - acquires historicity and would therefore be welcome beyond the sacred threshold of a museum.

This would not be possible for any of the works produced via the channels we have listed without the help of criminals specialised in the counterfeiting of supporting documentation. There is a strong relationship between fake works and international money laundering. As for Modigliani (but we could mention other comparable cases), the original paintings and sculptures, which are well known and have been included in Ambrogio Ceroni's catalogue, have been traced for over half a century. The various changes of ownership are known in many cases. On some occasions, the presumed origin is also recounted in fanciful tales.

A striking example concerns one of the two paintings seized in Palermo. D'Atanasio, now under investigation for forgery and fraud, elaborated on the story of the painting which was later impounded as he inaugurated the exhibition at Palazzo Bonocore. He even claimed that the canvas on which it was painted was a gift that Paul Alexandre had given to Amedeo on his return from the First World War. A sheet of canvas that came from the Moroccan legion. Unfortunately for D'Atanasio, it is now certain that the doctor and close friend of Modigliani had no further chance to meet the painter, after returning to Paris from the war.

Art, money laundering and tax havens

"Whether we like it or not, art is used to avoid taxes and for tax evasion. And it can be used to launder money. A lot of people are using it for this purpose. While art seems to be concerned only with beauty, when seen as a business it is a market full of shadows. That should be corrected, or it will be damaged." It was 2015 when in Davos, during the work of the International Forum, the economist Nouriel Roubini made these heavy accusations in a meeting sponsored by the Financial Times.[71] Since then nothing has been done to prevent cases of evasion and money laundering through works of art and archaeological finds from growing exponentially. In the meantime, and across the world, justice has little concept of the seriousness of this type of crime.

The Italian mafia which, if no longer the largest, is certainly among the most powerful criminal organisations on the planet, began to invest in this area by illegally selling archaeological treasures stolen from our country. Matteo Messina Denaro's father, Francesco, was considered a "grave robber" as well as a mobster. For many years, precious and rare archaeological finds from the South of Italy were shipped abroad and sold

---

[71] Francesca Sironi, *L'arte va offshore: così il commercio delle opere aggira il fisco*, «L'Espresso», December 13 2016.

to important museums through channels that proved capable of penetrating the international market through contacts with Switzerland.

In this area too, the mafia was a trailblazer. Many others queued up to access this channel for the illicit financing of criminal activity. Money laundering through works of art is a highway used by Italian and foreign organisations of all kinds in which the circuit of fake works is custom-made, allowing the proceeds of crime to reach their destination faster and with less risk. Mafias and traffickers of all sorts on the virtual market exchange any type of currency, information, drugs, weapons, true and forged paintings, finding a formidable ally in the "deep web".

The Carabinieri that uncovered and seized the alleged fakes of Genoa provided a template for an effective investigation methodology. However, in general, there is no easy connection between investigators across international boundaries, particularly those investigating the trafficking of works of art. International requests for cooperation for this type of offence are so rare as to be almost unique, and formulating them can be complex. There is no national catalogue of fakes that have been impounded, such as the many Modigliani forgeries mentioned earlier. And yet, it would be easier to produce one for Modigliani than for many others, considering the small number of works that can be definitively attributed to the Maestro due to the brevity of his life. When charges of forgery, fraud and receiving stolen goods lapse because of the statute of limitations, the works must be returned to the rightful owners even if they have been proven to be forgeries. Where cases are closed with a conviction, then by law, such works should be destroyed. But often they return to the circuit of worldwide sales instead, perhaps appearing in exhibitions organised on the other side of the planet.

The story of the well-known Chinese art dealer and business man Gao Ping[72] is emblematic. In 2007 a cultural association, the Fundación arte y cultura, opened in Spain. Meanwhile, in Beijing, he was among the owners of the Center of Contemporary Art Iberia which, at four thousand square meters, is one of the largest spaces dedicated to art in all of China. In

---

[72] Luca Rinaldi, *Un gallerista della «Madrid bene», era la faccia della mafia cinese in Spagna*, «Linkiesta», November 5, 2012.

Madrid, he had sponsored galleries and exhibitions, and also collaborated with Ivam (Valencian Institute of Modern Art). During one of these exhibitions, he was photographed with King Juan Carlos. In 2011, the Spanish magazine «Descubrir el Arte» honours him for the promotion of Spanish art abroad. Such a well-known man, powerful enough to be called "the emperor", ended up in jail in the Iberian Peninsula for colossal tax evasion and for money laundering exceeding one billion euros. In one of his warehouses, they found about 5 million euro in cash.

He had been seen as a patron of art galleries on his way to emulating the Guggenheim dynasty. He sponsored a football team and was head of a plethora of companies that imported goods from China without paying taxes. He evaded 17 million euros in taxes. Two policemen and a politician were arrested with him. The money was recycled through affiliates of Gao's holding company or kept in tax havens thanks to the help of compliant Spanish intermediaries. There are alleged to have been two hundred entrepreneurs who, availing themselves of his cover, exported capital to various tax havens, evading the Spanish tax system.

Money laundering through works of art is made easier by the countless paintings that come out every year from the so-called "City of forgers". Dafen Oil Painting Village is a neighbourhood in the city of Shenzhen, a metropolis in southern China.[73] It became famous in the nineties for the serial reproductions of works of great painters such as Vincent van Gogh, Salvador Dalí and Claude Monet. In those years, it was believed that about 60 percent of the world's production of fake oil paintings came just from Dafen. The products then took different routes depending on the skill of the artist and the quality of the work. From the Chinese province and world markets to the salons of the *nouveau riche* and the prestigious galleries of China; from there, to the rest of the planet.

Works of this kind are therefore also useful to criminals looking to invest money from illegal activities; when they launder it through art, they often give an exorbitant value to objects that do not have any. There are many

---

[73] Jamie Fullerton, *La nuova borghesia cinese trasforma la capitale dei «falsi» in un fervido laboratorio di opere autentiche*, «The Telegraph», June 13, 2018 (reproduced in Thema-international.it).

cases in the press that link works of art to laundering and to mafias. The 'Ndrangheta had used a leading exponent of a crime family from the Gallina district of Reggio Calabria, Gianluca Landonio, a fugitive arrested in Barcelona in 2016.[74] The family has always laundered its dirty money through paintings: Guttuso, Modigliani, Arman, Schifano are just some of the artists that the clan deals with. Not all of them originals and some produced by the "schools" rather than the maestros.

During the operation which leads to the arrest of Landonio, fifty-one paintings are seized, for a total value of over 60 million euro. Another Calabrian presumed to be a member of the 'Ndrangheta crime family is Gioacchino Campolo, who accumulated assets worth approximately 400 million euros with his slot machine business. He, one of the kings of video poker, was sentenced to sixteen years in prison for extortion. He invested in Ligabue, Fontana, Dalí, Sironi and De Chirico. Who knows whether they were authentic works or forgeries, just like the thirty-two artworks by Miró and Picasso seized at Malpensa Airport in 2015 after arriving from Medellín, Colombia on a private cargo plane which was heading for the rather surprising destination of Teramo.[75]

We have direct knowledge concerning the bankruptcy of the famed Hottinger, one of Switzerland's oldest private banks, since we worked on the case in a professional capacity. Its luxurious Geneva salons, where bankers would meet important investors, were shut down following the discovery of an international scam worth at least 100 million Swiss francs.

The show was orchestrated by Fabien Gaglio, a French national of Italian origin who was at the time a well-placed employee at the bank. Gaglio had been employed in the London office of Rothschild. After a conviction for falsifying his qualifications, he moved to Geneva taking with him some of his customers, including his own Milanese relatives: Alfonso Ziribotti and family. Before syphoning off the money (using a system that his lawyers

---

[74] *Arrestato Landonio pericoloso trafficante d'arte*, «Il Sole 24 Ore», December 22 2016.

[75] *Falsi Picasso e Miró fatti in Colombia sequestrati a Malpensa*, «Askanews», December 14, 2015.

have been attempting to characterise as a "Ponzi scheme",[76] but which is nothing of the sort), he prepared, or rather he refined, a dense network of money laundering.

Gaglio used a number of existing structures already employed by one of the most expert money launderers in Ticino, the Baron Filippo Dollfus de Volckersberg.[77] Hundreds of accounts, offshore companies and trusts, activated to bounce millions of euros from one part of the globe to the other. The network is so complex that it took a Swiss mathematician-physicist to reconstruct it; Andrea Galli, a Zurich-based financial investigator. Italy's investigative bodies are hampered because they lack access to such focused expertise and don't have the funds needed to complete the work quickly enough.

In the course of the investigation, we came across several transactions involving works of art. Gaglio has a childhood friend, the Nice-based artist Stéphane Cipre, who transforms pieces of scrap metal into works of art. His circle of friends includes the former captain of the French rugby team, Jean-François (Jeff) Tordo. Gaglio needs a document to make money disappear from a client's account and then to launder the money. He comes up with the idea of asking Cipre to make him a metal structure depicting the rugby player. Together with Tordo and other guests, he takes a trip to New Zealand, where the artwork is donated to the city of Wellington, which at that time was hosting the world championships. The cost of the whole operation, transferred via one of Gaglio's money laundering companies, is about one and a half million euros[78]. The money comes from the bank account of a defrauded customer who remains unaware that his money is being laundered for the benefit of others.

---

[76] A fraudulent economic system based on a sort of "chain" of investors who are asked for investments, with the promise of subsequent gains that, for most of them, will never come. It takes its name from the Italian immigrant to the US, Charles Ponzi, who first used such a system in 1920.

[77] Vittorio Malagutti, Leo Sisti, *Filippo Dollfus, chi è il barone del riciclaggio*, «L'Espresso», May 13, 2015.

[78] Denise McNabb, *New Zealand Heaved Under the Grip of Rugby World Cup Fever. To Celebrate the Event the French Gifted Two Sculptures. They Were Paid for with Stolen Money*, Interest.co.nz, March 6 2018.

Gaglio buys a certain number of artworks by contemporary artists, illegally taking the funds from his clients' accounts. Later on, he simply reports the theft of the artwork. He regularly visits important galleries and famous auction houses like Sotheby's in London. On at least two occasions, on January 17, and January 23, 2008, he transferred artworks to Milan, to Ziribotti's home address. A work by Alberto Burri was also delivered to the Ziribotti home; the Mazzoleni Art Gallery of Turin delivered it directly after receiving 2,300,000 euro on a numbered Swiss account. The beneficiary, as it appears from the private agreement, is Alfonso Ziribotti, while the payment, from one offshore account to another, is effected by one of Gaglio's shell companies. Obviously, whoever received the payment wanted to hide it from the tax authorities, and whoever made it likely did so with the proceeds from another crime.

Ethics, business and art critics

We have discussed forgeries and how easy it is to get a value assigned to them, and the well-oiled system of fake expert appraisals which take on a credit function similar to the bills of exchange and checks of the past. We have explained how progress in scientific research helping to achieve ever more authoritative judgment. Nevertheless, we also wonder what the role of an honest and competent critic or an art historian is. If we should continue to trust the eye of the experts or if it is preferable to rely on an aseptic and impersonal analysis, the cold response of the laboratories. In this regard, we sought the opinion of a professional who has been a student and lover of art for over forty years.

As Claudio Metzger told us:

Oscar Wilde said that "we live in an age where unnecessary things are our only necessities". When I was a boy, I collected Greek coins because of the feeling it gave me to hold them and reflect on them. I could admire bronzes and ceramics in museums, but a coin - which by nature was just one of many - I could also hope to hold one in my hand.

Once with great effort, I bought one from the reign of Alessandro the Great, from 320 BC; 17 grams of silver, issued in Babylon. I was thrilled by its beauty. I knew about the mints and typefaces used by the great

Macedonian and therefore I felt safe. But it was a fake. When I found out I was so upset, because it was exactly like I wanted it to be, but it was bogus, even though it looked much more beautiful than authentic ones.

I returned it to the seller, who refunded me. Shortly afterwards, one after another, the friends who I had told it was fake came to me asking me about the coin. I was sorry I had given it up, and immediately went back to the collector to whom I had returned it, but he never sold it back to me. The forger had been an artist in his own way, and had intrigued and attracted me, yes, because the love for objects has several aspects: curiosity, attraction, desire, fulfilment or frustration. If everything goes well, you can achieve true happiness! Oscar Wilde also wrote that happiness is not having what you want. It's wanting what you have.

The more depth there is in the object you love, the more value you find in it, the more knowledge of it increases that love. We describe as an "artist" one who can give shape to thoughts, dreams, emotions, prayers. When he is great, he depicts images that we could never have seen, thoughts we have never had and emotions of which we were unaware.

Amedeo Modigliani's greatness is not derived from some abstract excellence in painting. If he hadn't painted female portraits might well have been forgotten, but no one before had portrayed the woman as he did. He invented a completely new way of portraying that was unique and unmistakable; it conveys powerful emotions, calling to mind unconscious primordial images.

Beauty and uniqueness arouse our wonder, giving the author an identity, making him immortal. The artists best remembered were innovative, and their success means they are destined to be copied, out of admiration, contempt or mere speculation. Not all those who copy are counterfeiters. There are some who love the master as though they were his child, or his pupil; they copy his style, but they don't sign in his name. In more recent times renowned counterfeiters, in mockery of art critics, have sought to improve on the original, with the paradoxical and unconscious desire to themselves gain recognition. In the history of plagiarism, at least since Caravaggio, there is a growing concern that copies may on one hand testify to the success of the subject while, on the other, decreasing the commercial value of the original.

While coins minted since the 7th century BC have made efforts to prevent forgery, artists, from ancient times to the present, have never taken such precautions. Here, I would like to emphasise the fundamental difference between those who, by copying a work of art, provide a personal interpretation of it; you can think for example of *Judith decapitating Holofernes* by Louis Finson, based on the painting by Caravaggio, and who, for his part, simply wants to take advantage of the prestige of the artist who painted the original.

If we think that Michelangelo Buonarroti sculpted a Cupid in Roman style and then "aged" it underground and, according to Giorgio Vasari, copied ancient drawings and then smoked them over a green wood fire (to make them seem much older - ed), it is clear to us that everything is possible in art. But if there are innumerable students who copied out of veneration, even more are those who plagiarised, imitating styles and subjects. Seeing Caravaggio in Italy and imitating him in Flanders or in Spain was a guarantee of fame and success. All this has created a great deal of confusion and uncertainty, making it difficult to fully reconstruct the bodies of artistic work of the masters whose paintings have been emulated and falsified.

The result is an incomplete and distorted view of the artist. Since the phenomenon is not limited by value or importance or even timeframe, it is not only the artistic catalogues of giants like Rembrandt, Rubens, Caravaggio, Van Gogh or Modigliani that are under discussion, but also those of countless other authors, from the ancients to the contemporaries, all brilliant and successful in one way or another.

It is often debated whether it is more difficult to falsify a contemporary or an ancient piece. I think it's easier to copy those who you know and you have seen working. I think of the children and pupils of great masters, but also of Dr. Paul Gachet who copied Vincent van Gogh. I think of the painter friends of Amedeo Modigliani, Moïse Kisling *in primis*, who seem to have finished some of his unfinished works and later emulated him.

Nothing changes over the centuries: many unfinished paintings left in the workshops of twentieth century painters have subsequently appeared in catalogues and been sold as finished works. How is one supposed to recognise that someone else has intervened, when simple sketches can be the basis of plagiarism? It is useless and misleading to mention the possibility of scientific analysis, since in these circumstances the materials, iconography and painting technique will be at least similar to those of completely authentic works. How do you imagine that so many works of great quality left Pieter Paul Rubens' workshop without the consent of the "owner"? How can you not believe that Guercino would verify the quality of his workshop, personally intervening where he through it was needed to protect his own name? And so there is often debate, without evidence over versions that appear to be different authors of the same theme, or replicas. Or identical authors: copies. Or, reproductions by another hand: forgeries. Works performed in order to mislead people about the author: tributes. Or, finally, works that can be clearly recognised as being by another author.

You can overpay for building land, share certificates, a football team, a patent or a work of art: as long as there are elements of subjective evaluation. The beautiful view from that piece of land, the company's development prospects, the football team's expected advertising revenues, scientific development prospects or, for the work of art... well, numerous factors and considerations - but all very subjective.

In such a complex field, anything is possible. Andy Warhol believed it foolish to sign his works, which everyone could easily copy, but he commented, "People just don't buy things that aren't signed ... It's so stupid. I don't really believe in signing my works. Anyone could do the things I'm doing and I don't think they should be signed."[79] When they gave him forgeries of his own works, he signed them in felt-tip pen with the words: "It's not my work!", and his signature. In doing so, he rendered the fakes "authentic".

The chickens come home to roost

We have travelled through a century of history, starting with the common and well-known picture passed on by others of Amedeo Modigliani and his family. We believe we have portrayed a different picture, one with the

---

[79] Andy Warhol, interview with Robert Vaughan, in Annette Michelson (edited by), *Andy Warhol*, Mit Press, Cambridge 2001.

same frames, but a different composition. The magnifying glass through which we observed it, in an adventurous search that lasted over a year, placed facts before us that were very different from the ones we thought we knew. We found important answers that upended prevailing ideas. Nothing was as it had seemed.

It has been proven that the Modigliani racket exists, it is no longer just a theory. Some of the main players in this book belong to a group of actors who have pulled strings in this puppet show for a hundred years. Following the money, our intention when we began this investigation, we identified other truths far more disconcerting than those historically acknowledged. Who was behind it all, who got rich, who twisted and dishonoured the memory of Amedeo Modigliani? Today we can say it with some certainty; it was a network of crooked dealers.

In our opinion - which mirrors the one expressed by Margherita Modigliani, Modì's sister, on the very day of the artist's funeral - from the very moment of the artist's death, forgeries began to proliferate. Now they are included in famous art collections and, thanks to the historicity acquired through prestigious exhibitions, especially in the second half of the last century, they are universally considered authentic works.

Today, not much is actually left of the work of Amedeo Modigliani. According to the experts Isabella Quattrocchi and Carlo Pepi, even among the 337 works contained in the authoritative collection of Ambrogio Ceroni there are paintings and a sculpture that - by mistake, or perhaps not - are included despite being adjudged fake by the artist's daughter, Jeanne Modigliani. Who is responsible for the sullying and impoverishment of the Leghorn painter's cultural and artistic heritage? The usual profiteers.

Throughout all this, despite continuing appeals and questions, justice has been missing in action Both in Italy and in France. Everything we have discovered through a year of investigation - which we financed ourselves - could have been unearthed by any public prosecutor's office. In the reports and documents underlying a proliferation of legal proceedings could be found all the evidence to justify further in-depth investigation, expert appraisals and the verification of alibis.

Nobody paid attention to the detailed charges raised by Amedeo's last heir, Laure Modigliani. As we promised at the beginning of this book, we wanted to make a case, and we have done so. We have delivered the results to the competent authorities: the prosecutor's office, the ministry of cultural heritage, the Carabinieri. They all listened attentively, and in wonder. We hope they will also proceed with internal investigations to identify who is responsible for so many leaks, and for so much carelessness, neglect and complicity.

Appendix

studio benini
indagini su scritture e documenti

TECHNICAL-GRAPHOLOGICAL ASSESSMENT on Jeanne Modigliani's writings.
Summary points of the findings

As a technical consultant registered in the Court Register of Turin, I was appointed to carry out an expert investigation to ascertain the authorship of handwriting and signatures on three documents in photocopy, purportedly signed by Jeanne Modigliani. In case of forgery, I was asked to verify if the fakes were produced by the hand of a person named Christian Parisot.

These are:

- the letter with sender Jeanne Modigliani in the upper left, dated 23/09/1974 (from now indicated with X1);

- the letter on non-headed paper dated 09/10/1974 (henceforth indicated with X2);

- the letter on ARCHIVES LEGALES AMEDEO MODIGLIANI headed paper, with text typescript, front / back, dated 12 / 10-11 / 1982 (from now indicated with X4).

To carry out the first comparison phase, I was given writing samples in copy, attributable to Jeanne Modigliani, consisting of: a letter dated **11/11/1968** (published on *Modigliani, dal vero*, author Enzo Maiolino, ed. De Ferrari, 2016); a letter dated **26/04/1971** (published in the article *Il figlio segreto di Modigliani*, by Francois Mattei, in the weekly magazine Epoca, 04/06/1972); a letter on headed paper ARCHIVES LEGALES AMEDEO MODIGLIANI dated **03/10/1982**; a letter on ARCHIVES LEGALES AMEDEO MODIGLIANI headed paper dated **02/06/1984** (published on *Jeanne Modigliani racconta Modigliani*, ed. Graphis Arte, 1984); a typewritten letter on ARCHIVES LEGALES AMEDEO MODIGLIANI headed paper signed at the bottom, dated **26/07/1984** and with postmark 27/07/1984.
It is specified that:

- on the copies it was not possible to examine the quality of the graphic style in terms of dynamism, smoothness and elasticity, of pressure, which could only be appreciated on lines inked in the originals. The investigation was limited to the formal / compositional aspect, focusing the attention on elements of a typical nature;
- the lines in the copies are subject to distortion phenomena, which deform, to varying degrees, the original graphic style;

dott. Silvia Benini - Corso F. Brunelleschi 121/D - 10141 Torino
e-mail: silviabenini@beninistudio.com - web: www.beninistudio.com

- since these are reproductions - some of them in publications that are likely to be enlarged or reduced compared to the original - the verification of the size category of the gauge is also pending;

- for the above, the final assessments are considered to be expressed subject to verification on the originals, in compliance with the reference guidelines indicated by ENFSI 2015 (European Network of Forensic Science Institutes).

- the full version of all documentation has not been published due to space constraints, but it remains available for further verification and broader research.

The preliminary phase of the investigation took place on the internal comparison between the spellings under examination X1, X2 and X4.

Except for the two blocks saying "Christian Parisot 12/11/1982" that appear on the two pages of X4, it has been ascertained that the XX scripts come from the same hand.

The correspondence exists, on the basis of significant qualitative elements; its identification was facilitated by the compositional customisation and by the typicality of some letters. To give some examples among the characterising elements, taken from both handwriting and signatures: the formation of eyelets **a, o, d** and **g** in the version with head opening or cap opening and an attached stroke, or in the version with eyelet open at around 9 o'clock on the dial and internal curls, detached fore-end; the point **i** in the apostrophe; the curved thread at the end of **P**; the **r** with a wide upper plateau; the narrow **gli** group, elongated and hanging, with **g** open at the head; saddle hem of the **M**; rod of the **d** like a buttonhole.

dott. Silvia Benini · Corso F. Brunelleschi 12 /D - 10141 Torino
e-mail: silviabenini@beninistudio.com · web: www.beninistudio.com

Comparison between X1 – X2 – X4:

X1

X2

X4

dott. Silvia Benini - Corso F. Brunelleschi 121/D - 10141 Torino
e-mail: silviabenini@beninistudio.com - web: www.beninistudio.com

Comparison between X1 – X2 – X4:

X1

X2

X4

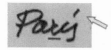

dott. Silvia Benini - Corso F. Brunelleschi 121/D - 10141 Torino
e-mail: silviabenini@beninistudio.com - web: www.beninistudio.com

The comparative group was also examined from within. This step is to ensure that, beyond the apparent reliability of the documents, the handwriting was actually written by the subject to which it refers, and meets the qualitative and quantitative suitability parameters expected by the expert protocol.

The five comparative documents appear contradictory. The handwriting in the letters **11/11/1968** - **26/04/1971** - **02/06/1984** is substantially incompatible with the handwriting in the letters **03/10/1982** - **07/26/1984**.

An aside about the letters **11/11/1968** and **02/06/1984**: contrary to what might be believed from observing the apparent general divergence between the two signatures, the origin matrix is in fact certainly the same

11/11/1968

02/06/1984

Over the course of about sixteen years, the gait has evidently undergone a natural involution; the handwriting of 1984 is simplified, calm, at times laboured, with some elements of difficulty, while that of 1968 is vigorous, dynamic, with ingenious links. A different thrust emerges in its execution which, however, does not prevent us from appreciating the stylistic equivalence, more perceptible from the handwriting, where a series of shared personalised literal elements are captured.

11/11/1968

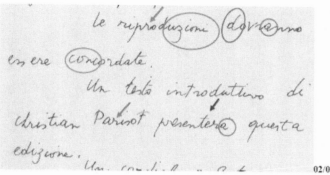

02/06/1984

In 1984, Jeanne was 66 years old and had been suffering from alcohol addiction since the 1970s; it is possible that the alterations in the balance of neurotransmitters have affected motor coordination of intricate movements, with repercussions on the writing process.

Returning to the comparison, in the letter **03/10/1982** we observe a clumsy and awkward handwriting, with amorphous elements, incoherent formations, coarse features, and unjustified and unnatural stops. Therefore it is a handwriting that is not convincing, which is already suspicious in itself.

03/10/1982

In the letter **02/06/1984**, after a lapse of only 20 months, the movements are on the other hand fluid, the gestures are lively, snappy, energetic, the overall appearance is harmonious.

dott. Silvia Benini · Corso F. Brunelleschi 121/D · 10141 Torino
e-mail: silviabenini@beninistudio.com · web: www.beninistudio.com

02/06/1984

The differences between the handwriting in XX and the signature, both from an overall viewpoint and from the individual internal details, were confirmed by the in-depth study of the signatures. For example, in the letter **02/06/1984** the eyelets **a**, **o**, **d** and **g** are closed counter-clockwise and with a terminal curl tending downwards; the dots on the **i** are precise and without smudging, while in the letters **03/10/1982** and **26/07/1984** the eyelets are open at the top and the **dots on the i** are long and drawn, like an apostrophe

02/06/1984

03/10/1982

26/07/1984

dott. Silvia Benini - Corso F. Brunelleschi 121/D - 10141 Torino
e-mail: silviabenini@beninistudio.com - web: www.beninistudio.com

studio benini
indagini su scritture e documenti

The group of confirmed signatures by Jeanne Modigliani is therefore made up of the three letters **11/11/1968 - 26/04/1971 - 02/06/1984** (respectively classified **A1 - A2 - A3**).

The letters **03/10/1982** and **26/07/1984** were on the other hand included in the group under review, thus chronologically ordered: **X1** - letter **23.09.1974**; **X2** - letter **09/10/1974**; **X3** – letter dated **03/10/1982**; **X4** - letter dated **12.10.1982**; **X5** - letter dated **07/26/1984**).

The five XX scripts are stylistically similar to each other:

studio benini

The comparison between group XX and Jeanne's autographs shows some apparent similarities with regard to more generic structures that are easy to reproduce such as the **Mo** group of Modigliani, but it denotes a substantial divergence with respect to less controlled gestures, which the hand of another would find difficult to reproduce.

studio benini

COMPARATIVE JEANNE MODIGLIANI

To sum up, the five XX come from the hand of the same forger and not from that of Jeanne Modigliani.

It was crucial at this point to proceed with the attribution of the forgeries, comparing them with the writing of a subject named Christian Parisot, for whom I was provided with abundant original documentation. As already mentioned, the fabrications are characterised by the typical artificiality inherent in the attempted forgery; in the act of producing another person's writing the forger intentionally intervened on his own natural graphic structures, disguising them to a great extent in order to depersonalise them. However, interesting details emerged during the investigation that recall the Parisot's style, which escaped from (his) conscious control due to their compulsive nature.

The frequent use of the **a** in script (lowercase block letters) is observed in the comparatives, which in the verifications were inadvertently used once in the word Paris in X1. Similar are also the **r** always in script and the **s** in the handwriting which has a flat plateau

X1

COMPARATIVE CHRISTIAN PARISOT

The **P** has a generic structure but the detail of the terminal curl offers a peculiar index of correspondence. I note the analogy in the s in script, detached, hanging on the right and increased in its dimensions with respect to the **i** that precedes it. I observe that the **s** finds affinity in the two variants, in italics with the flat plateau that can be seen above.

X1	X2	X4

COMPARATIVE CHRISTIAN PARISOT

dott. Silvia Benini - Corso F. Brunelleschi 121/D - 10141 Torino
e-mail: silviabenini@beninistudio.com - web: www.beninistudio.com

studio benini
indagini su scritture e documenti

The dot of the **i** of X1 from the copy appears to be drawn in a circle

X1

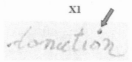

COMPARATIVE CHRISTIAN PARISOT

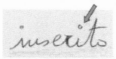

The **z** has bevelled profiles and a horizontal cut shifted to the right

X1

COMPARATIVE CHRISTIAN PARISOT

The **N** has a generic structure in capital letters, but the degree of spreading makes it typical of the angles and torsion of the upper apex; the **p** consists of only the lower slot without the body; the **f** has a double buttonhole and lacks a median cut

dott. Silvia Benini · Corso F. Brunelleschi 12/D · 10141 Torino
e-mail: silviabenini@beninistudio.com · web: www.beninistudio.com

studio benini

XI

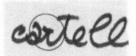

COMPARATIVE CHRISTIAN PARISOT

The **r** has an upper plateau, concave or rectilinear, and hints of small slots, as can be found in the comparative variants

COMPARATIVE CHRISTIAN PARISOT

dott. Silvia Benini - Corso F. Brunelleschi 121/D - 10141 Torino
e-mail: silviobenini@beninistudio.com - web: www.beninistudio.com

The **v** has a particular deviation in the direction of the cone

X2   X2

COMPARATIVE CHRISTIAN PARISOT

The **m** has the initial section with a characteristic hook apex

X2

COMPARATIVE CHRISTIAN PARISOT

dott. *Silvia Benini* - Corso F. Brunelleschi 121/D - 10141 Torino
e-mail: silviabenini@beninistudio.com - web: www.beninistudio.com

indagini su scritture e documenti

The occasional presence of the peduncle running to the right of the **o** is peculiar, and also present in some comparative cases

X2   X3

COMPARATIVE CHRISTIAN PARISOT

Note the correspondence of the **n** in script and of the two versions of **g**: with extension both stylised and complete in the handwriting, and eyelet opened / closed at the top

X1   X2

COMPARATIVE CHRISTIAN PARISOT

dott. Silvia Benini - Corso F. Brunelleschi 121/D - 10141 Torino
e-mail: silviabenini@beninistudio.com - web: www.beninistudio.com

Note the shape of the eyelet of **a** and **g**, open at the head with eyelet to the right; the lower length of **g** in some cases interrupts its connection with the next letter

X3   X2

COMPARATIVE CHRISTIAN PARISOT

dott. *Silvia Benini* - Corso F. Brunelleschi 121/D - 10141 Torino
e-mail: silviabenini@beninistudio.com - web: www.beninistudio.com

On the X5 there is the **i** with dovetail stitch, generated by the dynamic aerial movement escaped from dissimilatory control, in total compatibility with the comparative homologs

X5

Jeanne Modigliani

COMPARATIVE CHRISTIAN PARISOT

The **gl** group has a stylised composition in X5, akin to the more sober modality that Parisot uses in alternative to italics. The analogy relating to the straight and pending initial grip is also evident in the capital letter **M**

X5   X1

Jeanne Modigliani

COMPARATIVE CHRISTIAN PARISOT

dott. Silvia Benini - Corso F. Brunelleschi 121/D - 10141 Torino
e-mail: silviabenini@beninistudio.com - web: www.beninistudio.com

studio benini
indagini su scritture e documenti

The detail of the sharp-angled section of the **Mo** connection of some samples of XX is interesting, occasional but present in Parisot's signatures. Also similar is the initial straight and sloping leg of the capital **M** and the misalignment of the saddle moved to the left, particularly marked in X3

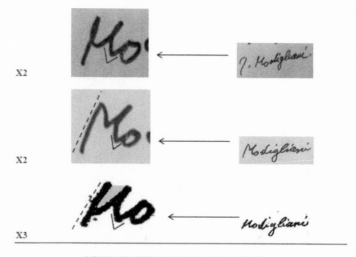

COMPARATIVE CHRISTIAN PARISOT

dott. Silvia Benini - Corso F. Brunelleschi 121/D - 10141 Torino
e-mail: silviabenini@beninistudio.com - web: www.beninistudio.com

In lower left in small print on document **X1**, a signature appears in the name of J. Modigliani which has a different **J**, one of a kind within the checks, with an upper straight plateau and spiral terminal. In the signatures, the Js have a similar structure. It is probable that this small signature was affixed with less control, which is exercised more heavily on the more visible large signatures

X1

COMPARATIVE CHRISTIAN PARISOT

As repeated, what is crucial from the demonstrative point of view is the convergence of small, less striking details, which in the demonstrative context are the most salient; beyond the generic form of **C**, the most significant element of attributive correspondence is the small initial superscript

X3   X3

COMPARATIVE CHRISTIAN PARISOT

dott. Silvia Benini - Corso F. Brunelleschi 121/D - 10141 Torino
e-mail: silviabenini@beninistudio.com - web: www.beninistudio.com

studio benini
indagini su scritture e documenti

The dilated eyelet has a particular shape with depression on the left and curls thrown inwards

XI

COMPARATIVE CHRISTIAN PARISOT

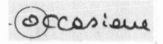

The figures were also compatible. I present as example the number 4, narrow, in a chair like shape

XI

COMPARATIVE CHRISTIAN PARISOT

The correspondence indicators emerging from the comparative spellings presented here constitute only a demonstrative sample of how many have been found.

dott. Silvia Benini - Corso F. Brunelleschi 121/D - 10141 Torino
e-mail: silviabenini@beninistudio.com - web: www.beninistudio.com

studio benini
indagini su scritture e documenti

I conclude with an overall parallel from which the lexical compatibility is also understood from the recurring use of the words *Ti prego* present on the X3 and on many Parisot's autographs

X3

dott. Silvia Benini - Corso F. Brunelleschi 121/D - 10141 Torino
e-mail: silviabenini@beninistudio.com - web: www.beninistudio.com

studio benini

At the end of the technical process, based on the significance of the elements of analysis and in relation to the qualitative indexes of the documentation examined, I respond to the request for an expert analysis by formulating the following conclusion: **the writings of texts and signatures in the apparent name of Jeanne Modigliani affixed to documents classified from X1 to X5 were apocryphal. The fakes are compatible with the comparatives provided as Christian Parisot's hand samples.** Subject to further study.

The Technical Consultant
(Dr. Silvia Benini)
(Professional graphologist disciplined pursuant to law 4/2013)

Turin, May 16 2019

dott. Silvia Benini · Corso F. Brunelleschi 121/D · 10141 Torino
e-mail: silviabenini@beninistudio.com · web: www.beninistudio.com

Afterword by Pietro Grasso

When the authors came to me to discuss *The Modigliani Racket* for the first time, about a year ago, I was struck by the light and the passion they had in telling this story: they felt they had found the "right track" to expand their investigation, to dig into the mysteries, scams and connivance within a system that degrades art and exploits artists and their name to earn hyperbolic sums and to launder money. I recognised that light because I had seen it - and experienced it - many times in my previous profession as magistrate.

The fruit of those investigations are found in this book, which recounts some incredible and well-documented stories and which, I am sure, will soon become documentaries, movies, TV series. In fact, in a few months, we will be celebrating the centenary of Modì's death; at last, the celebrations and interest such anniversaries typically draw will be based on solid foundations, rather than being just another opportunity for speculation.

The maze of stories and swindles that began on the day of Modigliani's funeral are enmeshed in the history of the twentieth century, from the drama of the Nazi persecutions to the cold war, a possible factor in the story of the "Modigliani heads" found in Livorno in 1984; it was a case too hastily dismissed as just a simple "hoax", and passed into the collective imagination as such, but one which acquires, in these pages, a new interpretation.

There are some phrases that give the exact measure of how many unscrupulous scammers revolved around the Leghorn artist: "Of Modigliani, it is said that he produced more in death than in life" is one of these. Compared to the 337 works registered in the most accredited catalogue, in fact, there are more than 1200 on the market. In practice, just one work out of four is original. So each of us who has visited his exhibitions in Italy and around the world has found himself staring in awe at forgeries, fake reproductions, even copies of fakes. The art lover, even the non-expert, may feel dizzy when delving into this revealing work: even the fakes vary in kind, and there are forgers so famous that they become renowned artists in themselves and are mentioned in other works (this is the case of Elmyr de Hory, among the main characters in the film *F for Fake* by the great Orson Welles).

On the other hand, the art market is such that it is sufficient to sell just one painting to earn millions of euros and change your own standard of living and that of your descendants. In order to be able to transform a forger's daub into a goldmine, however, a certificate of authenticity is required, and much of the Modigliani case revolves around the desire of its principal characters to have exclusive control over this process.

The trafficking of works of art, real or false, is in fact a sector considered to be low risk in terms of legal consequences, with high profits to be made particularly in the international market. All that is needed is a high degree of professionalism.

An entire criminal food chain has sprung from the looting of assets: from grave robbers to specialists art thieves and forgers. In the second act of this book, we meet the experts who evaluate and enrich the work before we move on to the marketing stage, one whose characteristics are also typical of money laundering: normally achieved via a sale though an auction house or a round of fictitious private sales helps to establish the price of the artwork.

Of course, these operations require an extensive degree of complicity. The painting or the artwork are nothing but justifications to shift large sums of money, they are treasures that move on a circuit that shadows the transparent and official one. This circuit is used by experts and merchants whose singularity lies entirely in the customers they serve.

The Bank of Italy included the "purchase of works of art at a value far exceeding their market price" among the indications of suspected money laundering after a consultation with trade associations, the stock exchange regulator and the insurance industry supervisor. Works of art are in fact assets that are of increasing interest to criminal organisations looking to launder their ill-gotten gains.

I was national anti-mafia prosecutor when Gioacchino Campolo, "the king of video poker" mentioned in the book, was arrested in 2009. Authentic paintings were his real weakness: when the officers from the

Guardia di Finanza, Italy's financial investigators, searched his house to notify him of a seizure of assets worth 300 million, they found themselves before an Aladdin's cave of art, with works by Salvador Dalí, Renato Guttuso, Giorgio de Chirico, Giuseppe Migneco, Antonio Ligabue, Lucio Fontana, Mario Sironi and Michele Cascella.

I also remember the case of Pepe Onorato, a Calabrian mob boss who ruled with an iron fist and sat on a mountain of money made from drug trafficking. But finance was his specialty. In his circle, there was also a gallery owner, Marco Semenzato, from the auction house of the same name. With his help, Pepe Onorato discovered the infinite possibilities of art, including using overvalued paintings, authentic or fake, to either make money through swindles or to hide it from prying eyes.

Thus it was that this investigation, with all the ingredients of any other anti-mafia investigation anywhere else in the world, revealed an entirely new phenomenon: the art dealer boss. It wasn't just the whim of owning an art work to show off status, but a branch of the business with attractive prospects which could be developed in parallel with the company's core business.

The agents found sixty-nine paintings, real works of art, including two attributed to Modigliani, *Portrait de jeune fille* and *Portrait de Rosalie*. None of the paintings was stolen, they were regularly purchased abroad and smuggled into Italy to prevent the money used in their acquisition from being traced. Here they received a valuation, from complicit appraisers, which was of course higher than the purchase price. This set the stage for the next sale, to the circuit of official art dealers. The final step was the sale of the paintings to the unwary buyer, the last link in the chain. Thus the path of the dirty money was hidden, and the boss got a nice profit. The *Portrait de Rosalie* was recovered at Orio al Serio airport when it was about to be shipped to the Netherlands. On the face of it, this was a chance find of an artwork with an estimated of 1.2 million euros; but in truth, it was a piece in an investigative puzzle that investigators had been patiently putting together.

The respect and admiration for a great artist like Modigliani must lead us to purge the catalogues from fakes of any kind, and to give lustre to his original works. This book, the fruit of old-fashioned field work, helps us to understand, and I am sure it will help investigators to reopen, important chapters of such investigations. It may help legislator to refine the rules to combat the phenomenon more effectively. In thanking the authors for this work, I conclude by pointing out a curious coincidence: I am writing this afterword on September 5, Antonino Caponnetto's birthday. It was at the foundation dedicated this great anti-mafia crusader that I first met the authors, and I would like to spare a grateful and affectionate thought for "Nonno Nino" (as Antonino Caponnetto is affectionately remembered - ed), whose teachings, evidently, continue to bear fruit.

Acknowledgments

We must give credit to those offered their help during this investigation, some out of true generosity and a thirst for justice, others out of self-interest, a desire for revenge or just plain mischief.

Many people provided us confidential documents. Our thanks also go to them for their help.

However, please note that what we have written derives from our own independent evaluation. We did not let anyone influence us. Those who attempted to do so were soon rebuffed.

In particular, we thank those who believed in this project even though it promised to be both challenging and lengthy.

Thank you also to Pietro Grasso, president of the Antonino Caponnetto Foundation, who welcomed us into his distinguished study with a smile and encouraged us to move ahead with this project, giving us valuable advice as a magistrate, and as a man on the side of legality.

Finally, thank you "Nonno Nino", the judge Antonino Caponnetto who, through the memory handed down by the foundation that bears his name - of which we are proud members - inspired and spurred on our efforts.

We believe that commitment pays off. We feel fulfilled by what we believe is a fine outcome. However, this book is fruit also of a great collective effort. Thank you to all the main characters in this story: to the brothers Giorgio and Guido Guastalla; to Michele Caturegli; to Alessandro Bulgini; to Massimino Filippelli; to Christian Parisot; to Maria Stellina Marescalchi. Thank you also to those who worked to uphold the law: Marc Restellini; Marc Ottavi; colonel Nicola Candido; captain Fabio Castagna; lieutenant Andrea Dentale; the deputy prosecutor Pierluigi Cipolla; Emilie Modigliani; and the journalist Luisa Nannipieri. A special thanks to those who put their experience and professionalism at our disposal: the lawyer Lavinia Savini; the art historian Claudio Metzger; the art historian Sira von Waldner; the painter Ernando Venanzi; the graphologist Silvia Benini; professor Sylvie Pipari; Dr. Riccarda Giraudi, medical examiner; and the professor and consultant to the public prosecutor's offices Isabella Quattrocchi.

A warm hug, more than a thank you, to Carlo Pepi who inspired us in this enterprise against wrongdoing. We were proud to walk by his side after his decades of lone struggle. Our last thoughts return to the place where it all began: the nude school in the academy of rue de la Grande Chaumière. Here for a few minutes we bathed in history... we entered the world of Amedeo Modigliani.

Names Index

Guy Vincent Chastenet; 164; 215
Hanka Zborowska; 165; 166
Isabella Quattrocchi; 15; 153; 156;
 168; 169; 170; 171; 175; 188;
 189; 190; 191; 214; 264; 296
Isacco Garsin; 18
Italo Zannier; 71
Ivo Cozzi; 138
Jacques Lipchitz; 211
Jean Leymarie; 149
Jean Olaniszyn; 154; 160; 165; 186;
 188
Jean-François (Jeff) Tordo; 259
JEANNE HEBUTERNE; 24
Jeanne Modigliani; 15; 17; 26; 27;
 39; 43; 44; 49; 50; 54; 60; 67; 74;
 75; 82; 84; 86; 93; 95; 97; 99;
 101; 103; 105; 109; 112; 119;
 124; 129; 134; 140; 144; 149;
 151; 154; 184; 189; 193; 201;
 216; 225; 226; 227; 229; 230;
 231; 232; 235; 237; 244; 245;
 264; 268; 275; 277; 289
John Connolly; 213
John Papi; 169
Jonathan Zebina; 189; 217
Joseph Guttmann; 153; 156; 163;
 166; 169; 175; 178
Joseph Lanthemann; 83; 86; 93; 95;
 103
Joseph Laposata; 112; 113; 131
Kenan Evren; 239
Kenneth Clark; 209
Klaus Perls; 86; 112; 134; 141; 143;
 148; 149; 151; 165; 167; 203;
 205; 213; 214
Kurt von Behr; 202
Lamberto Vitali; 149; 192
Laure Modigliani; 50; 54; 59; 61;
 83; 90; 91; 93; 98; 223; 227; 264

Lavinia Savini; 89; 295
Léopold Zborowski; 18; 20; 162;
 207; 209
Lido Bellandi; 112; 114; 129; 137
Lorenzo Bocchi; 238
Lorenzo Guerrini; 123
Luc Prunet; 60; 93; 109; 235
Luca Borzani; 159; 176
Luciano Renzi; 50; 57; 58; 59; 76;
 86; 93; 108; 189; 193; 194; 195;
 219; 223
Luciano Scala; 69
Ludovico Ragghianti; 123
Luisa Nannipieri; 237; 295
Lunia Czechowska; 17; 28; 35; 96;
 166
Marc Ottavi; 153; 155; 156; 161;
 162; 295
Marc Restellini; 70; 153; 155; 156;
 161; 177; 184; 199; 295
Marco Franzini; 124
Marco Semenzato; 293
Marella Ferrera; 64
Margherita Modigliani; 199; 264
Marguerite de Rochechouart; 193
Maria Marevna; 164
Maria Stellina Marescalchi; 49; 50;
 51; 52; 53; 54; 56; 91; 96; 108;
 181; 183; 185; 188; 295
Mariastella Margozzi; 153; 156;
 168; 169
Marie Pierre Etcheverry; 156
Marika Rivera; 164
Mario Camici; 138
Mario Schifano; 173
Marisol Monica Rossetti; 71
Marta Massaioli; 173
Martin Dannenberg; 203
Massimino Filippelli; 111; 135; 137;
 140; 151; 295

Printed on December 2020
by Graphot, Turin - Italy